Game Development Patterns with Godot 4

Create resilient game systems using industry-standard solutions in Godot

Henrique Campos

‹packt›

Game Development Patterns with Godot 4

Copyright © 2025 Packt Publishing

Group Product Manager: Rohit Rajkumar

Publishing Product Manager: Neha Pande

Book Project Manager: Arul Viveaun

Senior Editor: Rakhi Patel

Technical Editor: K Bimala Singha

Copy Editor: Safis Editing

Indexer: Rekha Nair

Production Designer: Nilesh Mohite

DevRel Marketing Coordinator: Nivedita Pandey

First published: January 2025

Production reference: 3041225

Published by Packt Publishing Ltd.

Grosvenor House

11 St Paul's Square

Birmingham

B3 1RB, UK.

ISBN 978-1-83588-028-9

www.packtpub.com

To my Lord and Savior, Jesus Christ, who gave me the strength and faith to dedicate my efforts to writing this book, knowing it will be used for great things. And to my family: Sheila, my mother, Claudio, my father, and Ráisa, my sister, who have always been by my side on my journey in the video game industry. In memory of my uncle Wemerson, who made great investments in my dream. With all my heart.

– Henrique Campos

Contributors

About the author

Henrique "Ludonaut" Campos is an indie game developer and game designer working in the industry for years. Started as a University teacher in 2015 in the Computer Graphics and Artificial Intelligence chairs and working in the GDQuest team from 2018 to 2022, Henrique is also an independent consultant for studios and schools. Under the alias of Ludonaut, Henrique creates game development content on his YouTube channel making games, assets, ebooks, and courses that can be found in his itch.io profile.

Being the author of *The Essential Guide to Creating Multiplayer Games with Godot 4.0*, Henrique paved the way for Godot users to make incredible shared online experiences while helping them discover the engine's bleeding edge features.

I want to thank everyone who is working to create great open source software such as Godot; you are building a better world. Special thanks to my family and friends, especially Arthur, Luan, and Tumeo for being by my side and believing in my dream. I also want to thank my supporters, who have followed every step of this journey, especially Laurence Bannister and Kyle Szklenski. Lastly, thank you to my brothers in Christ for all the support they've given me.

About the reviewers

Jonathan Reeves is a multi-faceted software engineer with more than 6 years of professional experience. He has a wealth of experience, ranging from full-stack development to video game development, and he has a passion for technical education. He's adept at building engaging user interfaces for both consumer-facing and internal web applications. Beyond the frontend side of things, he has developed a few games and published them on web and mobile platforms. Previous technical works he has worked on are *React 18 Design Patterns and Best Practices, 4th edition* by *Carlos Santana Roldán*and *React and React Native, 5th edition* by *Mikhail Sakhniuk and Adam Boduch.*

Ryan Hinds is an independent game developer, the founder and CEO of Industrial Llama, and a teaching assistant for courses such as *Godot 4 C# Action Adventure: Build your own 2.5D RPG* through GameDev.tv. He was born in Alberta, Canada, where he resides with his wife and their daughter. He has recently started reviewing and editing educational books on programming in his free time to help others learn the trade. Currently, he is a student in Advanced Game Development at Bow Valley College in Calgary, Alberta.

Table of Contents

Preface   xiii

Free Benefits with Your Book   xix

Part 1: Object-Oriented Design Principles

1

Understanding Object-Oriented Design   3

Technical requirements   4   Turning your design into an object in
Learning the basics of OOP   4   Godot Engine   10
Complying with the principles of OOP 6   Summary   17
Designing games with OOP   8

2

Learning the Four Fundamental Pillars   19

Technical requirements   20   Extending an object's behaviors with
 Simplifying complex systems with   inheritance   25
abstraction   20   Maintaining compatibility with
Scoping properties and methods with   polymorphism   31
encapsulation   22   Summary   34

3

Creating SOLID Design Solutions   35

Unbloating objects with the SRP   36
Maintaining and extending objects
with the OCP   38
Ensuring compatibility with the LSP   39

Creating components with the ISP   40
Making high-level abstractions with
the DIP   41
Summary   43

4

Favoring Composition Over Inheritance   45

Technical requirements   46
Understanding the composition
approach   46
Creating complex scenes by
composing with nodes   48
Turning a behavior into a component   49

Making games by composing with
scenes   52
Creating the LootBumpingPig   53

Summary   57

Part 2: Basic Design Patterns

5

Maintaining Global States with the Singleton Pattern   61

Technical requirements   62
Understanding the Singleton pattern   62
Spotting use cases of singletons in
games   63
Maintaining players' data throughout the
game states   63
Playing background music without
interruptions   65
Using third-party APIs and plugins   65

Accessing the engine's built-in features   66
Implementing the Singleton pattern
in Godot   66
Understanding the designer's request   66
Creating the score system   68
Implementing the multi-door teleporting system 78

Summary   82

6

Decoupling Objects with the Observer Pattern   83

Technical requirements	84	Implementing the Observer pattern in Godot	87
Understanding the Observer pattern	84	Integrating the player's health interface	89
Spotting use cases for the Observer pattern	86	Summary	93

7

Spawning Game Objects with the Factory Pattern   95

Technical requirements	96	Implementing the Factory pattern in Godot	99
Understanding the Factory pattern	96	Creating the Node2DFactory class	100
Spotting use cases for the Factory pattern	97	Using Node2DFactory in our game	104
		Summary	113

8

Changing Object Behavior with the State Pattern   115

Technical requirements	117	Godot	121
Understanding the State pattern	118	Understanding the designer's requirements	121
Spotting use cases of the State pattern in games	119	Implementing an FSM with animations	123
Implementing the State pattern in		Handling state-specific behaviors with the State pattern	136
		Summary	154

9

Designing Actors with the Command Pattern   155

Technical requirements	156	Understanding the Command pattern	156

**Spotting use cases for the
Command pattern** 158

Using commands such as undo/redo in level
editors 158

Queuing commands in real-time strategy
games 159

Creating strategic encounters in role-player
games 159

Making template behaviors in RPGs 159

Backtracking actions in tactical RPG battles 160

**Implementing the Command pattern
in Godot** 160

Evaluating the game designer's changes 161

Creating the BumpingPig commands 168

Using commands with buttons 169

Implementing the concrete commands 171

Mapping the commands to buttons 177

Designing the Bumping Pig brain 181

Summary 188

Part 3: Advanced Design Patterns

10

Implementing AI with the Strategy Pattern 191

Technical requirements 192

Understanding the Strategy pattern 192

**Spotting use cases for the Strategy
pattern** 194

**Implementing the Strategy pattern
in Godot** 196

Creating the InteractionStrategy family 198

Using the target object to provide a strategy 199

Cleaning up the Brain class with strategy
executions 202

Implementing interaction strategies 205

Summary 208

11

Creating a Power-Up System with the Decorator Pattern 211

Technical requirements 212

Understanding the Decorator pattern 212

**Spotting use cases for the Decorator
pattern** 213

**Implementing the Decorator pattern
in Godot Engine** 215

Turning properties into the Stats class 217

Creating our StatsDecorator class 224

Wrapping Stats with the power-ups Singleton 227

Using Diamond objects to add power-ups 232

Summary 237

12

Cross-Fading Transitions with the Service Locator Pattern   239

Technical requirements   240   pattern in Godot Engine   243

Understanding the Service Locator   Creating the BackgroundMusic
pattern   240   Service Locator   245

Spotting use cases for the Service   Using the BackgroundMusic Service Locator   250
Locator pattern   242   Summary   255

Implementing the Service Locator

13

Improving Game Feel with the Event Queue Pattern   257

Technical requirements   258   Implementing the Event Queue

Understanding the Event Queue   pattern in Godot   264
pattern   258   Storing input events with an input buffer   266

Spotting use cases for the Event   Buffering and processing jumps   271
Queue pattern   260   Summary   272

Index   275

Index   275

Other Books You May Enjoy   280

Other Books You May Enjoy   280

Preface

Hello there! I'm Henrique Campos, also known as *Ludonaut*, and in this book, we will talk about a topic that always intrigues me: design patterns. Specifically, in this book, we will talk about object-oriented programming design patterns. The idea behind this is that there are numerous problems regarding design that are common, so instead of reinventing the wheel, we can stand on the shoulders of giants and rely on tested, time-proven solutions. But in doing so, we are going to take a non-conventional path. You will learn the following from this book:

- Create reusable and scalable code that follows SOLID principles

- Identify common game development issues and apply industry-standard solutions

- Understand feature requests and how to turn them into concrete solutions leveraging design patterns

- Analyze game development pathologies to figure out underlying issues

- Architect reliable systems that are understandable, intuitive, and scalable

- Structure professional, collaborative game systems that are easy to maintain

We will use our imagination by role-playing a game mechanics engineer who is responsible for implementing requests from a fictional game designer. This allows us to work in a similar context to real life, where a designer responsible for the creative direction of a game, comes with game design requests that a programmer should implement. In this process, we will create a complete platformer game with a player, an enemy with complex artificial intelligence, interactive objects, multiple levels, music, and more.

By the end of this book, you will have a solid knowledge of how to create reliable architectures for your game's code bases that you can scale and reuse knowing exactly what its points of pressure are and how to solve potential problems. You will also understand that design patterns should not be used as an initial approach to implementing features; instead, they are used as solutions for problems that arise as we develop our games. In this process, you will learn refactoring techniques that will save you time and energy.

As a friend of mine says: an amateur knows how to create new code, and a professional knows how to fix old code. In that sense, the skills you will learn from this book will help you avoid the urge to make things from scratch and instead deal with ugly and messy situations, thriving through them and leaving a trail of elegant and scalable solutions.

Throughout the book, we will use Godot Engine 4.3, by the time of writing, the latest version of the rising star open source project that has been getting the industry's eyes. To make the onboarding easy, we will use the built-in text editor and GDScript as the main tools. Godot has many built-in features that help us implement the design patterns we are going to see. In some cases, such as the Observer pattern, Godot provides the implementation and all we have to do is use it, but we must understand the principles behind it.

Who this book is for

This book is for anyone with sufficient knowledge to understand what variables and methods are. As we introduce basic programming and object-oriented programming concepts, most of the content in the book can be used by intermediate to advanced programmers. People who have experience with GDScript and the Godot Engine editor will take the most out of this book as the main focus is to present the design patterns themselves. People with no programming background will have trouble understanding the core concepts and how each pattern helps to solve specific issues.

The three main skills our audience must have in order to make great use of this book are as follows:

- Understanding the nodes and resources philosophy behind Godot Engine's design

- Basic knowledge of the GDScript language's syntax

- Experience with programming concepts such as functions, variables, constants, algorithms, and procedures

To summarize it all, if you have already made one or two games with Godot Engine or similar applications, you will be able to understand the concepts presented in this book and the problems that we face throughout the process of making a game. Understanding these problems is fundamental to understanding the value of using the design patterns we will introduce in this book. But if you have good abstract thinking and can intuitively understand how one approach can generate issues as projects scale, then you will also be able to engage with this book's value proposition.

What this book covers

Chapter 1, Understanding Object-Oriented Design, explains the philosophy behind writing programs from an object-oriented perspective.

Chapter 2, Learning the Four Fundamental Pillars, discusses the tools object-oriented programming provides to write object-oriented code.

Chapter 3, Creating SOLID Design Solutions, guides you through five core principles of writing good, reusable, and scalable object-oriented code.

Chapter 4, Favoring Composition Over Inheritance, explains that inheritance is a powerful but dangerous tool in object-oriented programming, so we must use it responsibly. In this chapter, you will explore the issues behind inheritance and the composition alternative to achieve code reusability.

Chapter 5, Maintaining Global States with the Singleton Pattern, begins implementing the Singleton pattern for a common issue in game development: global data that multiple objects should have access to.

Chapter 6, Decoupling Objects with the Observer Pattern, discusses coupling, which is a major issue in programming, but it's unavoidable. But with the Observer pattern, we can make objects communicate without coupling them by using a notification system.

Chapter 7, Spawning Game Objects with the Factory Pattern, covers creating new objects in the game world, which is a skill every game developer needs to master. Using the Factory Pattern can help you do that in a reliable and reusable fashion.

Chapter 8, Changing Object Behavior with the State Pattern, discusses handling object states, which can lead to a chaotic monolith code base that handles state machines and multiple states in a single class. The State pattern is a way to extract this code from the context class with the double benefit of encapsulating each state as an independent object.

Chapter 9, Designing Actors with the Command Pattern, explains that a method, or function, doesn't leave footprints when called, and this can be an issue. By turning requests into objects, we can store them in memory, store their parameters, pass them around, delay their execution, queue them, execute them in a specific order, and even undo them, and all that is possible using the Command pattern.

Chapter 10, Implementing AI with the Strategy Pattern, explains that using conditional statements to alter the behavior of your code based on specific parameters may not be scalable. The Strategy pattern proposes that, instead, we use objects called strategies that perform different behaviors and adapt the context in real time by passing these objects.

Chapter 11, Creating a Power-Up System with the Decorator Pattern, explores wrapping objects within objects, which is a common practice in programming. The Decorator pattern proposes that we can wrap objects within objects of the same type, allowing us to add new functionalities to them in real time. With this in mind, we create an interesting power-up system for our project, wrapping objects with power-ups.

Chapter 12, Cross-Fading Transitions with the Service Locator Pattern, discusses one way to protect our code from coupling, which is by using a mediator object as an interface to interact with other parts of the game. The Service Locator pattern allows us to perform procedures, such as changing the game music, without leaking implementation and maintenance details on user classes.

Chapter 13, Improving Game Feel with the Event Queue Pattern, explores situations when we need to store events such as keystrokes to be handled in the future. An example is checking whether the player has jumped while in mid-air in the last few milliseconds so that the character performs a jump when they land on the ground. We can achieve this kind of functionality with the Event Queue Pattern.

To get the most out of this book

In order to fully engage with the exercises and examples provided in this book, you will need to download and install Godot Engine 4.3. This version of the engine introduces key features and updates that are essential for understanding and implementing the techniques we cover. Whether you're new to Godot or have experience with earlier versions, it's important to work with version 4.3 to ensure compatibility with the projects and concepts discussed throughout the book.

You can easily download Godot Engine 4.3 from the official website at `godotengine.org`. The installation process is straightforward, and the engine is available for Windows, macOS, and Linux. Be sure to follow the instructions for your operating system, and once it is installed, familiarize yourself with the interface. By using the same tools and environment that we explore in this book, you will have the best learning experience and will be able to follow along with the code examples smoothly.

Software/hardware covered in the book	Operating system requirements
Godot Engine 4.3	Windows, macOS, or Linux

If you are using the digital version of this book, we advise you to type the code yourself or access the code from the book's GitHub repository (a link is available in the next section). Doing so will help you avoid any potential errors related to the copying and pasting of code.

Download the example code files

You can download the example code files for this book from GitHub at `https://github.com/PacktPublishing/Game-Development-Patterns-with-Godot-4`. If there's an update to the code, it will be updated in the GitHub repository.

We also have other code bundles from our rich catalog of books and videos available at `https://github.com/PacktPublishing/`. Check them out!

Conventions used

There are a number of text conventions used throughout this book.

`Code in text`: Indicates code words in text, database table names, folder names, filenames, file extensions, pathnames, dummy URLs, user input, and Twitter handles. Here is an example: "Add a new `AudioStreamPlayer` node as a child of the `BackgroundMusic` node."

A block of code is set as follows:

```
extends Area2D
class_name AmbienceArea2D
@export var background_music: AudioStream
var previous_background_music: AudioStream
```

Any command-line input or output is written as follows:

```
$ mkdir css
$ cd css
```

Bold: Indicates a new term, an important word, or words that you see onscreen. For instance, words in menus or dialog boxes appear in **bold**. Here is an example: "Then, drag and drop a piece of cool music to the **Background Music** property on the **Inspector**."

> **Tips or important notes**
> Appear like this.

Get in touch

Feedback from our readers is always welcome.

General feedback: If you have questions about any aspect of this book, email us at customercare@ packtpub.com and mention the book title in the subject of your message.

Errata: Although we have taken every care to ensure the accuracy of our content, mistakes do happen. If you have found a mistake in this book, we would be grateful if you would report this to us. Please visit www.packtpub.com/support/errata and fill in the form.

Piracy: If you come across any illegal copies of our works in any form on the internet, we would be grateful if you would provide us with the location address or website name. Please contact us at copyright@packt.com with a link to the material.

If you are interested in becoming an author: If there is a topic that you have expertise in and you are interested in either writing or contributing to a book, please visit authors.packtpub.com.

Subscribe to Game Dev Assembly Newsletter!

We are excited to introduce Game Dev Assembly, our brand-new newsletter dedicated to everything game development. Whether you're a programmer, designer, artist, animator, or studio lead, you'll get exclusive insights, industry trends, and expert tips to help you build better games and grow your skills. Sign up today and become part of a growing community of creators, innovators, and game changers. `https://packt.link/gamedev-newsletter`

Scan the QR code to join instantly!

Free Benefits with Your Book

This book comes with free benefits to support your learning. Activate them now for instant access (see the "*How to Unlock*" section for instructions).

Here's a quick overview of what you can instantly unlock with your purchase:

PDF and ePub Copies

Next-Gen Web-Based Reader

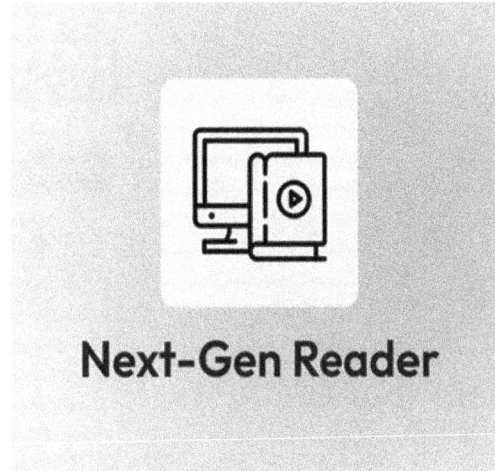

Access a DRM-free PDF copy of this book to read anywhere, on any device.

Use a DRM-free ePub version with your favorite e-reader.

Multi-device progress sync: Pick up where you left off, on any device.

Highlighting and notetaking: Capture ideas and turn reading into lasting knowledge.

Bookmarking: Save and revisit key sections whenever you need them.

Dark mode: Reduce eye strain by switching to dark or sepia themes

How to Unlock

Scan the QR code (or go to packtpub.com/unlock). Search for this book by name, confirm the edition, and then follow the steps on the page.

UNLOCK NOW

Note: Keep your invoice handy. Purchases made directly from Packt don't require one

Share Your Thoughts

Once you've read *Game Development Patterns with Godot 4*, we'd love to hear your thoughts! Scan the QR code below to go straight to the Amazon review page for this book and share your feedback.

https://packt.link/r/1835880290

Your review is important to us and the tech community and will help us make sure we're delivering excellent quality content.

Part 1: Object-Oriented Design Principles

Object-oriented programming is a programming paradigm with its own approach and way of thinking. To design systems using the tools that object-oriented programming offers, we need to understand what we have at our disposal and how to take the most out of it by following good principles. In this part, you will be introduced to the general philosophy behind programming, object-oriented programming, the four major instruments we use in object-oriented programming, the SOLID principles, and how to favor composition over inheritance and avoid misusing inheritance, a major critique that this paradigm receives from professionals across the industry.

This part includes the following chapters:

- *Chapter 1, Understanding Object-Oriented Design*
- *Chapter 2, Learning the Four Fundamental Pillars*
- *Chapter 3, Creating SOLID Design Solutions*
- *Chapter 4, Favoring Composition Over Inheritance*

1

Understanding Object-Oriented Design

Let's commence our journey by learning about what **Object-Oriented Programming (OOP)** is first because as we start implementing different patterns throughout the book, they will all approach the presented problems from an OOP perspective. For example, you will notice that the *State pattern* turns an object's states into other objects. The *Command pattern* turns an object's functions into objects. The Strategy pattern turns an object's logic branching into objects. So, it's important to understand what OOP is and why it is the main programming paradigm for developing games.

In this chapter, we will explore this paradigm from a unique standpoint that will help you understand it better and even approach programming and coding from a different perspective. We will approach it from the perspective of the philosophy of language. The reason for this is that as human beings, the way we solve problems is by structuring them using formal syntax to understand what each step of a proposed solution tries to achieve.

I am not going to teach the basics of programming as this would take a whole new book. Instead, we will understand how OOP helps us structure our thoughts.

In this chapter, we will cover the following topics:

- Learning the basics of OOP
- Complying with the principles of OOP
- Designing games with OOP
- Turning your design into an object in Godot Engine

Free Benefits with Your Book

Your purchase includes a free PDF copy of this book along with other exclusive benefits. Check the *Free Benefits with Your Book* section in the Preface to unlock them instantly and maximize your learning experience.

Technical requirements

Throughout this book, we will use the projects presented in the official repository. Each chapter has its distinct folder named after the chapter. Inside the chapter's folder, you will find two sub-folders:

- `start/`
- `final/`

To follow along with the chapter's instructions, use the project files available inside the `start` folder. You can use the files presented in the `final` folder as a reference in case you feel lost or get errors or bugs through the process of following the instructions. You can download the repository files at `https://github.com/PacktPublishing/Game-Development-Patterns-with-Godot-4`.

For this book, you will also need, of course, Godot Engine version 4.3 and beyond, which you can find at `https://godotengine.org/download/archive/4.3-stable/`.

On top of that, it's recommended that you have a computer with dedicated video drives due to Godot Engine's Vulkan render. All the projects are under the **Compatibility** render option, so it's not absolutely necessary that you have a dedicated GPU. You may follow along with any hardware that runs Godot Engine.

With that said, you have everything in place to get started with the amazing journey that will lead to having great tools in your game development toolkit, on top of knowledge about the best practices regarding game development architectures.

Learning the basics of OOP

When we talk about programming, we are trying to convey the idea of a structured formalization of a solution to a given problem. This is what an algorithm is, and to program is to be able to formalize such solutions in such a way that everyone can follow the steps and get the same result. In that sense, programming is almost a science. However, the philosophical aspect of this craft is that we work with how each individual approaches the problem. Drawing from their own knowledge and experiences, they implement a variety of solutions, all of which can achieve the same goal.

The computer comes in to automate the implementation of the solutions that we created. Computers are pretty standard when it comes to reasoning, so they are perfect for following instructions as they won't pollute the solution with subjective matters and will be as accurate as the instructions allow. Note that we are going to avoid the engineering aspects of computing here. I don't need you to understand computers, how they work, how electricity turns into bits, or any of these aspects. I want you to become an excellent problem solver who can look at a problem, think about a solution, and formalize it. Nonetheless, to code these solutions, you will need to write them in a language that the computer can understand, so keep that in mind. First, you must think about a solution from a human perspective, then translate it into code so the machine can understand and test it for you.

The main way to write your solution using a formalized programming language is to abstract everything as data and procedures that work with and change this data. In that sense, OOP is a paradigm that allows you to bundle these procedures and the data they work with into a single *super data type* that we call a **class**.

I want you to approach classes in the following way: they are how you describe how you would solve a given problem. They have the data that you think is necessary to approach the problem and how, mutating this data, you reach the solution. **Mutation** is just an OOP term for changing the value of a variable.

Once you have a class in place, you can test your solution. For that, we have **objects** that you can approach as instances of your solution that are put into different contexts. The fact is that each individual object is called an instance of a class, and to create a concrete instance of a class, you *instantiate* it.

When you create a class, you are establishing all the terms and conditions for how its data mutates. To that, we give the name of **behavior**, and for the data, **properties**. When objects are instantiated, they will always have the same behavior and properties, but the idea is that there will be different mutations depending on how they react to the context they were put into. This is how we put our solutions into context, test them against different scenarios to see how they will behave, and see whether we will get the results we desire.

Now, something interesting about OOP is that it allows us to reference these bundles of data and procedures in run time, which we can use to leverage previous solutions and focus on specific scenarios. For instance, one trademark of OOP is inheritance, whereby we can create a new class that extends the behavior and properties of a previous class. This allows you to create specialized solutions as opposed to generic ones.

More important than referencing a class is being able to reference objects. This allows us to make multiple solutions work together in some kind of assembly line where each one specializes in a very specific task and works together with other objects to solve complex problems.

You can think about objects as little robots that pass small and simple data between each other. In that sense, a program, application, or game is made of millions of robots working together with small, simple solutions to mutate data in specific ways and pass that data around. However, in the big picture, you have a complex emergent behavior that is what you would expect from your game. This is one thing to keep in mind when programming with OOP: it is always better to compose your application with many tiny solutions instead of big monolithic classes or deep hierarchies of inheritance. Just create numerous small, specialized robots and have them work together.

This ability to reference objects is especially useful when we start to abstract solutions into objects that other objects should use. It was through this approach that design patterns started to appear. To this relationship, we give the name of *user class*, or just *user*. It can also be described as when a given class uses another class in its behavior. For instance, the *Mediator pattern* is an object that specializes in turning one data structure into another. Two or more classes use them to mediate their data processing. It's usually used when your architecture relies on third-party solutions.

To summarize, OOP is a programming paradigm that helps you abstract your solutions into bundles of properties and behaviors that mutate data in specific ways and then pass it around, ultimately creating emergent behaviors. This paradigm is useful because it helps you break problems down into small solutions and build up complex behaviors by making objects work together.

With the basics of OOP in mind, let's move on with our journey. In the next section, we are going to talk about the fundamental principles of the OOP paradigm.

Complying with the principles of OOP

When it comes to OOP, things can get messy quickly. OOP is a powerful paradigm to work with that allows us to leverage our own code to increase productivity while developing software. As we will see throughout *Part 1*, especially in *Chapter 2*, working with OOP demands that we approach it with the correct mindset so we don't get side-tracked and end up with code that is inferior to what we would achieve with other paradigms.

We are going to see in *Chapter 2*, that OOP has four main tools to help us build good, reusable, and scalable code. When we get into *Chapter 3*, you will also learn that there are design principles to prevent some common issues that can hurt your code's base health. These will become second nature to you as you become more experienced. To be honest, once you understand what they mean and why it's important to follow them, you will see that they make a lot of sense and are actually pretty obvious.

However, I want to make sure that from the beginning, you are able to understand the overall approach to OOP and comply with the principles that we are going to see in the upcoming chapters. So, let's talk about how to get into the right mindset to create good code with OOP.

First of all, we are going to get into more detail about this principle in the next chapter, but keep in mind that **abstraction** is the mother of great design. Every other principle relies on the ability to properly abstract a problem into a solution that makes sense for its purpose. When we are designing, the actual programming, and therefore the coding, is the least significant (and honestly easiest) step. First, we need to *analyze* the problem we are trying to solve to understand what we need to get done and what is expected from the solution. We might even decide, through good analysis, that OOP might not be the best approach for a given system or part of our game.

Then, after analyzing and understanding the domain in which we are going to implement the solution, we actually design the solution. At this point, we can assume that we are going to use OOP, so we need to approach the problem from an OOP perspective. This means abstracting a solution into objects, as mentioned before. That means that we are going to have little robots that will process data and pass it around to other objects until we get to the system's goal. In that sense, it's of fundamental importance that we know how to ensure that each part of the system has just one responsibility so we know where to improve and where to focus when issues related to that problem appear. For that, I recommend studying *responsibility-driven design*. It's a design approach by Rebecca Wirfs-Brock that considers OOP from the perspective of *roles, responsibilities, and collaboration*.

Roles are a collection of related responsibilities. We usually approach roles as the "outside view" of what is expected from a system or the service it provides. A responsibility is an obligation that an object has to do or know something – in other words, its behavior and data. Finally, collaboration is exactly that: it describes how objects and roles interact. I highly recommend reading more about this design approach, as it helps us comply with one of the most important SOLID principles: the single-responsibility principle. You can find more about responsibility-driven design in the original book, *Object Design: Roles, Responsibilities, and Collaborations*, which is available on Amazon at `https://www.amazon.com.br/Object-Design-Roles-Responsibilities-Collaborations/dp/0201379430`.

Keep in mind that when we are designing objects, we are not trying to create a digital representation of, or mimic, a real-world object. I need to make this more evident; an object is simply a class put into context. In that sense, it is just a concrete instance of your solution to a problem that is fed with data. Don't try to create hierarchies of classes that mimic the real world for no reason. The *cow/cat/dog→mammal→animal* example, which is often used to explain hierarchies and inheritance, is the worst thing people have been teaching programmers. Class inheritance is about maintaining a given responsibility while specializing a class' behavior, or in other words, extending the class to specific contexts.

As I mentioned before, approach classes as solutions to a problem. Do you need to represent a cow? Then instead of making a `Cow` class, what about having a class to emit sounds, one to listen to sounds and react, one to eat that can be specialized further on into a class that specifically eats grass, one that ruminates, one that turns water and fat produced by the other classes into milk… and then combining them? This is also how you can comply with one of the most fundamental principles that we are going to talk about in *Chapter 4*.

This approach of breaking big problems into smaller ones is the best approach you can use to create good code bases. Once you have general small solutions, you can combine them and solve specific problems while keeping them generic enough to be used in other contexts, even within the same application (or game, in our case). For instance, look at how many nodes we have available in Godot Engine. We could definitely have a single class meant to represent a player that moves around and collides with things. However, isn't it more intuitive to break this down into a `CharacterBody2D` node, a `CollisionShape2D` node, a `Sprite2D` node, an `AnimationPlayer` node, and some `AudioStreamPlayer2D` nodes, and then combine these classes to build a class that, using these classes together, represents the player's avatar? This also allows us to create other objects with graphics using the same `Sprite2D` class. To have sounds in our game's levels, use the `AudioStreamPlayer2D` class. To have static and moving obstacles, use the same `CollisionShape2D` class to collide with the player, and so on.

See how tackling one problem at a time helps you tackle more problems by combining previous solutions? This is the power of complying with composition.

In the next section, we will put this to the test and design a new feature for our game. You will see that, besides being rigid and looking quite demanding, complying with these principles is more natural than you think, especially because we can rely on Godot Engine's design and features to help us use this approach and not get sidetracked unless we deliberately want to break these principles.

Designing games with OOP

It's time to put our knowledge into practice. In this section, we will design an object based on a prompt made by a fictional game designer. The goal is to understand the demands of the game designer, as well as to identify the data and behaviors that an object would need in order to fulfill the request.

OOP is especially useful in game development due to the intricate nature of games. When it comes to applications, other paradigms can often better fulfill the requirements. Think about it for a second. In many applications, as long as some data comes from the user's input and the application provides those users with the desired output, it's OK. The idea of maintaining and mutating states is unnecessary in most cases. Now, in games, it's important that objects are kept in memory and react to each state of the application. We can't simply render a page and wait for players to react to it. Games have a game loop, where everything is processed 30, 60, or more times per second. Things can react to each other in unpredictable ways. Games need mutations, in the sense that the same algorithm must react to different emergent contexts 30, 60, or more times per second. It's different from most applications, which can stay on standby without performing any processing while the user isn't interacting with them. So, for games, OOP is the most natural way to implement a given game design.

OOP aligns well with the nature of game development, which often involves creating complex, interactive systems that can evolve over time. The principles of OOP help manage this complexity and foster an environment where creative and technical requirements can be met more efficiently and effectively.

As we progress through this section, you will notice that most of the requirements are already available through Godot Engine's built-in features, but don't get caught up by the technical details of the solution. At this point, we will only focus on understanding the design process, especially the abstraction, which is the most fundamental aspect of any design process.

Now, I want you to imagine that you are the engineer of a game development studio. The lead game designer comes to you after playtesting the game's current iteration. They notice that it's lacking some visual feedback regarding the scoring when players pick up diamonds. This is their request:

"I see that when players collect diamonds, the diamonds disappear. However, we need to communicate visually that this is a positive action that leads the player closer to the level's goal."

"Picking up diamonds increases the player's score, but there is no visual cue to communicate that. We need to show text on the screen that displays the points a player gets when they perform an action. The text should pop up on the screen with a punchy animation at the very position of the object the player picked up, so they understand that the object and the points are directly correlated. After popping up, the text fades, disappearing from the screen. I think we can use the same feedback approach to communicate other messages to the player as well, such as maybe damage when we set the combat system, so I need to be able to directly change the text to any word, phrase, or number when I create it."

Note that this is an experienced designer, so there is a lot of good information in their prompt. First of all, they talk about something visual. This means that we are going to display something on the screen, meaning that this will require a position on the screen. The main feature is being able to display text. Therefore, our object needs a property to store this text so we can render it. They also mention a punchy pop-up animation, which makes me think that the object should appear on the screen like in videos where the subtitles appear, scaling up and then down quickly as if the words had appeared from somewhere deep within the screen. This makes me think that we will need to play with the animation's depth, and since we are talking about a 2D environment, this means playing with the object's scale. So, our object will need a scale as well. The final requirement is that it fades away at the end. This makes me think that we are going to play with the object's color to make it become transparent over time. So, this is the list of requirements that the object should have:

- It has a *position* and *scale*
- It displays *text*, so it may also need a *font*
- It has *color* with *alpha*
- It *animates* these properties to perform a *pop* animation
- User classes should be able to set the object's *text* and *position*
- User classes should be able to tell the object when to *pop*

Nice, these are the overall requisites of our object. This means that by fulfilling these, we can deliver them to our team's game designer and expect them to be satisfied. Now, how do we turn this into an object design?

Did you notice that we can clearly define that our object has some properties and does some actions? Everything the object has is its properties, meaning data. Everything the object does is its behavior – in other words, procedures it performs upon its data.

We start our object design by establishing its responsibility, which is to pop a text on the screen. Note that it doesn't need to access where this text comes from. It also doesn't need to know who is asking to pop it, or whether the text is positive or negative. It has a simple and single responsibility: it pops the text on the screen. This helps us keep it simple by establishing its boundaries on the system. Everything else regarding its behavior that is not related to popping the text on the screen should be provided by user classes, including the text content itself.

Why is this important? That's because this way, we can focus only on what matters for the scope of this object. In that sense, our object simply asks for the text it needs to display and where it should appear. This means our object has a single method that requires a string that will be the text displayed, and the position in which it should appear. The method's signature is the following:

```
func pop(text: String, position: Vector2) -> void: pass
```

Note that we didn't talk about any implementation details here. We don't know how it animates its properties, its parent class, or anything else. We just created an interface for user classes to request the object to perform its responsibility. This is how we usually abstract our classes. We think about how the user classes will communicate with this object, taking their perspective, or how they see the object from their point of view, into account. In that sense, they don't need to know how the popping happens.

Also, notice that this specific class doesn't return any data from its behavior, so we can simply say that this is a void method. Remember: here, objects are small robots that process data and pass it around. When an object's behavior doesn't output any data directly, we can say that it is on the tip of the system, accomplishing a high-level behavior. This is the ultimate abstraction level we expect to reach in our designs.

You will see, as we get deeper into complex topics, that objects will most commonly pass data around one to the other in low-level behaviors until they reach the point where the object performs the high-level behavior expected from the system itself. This is how responsibility-driven design helps us define and implement roles and collaborations.

Anyway, now that we have a good abstraction of our object, it's time to implement it in Godot Engine. We have seen, thus far, its essential properties and behaviors, and we have even created our first interface. In the next section, we will make the concrete implementation of this design using Godot Engine's built-in features.

Turning your design into an object in Godot Engine

After creating an interface for our class, we can dive into the implementation details. In this section, we will create a PopLabel object, which is an object that pops up on the screen displaying text and then fades away. If you have some experience with Godot Engine, you may already have some solutions in mind, right? However, let's follow the steps in this section to get the following results:

Figure 1.1 – Text popping up on the screen after the player collects diamonds

With the repository on your computer, open the project in the `01.understanding-object-oriented-programming/start/` folder and then follow these steps:

1. Create a new scene using a `Node2D` node as the root node. Remember, our object needs position, scale, and some way to change its alpha color, which the Node2D's `Modulate` property allows us to do.

2. Rename it to `PopLabel`, since ultimately we will use a `Label` node to display text.

    Properly naming your classes, objects, variables, methods, and so on is a fundamental skill we need to develop as programmers. The more information you can pass through names and the more accurate this information is, the better. Remember, you are writing down the solution to a problem, so people should be able to understand it by reading your code. Your code should be like prose. Readers should naturally read it and understand what's going on. If necessary, add comments to explain why you coded something in a given way, not what the code means.

3. Then, we will add a `Marker2D` node as a child of the `PopLabel` node and rename it to `PivotMarker2D`. This will work as the pivot for the `Label` node we are about to add. It will be through this node that we will animate some properties to perform the pop animation.

4. Speaking of animation, add an `AnimationPlayer` node as another child of the `PopLabel` node. We will use it to mutate the properties we need to perform the desired animation.

    This is an important topic to take notes on. Animations, in general, are a way of programming as well. So, especially if you don't need to access properties in run time to perform a behavior, and especially if the behavior is time-dependent, try to use animations instead of blocks of deterministic code.

5. Add a `Label` node as the child of `PivotMarker2D` node. This, of course, is the star of the show. It will be through this node that we will display the text and visually give the desired visual feedback.

6.   Finally, attach a script to the `PopLabel` node. Save the scene and the script as `res://Interface/PopLabel/PopLabel.tscn` and `res://Interface/PopLabel/PopLabel.gd`, respectively. After that, your scene's hierarchy should look like the following:

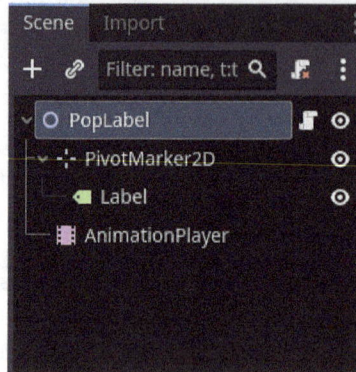

Figure 1.2 – The PopLabel node's scene node hierarchy

All right, we have everything we need to implement the requested object. Now, let's implement its behavior. For that, we will use `AnimationPlayer` to create the base animation that will pop the object on the screen and fade it. For that, let's follow these steps:

1.   Select `AnimationPlayer` and create a new animation called `pop`.

2.   Set the animation's length, in seconds, to `0.4`.

3.   Set the PivotMarker2D's scale to `0.0` on both the *x*- and *y*-axes and then add a key for this property.

4.   Set the key's **Easing** option to **Ease Out**, as shown in the following figure:

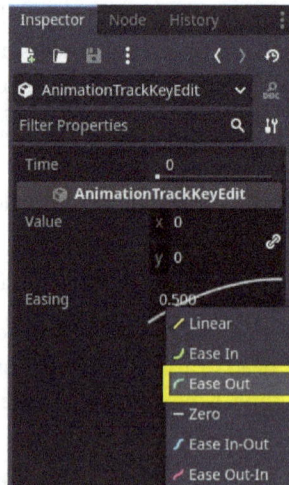

Figure 1.3 – PivotMarker2D's Scale key Easing option set to Ease Out

5. Move the animation's timeline cursor to 0.03 seconds, then set the **Scale** property of **PivotMarker2D** to 1.5 on both axes and add another key to the property's track.

6. Move the animation's timeline cursor to 0.05, then set the **scale** property of **PivotMarker2D** to 1.0 on both axes and add another key to the property's track.

At this point, we have the pop animation ready! Play the animation and see how this goes. Now, it's time to make it fade away and disappear. Let's continue the animation:

1. Move the animation's timeline cursor to 0.2, then set the **position** of **PivotMarker2D** to 0.0 on both axes and add a key to this property's track.

2. Then, set the **Modulate** property of **PivotMarker2D** to fully opaque white, in other words, 255 on all the properties in the RGBA format, or ffffff in hexadecimal format. This is shown in the following figure:

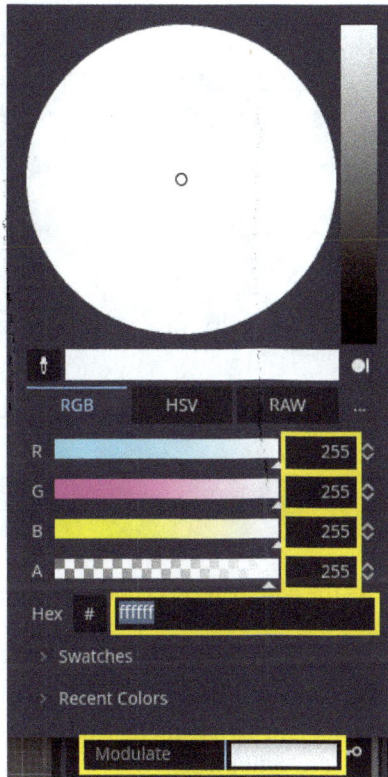

Figure 1.4 – PivotMarker2D's Modulate Color settings

3. Add a new key to the **modulate** property track of **PivotMarker2D**.

4. Move the animation's timeline cursor to 0.4 seconds.

5. Set the **Position** property of **PivotMarker2D** to -192 in the *y*-axis and add a new key to this property's track.

6. Set **PivotMarker2D**'s **Modulate** property **Color** value to a completely transparent white. In other words, set the alpha to 0 or the hexadecimal code to ffffff00, then add a new key to this property's track.

7. Now, add a new **Call Method** track for the **PopLabel** node and create a new key calling the queue_free() method. This will completely free the **PopLabel** node from memory after the animation finishes. See how powerful the Godot Engine's animation system is? We can even call methods using it, so it allows us to create really complex behaviors for our objects, all without writing a single line of code, but still programming.

Your animation timeline settings should be like the one in the following figure at this point:

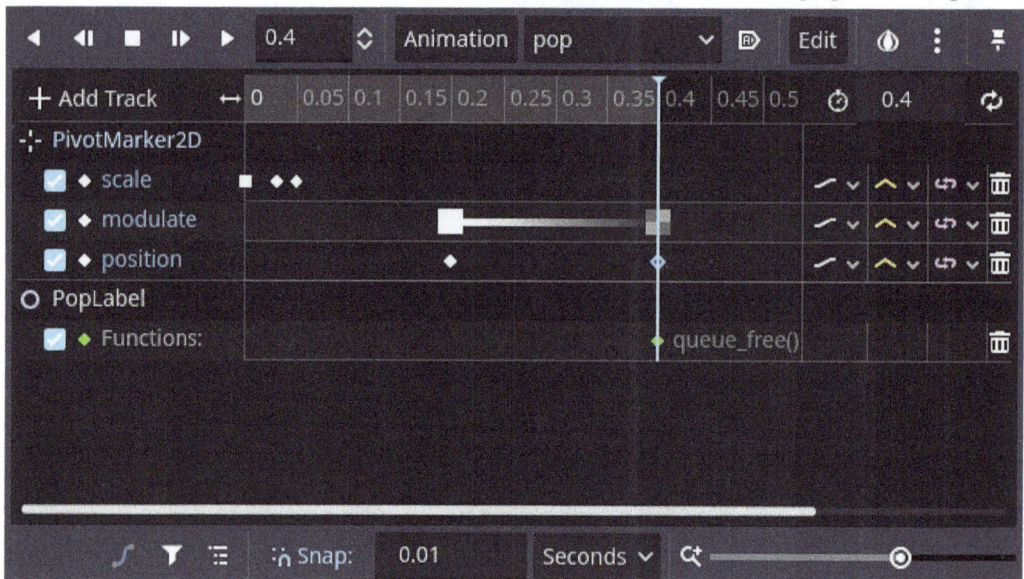

Figure 1.5 – The pop animation's tracks and keys

Now that we have the main behavior in place, it's time to allow user classes to pass the **PopLabel** node the proper data it needs to display the text at the desired position in the game. Open the res:// Interface/PopLabel/PopLabel.gd script and make the concrete implementation of the pop() method. For that, follow these instructions:

1. Create an @onready variable to store a reference to the AnimationPlayer node:

    ```
    extends Node2D
    @onready var animation_player := $AnimationPlayer
    ```

2. Create another `@onready` variable to store a reference to the `Label` node:

    ```
    extends Node2D
    @onready var animation_player := $AnimationPlayer
    @onready var label := $PivotMarker2D/Label
    ```

3. Create a function named `pop()`. As mentioned before, its contract requires that the user class passes `text` and `pop_position` as arguments and it won't return anything. The function signature is the following:

    ```
    func pop(text: String, pop_position: Vector2) -> void:
    ```

4. Then, inside the function, let's set `global_position` of **PopLabel** to `pop_position`:

    ```
    func pop(text: String, pop_position: Vector2) -> void:
        global_position = pop_position
    ```

5. After that, we set the `label.text` property to the `text` argument that the `pop()` method received:

    ```
    func pop(text: String, pop_position: Vector2) -> void:
        global_position = pop_position
        label.text = text
    ```

6. Finally, we play the pop animation on `animation_player`:

    ```
    func pop(text: String, pop_position: Vector2) -> void:
        global_position = pop_position
        label.text = text
        animation_player.play("pop")
    ```

With that, our `PopLabel` class is done! Now, you might be asking yourself whether it does what it proposes, right? We are confident that it does, so let's use it! When I say *use it*, I mean creating a user class! For that, open the `res://Objects/Diamond/Diamond.gd` script and make some changes so it instantiates a `PopLabel` node when the player interacts with it. For that, we will do the following:

1. Create an `@export` variable that will preload the `PopLabel` scene file:

    ```
    extends RigidBody2D

    @export var pop_label_scene = preload("res://Interface/PopLabel.
    tscn)
    ```

2. Then, create another `@export` variable to allow us to set the `Diamond` object's score amount. This represents the points the players will get by picking up this `Diamond` object:

    ```
    extends RigidBody2D

    @export var pop_label_scene = preload("res://Interface/PopLabel.
    tscn)
    @export var score = 175
    ```

3. Then, inside the `_on_interactive_area_2d_interaction_available()` callback, before calling the `queue_free()` method, we will create an instance of the `PopLabel` scene:

    ```
    func _on_interactive_area_2d_interaction_available():
        var pop_label = pop_label_scene.instantiate()
    ```

4. In Godot Engine, nodes are only processed if we add them to the `SceneTree` object, and to do that, we need to add the node as a child of another node. Since the `Diamond` object will be freed upon interacting with the player, we can't add the `PopLabel` node as its child. So, let's find the `Level` node and add a `PopLabel` instance as its child instead:

    ```
    func _on_interactive_area_2d_interaction_available():
        var pop_label = pop_label_scene.instantiate()
        find_parent("Level").find_child("PopLabels").add_child
        (pop_label)
    ```

> **Note**
>
> Adding a node based on physics events, such as detecting overlapping areas like we are doing, may cause Godot to throw a 'Can't change this state while flushing queries' error. If this causes any issues, use `call_deferred("add_child", pop_label)` as suggested by the console.

5. Now that the `pop_label` instance is being processed, we can call its `pop()` method. For that, we will pass the `score` variable converting it to a string type using the `str()` method, then for the second argument, we will use the `Diamond global_position` property so the `PopLabel` appears on top of it.

    ```
    func _on_interactive_area_2d_interaction_available():
        var pop_label = pop_label_scene.instantiate()
        find_parent("Level").find_child("PopLabels").add_child
        (pop_label)
        pop_label.pop(str(score), global_position)
    ```

6. Finally, we can call the `queue_free()` method to free the `Diamond` object from memory when the player interacts with it:

```
func _on_interactive_area_2d_interaction_available():
    var pop_label = pop_label_scene.instantiate()
    find_parent("Level").find_child("PopLabels").add_child
    (pop_label)
    pop_label.pop(str(score), global_position)
    queue_free()
```

That is it! If you playtest the `res://Levels/Level.tscn` scene, you will see that when the player collects the `Diamond` objects, a `PopLabel` node pops on the screen right on top of the `Diamond` object displaying the amount of points the player got by picking up the `Diamond` object. So, we have successfully designed and implemented an object using Godot Engine's built-in features.

Note that by doing this, we applied the principles of OOP, especially abstraction, inheritance, and encapsulation. Be proud of yourself.

Summary

In this chapter, we learned that OOP is foundational to understanding and applying the design patterns that will be discussed throughout this book. With a unique approach from a philosophy of language perspective, this paradigm is emphasized as crucial for structuring solutions to problems in a way that aligns with human problem-solving processes. The essence of OOP allows us to abstract our solutions into classes, where each class is a blueprint of how to solve a problem, including the necessary data and the methods to manipulate this data. This abstraction enables us to think about solutions in a more structured way, making it easier to test these solutions in various contexts by creating instances (or objects) of these classes.

Furthermore, the chapter delved into the basics of OOP, stressing the importance of understanding programming as a structured formalization of solutions to problems. By treating classes as *super data types* that encapsulate both data and the procedures to operate on this data, OOP allows for a powerful way of organizing and structuring code, as we learned in this chapter. Then, we also saw how we can use the concepts of OOP as a framework to abstract the required features that our team may demand from us. We saw how a designer may communicate a demand, as well as how we can turn this demand into an abstract set of data and procedures that we can turn into a class, and further, into an object.

With the system rules in place, we saw how to turn our abstraction into an actual class in Godot Engine using GDScript. We saw how we can implement properties and methods, as well as how we can instance and reference an object.

In the next chapter, we will delve into the details of each of the four pillars that comprise the core features of OOP: abstraction, inheritance, polymorphism, and encapsulation. These are the fundamental principles to keep in mind when designing and implementing OOP solutions. So, get ready to sharpen your skills!

Get This Book's PDF Version and Exclusive Extras

UNLOCK NOW

Scan the QR code (or go to `packtpub.com/unlock`). Search for this book by name, confirm the edition, and then follow the steps on the page.

Note: Keep your invoice handy. Purchases made directly from Packt don't require an invoice.

2

Learning the Four Fundamental Pillars

Now that you understand what object-oriented design and **Object-Oriented Programming** (OOP) are, and what the approach we are taking toward them is, it is time to present the four fundamental pillars that allow us to design and implement OOP solutions to you.

In this chapter, we will understand why abstraction is the very core of design and how to create good abstractions so you can focus on the class goal instead of wasting time and energy thinking about implementation details.

We will also see how encapsulation walks hand-in-hand with abstraction by preventing user classes from accessing implementation details on the designed class. Furthermore, we'll see why we should also prevent user classes from directly making mutations on the class.

Then, we will talk about inheritance, a topic that causes the most heated debates about OOP. Inheritance is both OOP's core feature and its nemesis unless you understand its underlying principles and learn how to use it properly.

Finally, we will learn polymorphism, which is, in my opinion, the most powerful of the four pillars. With polymorphism, you learn how to override class behaviors while maintaining their compatibility with user classes. It goes hand-in-hand with inheritance, so it's important to lay the foundation with inheritance first so we can make the most out of polymorphism.

Throughout this chapter, we will implement each of the four fundamental pillars of OOP to create the design of a new class for our project. By the end of the chapter, we will have created an extended version of a crate object that has a chance to drop diamond objects. Let's get started!

In this chapter, we will be covering the following topics:

- Simplifying complex systems with abstraction

- Scoping properties and method with encapsulation

- Extending an object's behaviors with inheritance

- Maintaining compatibility with polymorphism

Technical requirements

To follow along with the chapter's instructions, use the project files available inside the `start/` folder of the `02.learning-the-four-fundamental-pillars/` project. You can use the files presented in the `final/` folder as a reference in case you feel lost or get errors or bugs through the process of following the instructions. If you didn't get the repository yet, download the repository files from the following link: `https://github.com/PacktPublishing/Game-Development-Patterns-with-Godot-4`.

That said, let's start with understanding how we can use abstraction to simplify the concepts we are working with in our projects.

Simplifying complex systems with abstraction

Abstraction is unarguably the most fundamental skill anyone in any design area must develop. It is through abstraction that you identify the relevant aspects of the application, or in our case, the game. It's especially by using good abstractions that we design good classes by understanding what should be exposed and what should be hidden from user classes and other peers on the team.

For instance, when we are making a game project in Godot Engine, the actual implementation details in C++ of each feature, node, or class are not relevant. What matters the most is what is exposed to us by the Godot Engine's API. Another example is shaders. It's not important to know how a GPU works on a hardware level in terms of how electricity turns into graphics, but rather, what is available through a shaders API so we can create nice-looking visual effects for our games.

Abstraction is about knowing the goal of the class and what people will use it for. Another example is a remote control that simply turns a TV on and off. Do we need to expose the entire hardware and how the electronic components work together until a signal is emitted and turns on or off the TV? Or should we create an interface with a button that, once pressed, toggles the TV on and off? The answer is clear, right? This is the same with abstraction. We are always thinking about how the class will be used and how we can create a nice and intuitive interface to allow other classes to interact with the one we are designing.

That said, let's put that into practice. Consider the following scenario: your team's game designer has discovered that breaking crates lacks positive incentives if players don't get anything in return. As a solution, he suggests introducing a new crate type, known as a loot crate, which can contain diamonds. However, he cautions against always guaranteeing diamond drops, as this may lead to predictable rewards. Instead, he advocates for an intermittent reinforcement approach, where diamonds may or may not drop based on chance. He emphasizes the importance of being able to adjust this chance, particularly for scenarios such as treasure rooms, where crates may have a higher chance of diamond drops. On top of that, he mentions the possibility of introducing additional rewards beyond diamonds as the game progresses.

Now, to abstract that, we can point out three main things:

- The proposed object is a `Crate`
- It drops an item
- It needs a property to define the drop rate

So, in this abstraction, we can say that this object will extend the functionalities of the `Crate` object. It will need a method that will be responsible for creating an instance of an item in the game world only if the player is lucky. So, we can say that this object needs a `drop_rate` property that determines the chance of dropping the item. We also need a property to store which item it will drop; we can call it `loot`. Finally, we also need a method that we can call to execute this behavior. We can call it `drop()`. Our `LootCrate` object design will look as follows:

```
extends Crate

@export var loot_scene
@export_range(0.0, 1.0) var drop_rate

func drop():
    pass
```

Notice that we don't go into the intricacies of how it will calculate the player's luck, or how it will actually instantiate `loot_scene`. At this point, there's no technical implementation detail. We just made a rough sketch of what this class will look like in order to fulfill its purpose. This means that, if the game designer decides to use this class, they will be able to change `loot_scene` and instantiate other items. They will be able to change `drop_rate` to whatever they want, where `0.0` is no chance to drop and `1.0` is a 100% chance to drop the item. They can even tell when the drop happens by calling the `drop()` method.

This is what is most important when designing a class: to ensure that it fulfills its purpose. The abstraction helps us understand what is and isn't important for the fulfillment of the class' purpose. Ideally, by doing good abstractions, we would reach out to the person who requested the feature and ask them whether the abstraction accomplishes the need, as well as whether they will be able to use it on their own. Then, with their approval, we follow with the actual implementation of the class.

Up until now, we have reinforced the most important principle of any programming paradigm, especially OOP. We saw that abstraction helps us create good interfaces for users so they can accomplish their goals with the class. We saw that with a good abstraction, we don't need to care about implementation details, but rather focus on what matters the most, which is to create a good backbone structure for the class so that we and others can understand what it does and how to use it.

Now, imagine that the game designer approved the interface you created for the `LootCrate` object but requests how they can quickly test the `LootCrate` object behavior if the only current way to break a crate is when it gets hit by the player's avatar. We are going to see how we can use encapsulation not only as a principle to prevent undesired or unintended mutations in a class but also as a tool to create good and quick tests in the next section.

Scoping properties and methods with encapsulation

Encapsulation is another fundamental principle that will help us design scalable and easier-to-maintain classes. I prefer to define encapsulation as similar to abstraction but with a greater emphasis on safeguarding the internal state of the object. Image a medicine capsule. It has a bunch of chemical components that accomplish a given goal. We take a cup of water and swallow the capsule. The capsule will do its job once it is inside our body and all its components will perform their purposes. However, for us, the capsule is a single thing. We just call it a "capsule of", followed by its name. We don't list all its components. This analogy illustrates a practical approach to encapsulation. However, I'll provide a more detailed definition to ensure clarity.

The idea of encapsulation is to protect the object's internal states from user classes and expose only the necessary properties and methods to allow the object to do its job. In many languages, several features allow the programmer to implement levels of access to their object. One of them is the idea of private properties and methods. Such ability would allow the programmer to implement necessary variables, auxiliary functions, and other member data that would allow the object to perform its designed behavior while only exposing the properties and methods established by the abstraction made earlier. With encapsulation, we are preventing the implementation details from leaking outside the class and messing with the object's interface.

Now, in GDScript, the concept of private variables or methods doesn't exist. I particularly love that, because it allows us to come up with creative ways to work around this limitation while also maintaining the freedom to have everything publicly available for other classes to use if the user decides to take the risk. There is a way to control how mutations will impact a class, though.

GDScript offers the ability to use setter and getter methods to create routines that happen when a variable is accessed. Previously, in Godot Engine version 3.x.x, this would allow the class to dictate how interactions from user classes impact its states while allowing the class itself to bypass the setter and getter routines and manipulate the class mutations freely. This allowed us to create *pseudo-private* variables by using the `setget` features together with the `assert` features and ultimately prevent user classes from accessing said variables.

In Godot Engine 4.x.x, this changed. By using the setter and getter features, the very class itself will also trigger the setter and getter routines, so we can't implement private or protected features to our variables. Nonetheless, the ability to use setters and getters still allows us to create routines for accessing variables, which gives us control over the mutations expected within the class' scope. For instance, let's say that we want a `String` variable to only accept `String` variables that don't contain numbers and are eight characters long at most. In that case, we can do the following:

```
var example_string := "mystring":
    set(value):
        var regex = RegEx.new()
        regex.compile("\\d")
        assert(value.length() < 9 and
        regex.search(value) == null
```

Note that this is an aggressive approach to prevent your team or anyone using this class from mutating `example_string` out of these boundaries. However, you may want to approach it defensively by throwing a warning message and not assigning the new value to the variable. Yes, when you use setters, you can control whether the variable will or won't accept the mutation. In the case of a getter, you can control how it will handle the access to the variable's value. For instance, the following code will throw warning messages and won't assign the value to the variable if the new value is over eight characters long or has numbers. Otherwise, it will assign the value to the variable:

```
var example_string := "test":
    set(value):
        var regex = RegEx.new()
        regex.compile("\\d")
        if value.length() > 8:
            push_warning("Value not assigned to `example_string`.
Avoid values beyond 8 characters long")
        elif not regex.search(value) == null:
            push_warning("Value not assigned to `example_string`.
Avoid using numbers")
        else:
            example_string = value
```

Personally, I don't like using setters or getters. They pollute the code and may create unnecessary restrictions on interactions between objects on top of adding extra layers of complexity to an object. When I think about people using my solutions, I don't know what exactly they want to achieve; restricting them may not be the best way to handle edge cases or unpredictable behaviors. Adding setter or getter procedures may mislead people. For instance, if I set the value of a variable, I don't expect that this will trigger anything other than changing the variable's value. Many people use setters and getters to emit signals when the value changes. It's a good use case, but still, I would avoid that.

1. Encapsulation is all about maintaining boundaries between object interactions, which will lead to decoupling and further healthy and maintainable code. It's about making objects interact in a controlled manner and preventing user classes from knowing more than they need about the object. A practical example in the `Crate` class is how other classes assume they should interact with the `Crate.health` property. Since there is no method exposed to dictate the designed interactions with the `Crate` class, users may assume they can set the `health` property to whatever value they want. Not only that but they can assume that `Crate` class will still behave properly, for example, shattering when its `health` value goes below 1. However, this is not true. So, let's refactor this class by following these steps. First, you've got to open the `res://Objects/Crate/Crate.gd` script. Then you can do the following:

2. Create an interface so user classes can interact with the `Crate` class' `health` property. First of all, the main interaction is to damage the `Crate` instance, so let's create a `damage()` method that receives _damage that represents the amount of damage caused to the `Crate` instance:

```
func damage(_damage: int) -> void:
```

3. Then, let's extract the logic inside the `_on_hurt_box_2d_hurt()` callback to the `damage()` method and call the `damage()` method, passing the _damage value passed via the `_on_hurt_box_2d_hurt()` callback as argument:

```
func _on_hurt_box_2d_hurt(_damage: int) -> void:
    damage(_damage)
func damage(_damage: int) -> void:
    health -= _damage
    if health < 1:
        broke.emit()
        animation_player.play("break")
    else:
        animation_player.play("hit")
```

4. Note that we may want to shatter an instance of the `Crate` class without necessarily applying damage. A use case for that is when a `Bomb` object explodes, it may deal 1 damage to the player, but shatter `Crate` instances. Another use case is in a cutscene if we want a `Crate` instance to shatter. So, let's create a `shatter()` method and extract this behavior from the `damage()` method:

```
func damage(_damage: int) -> void:
    health -= _damage
    if health < 1:
        shatter()
    else:
```

```
            animation_player.play("hit")
func shatter():
    broke.emit()
    animation_player.play("break")
```

Note that now, we have given a name to a procedure that otherwise was just a sequence of steps that people could assume would perform a shattering behavior. Remember: we are trying to create code that people will read, understand, and reuse. So, giving names to procedures is one of the best ways to communicate your solution to your peers. It's similar to the way that giving names to feelings helps you communicate them and create strategies to deal with them.

In this section, we saw that encapsulation is a fundamental concept to create good object designs. Conceptually, encapsulation is like a layer that we create to shield the object's internal state from undesired or unintended interactions. Good encapsulation is like a medicine capsule: from the outside it is simple, and its purpose is obvious. Its insides are hidden behind an intuitive interface. We also saw how to apply encapsulation using GDScript in Godot Engine. We learned that private properties and methods are not supported, and that we can apply encapsulation using high-level abstractions to create clear boundaries that lay out the intended interactions for our object. We also saw how to use setters and getters to trigger routines when accessing and changing a variable's value. With that in mind, let's learn about one of the most controversial aspects of OOP: inheritance.

Extending an object's behaviors with inheritance

Here we are at our discussion of one of the core features of OOP. The ability to reference and implement a class by simply inheriting its behaviors and properties is what we'll be talking about here. Loved by few, criticized by many, inheritance is usually what comes to developers' minds when we talk about OOP, even though this paradigm is more about bundling data and procedures into the same data structure. Inheritance is the trademark feature of OOP.

One of the main critiques of inheritance is that, by definition, it creates a hard coupling between classes, namely the super-class and the subclass (or parent class and child class, or general class and specialized class). Usually, people are against coupling classes because it makes it harder to maintain them once the project starts to scale. A simple change in a class may break its user classes' code. This can be mitigated with good interfaces. Again, abstraction and encapsulation play a core role in this process. However, it's still difficult to have perfectly decoupled classes in any project. Let's learn about what inheritance really is so we know when and how to use it.

Inheritance is a mechanism that allows a new class, usually called a subclass or child class, to implement properties and behaviors from an existing class, usually referred to as a super- or parent class. This means that the subclass can reuse existing code and functionalities from the superclass by simply extending it. It doesn't need to explicitly import or make reference to it as an object instance in order to use its code. Ultimately, a subclass is a user class of its superclass with one major issue: by inheriting a class, the subclass gains access to all the implementation details of its superclass, completely breaking the purpose of encapsulation. For instance, in most languages, it can access private and protected variables and methods and can bypass setter and getter routines. Do you see where all the concerns come from?

The main tip I can give regarding inheritance is to avoid mimicking real-world hierarchies. Things such as the "cat, dog, cow, mammal, animal" example that people usually abuse to teach inheritance are to be avoided. The "job, rogue, warrior, mage" or "car, bus, truck, vehicle" examples should also be avoided. Don't fall into this trap. It's very tempting to think that this is a good approach to inheritance. Instead, think about it from the perspective of generalization and specialization. Think about it this way: we stand on the shoulders of giants. In order to accomplish specific tasks, we need to solve generic problems. For instance, in order to render a sprite on the screen, we need to first be able to tell where it should render, as well as its scale and rotation. Then we can think about how to render and modulate an image.

Something people usually do wrong when designing classes is to use inheritance as a starting point, but I want to suggest that you use it as a refactoring technique whenever possible. With that, I mean that you should create a class solving a specific problem. Then, when you need to solve another specific problem that can take advantage of some of the solutions you implemented in the first problem, you create a generic class that both inherit from. This way, only the necessary code is shared between the subclasses and we can keep their responsibilities self-contained in their own code as much as possible.

When done right, inheritance is a powerful tool to create good interfaces as well, especially when allied with polymorphism, which we are going to talk about in the next section. In fact, inheritance is imperative for most design patterns, especially the ones presented in this book. This is true to such an extent that it's part of the very definition of some design patterns, such as the Strategy Pattern.

We are going to see, in *Chapter 3*, that a good superclass is open for extension, or specialization, but closed for modification. This means that after a class goes into production, the best way to implement new features is to create subclasses that will extend its behavior. This is exactly what we do in Godot Engine, for instance, by extending nodes to implement the specific behaviors we need them to perform in our games while relying on their general implementations offered by the engine's API.

Another principle related to inheritance and its core to follow, to the point it is enforced in most languages, is the *Liskov Substitution Principle*. We will talk more about it in *Chapter 3*, but know that this principle is all about avoiding compatibility breaks with the superclass user classes, also known as client classes. This principle is more related to polymorphism, but since polymorphism is tightly related to inheritance, it is also important to understand that you should never change the contract made by the superclass. A contract is essentially what the class demands and offers in its relationships with other classes, for instance, the class' function signatures. If the superclass states that it needs a set of arguments of a specific type in order to perform its behavior and will output data of a specific type, the subclass cannot change this contract by any means. It can ask for more generic types as arguments and return more specialized types, but never the other way around. This is important to keep in mind, especially when creating interfaces for your classes.

In Godot Engine, inheritance is natural. The engine's design itself relies on and leverages object-oriented design. For instance, you can not only inherit, or rather, extend a class in GDScript but you can also create what are called *Inherited Scenes*. These are fundamentally sub-scenes of a super-scene, or specialized scenes from a generic scene. Conceptually, it's the same thing as inheriting a class with code. This is exactly what we are going to use to create `LootCrate` class, so get ready and follow these steps:

1. From the editor's top menu, go to **Scene | New Inherited Scene**. From the open base scene menu, choose the `res://Objects/Crate/Crate.tscn` scene. A new scene will be created with the same structure as the `Crate` scene.

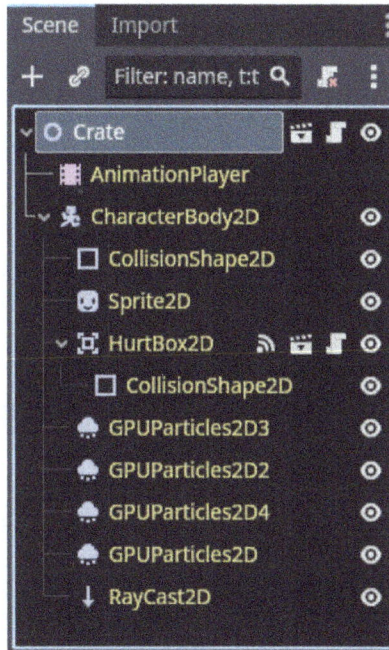

Figure 2.1 – The scene hierarchy of the new scene inherited from the Crate scene

2. Save this new scene as `res://Objects/Crate/LootCrate/LootCrate.tscn`.

3.   Right-click on the root node. From the drop-down menu, select the **Extend Script…** option.

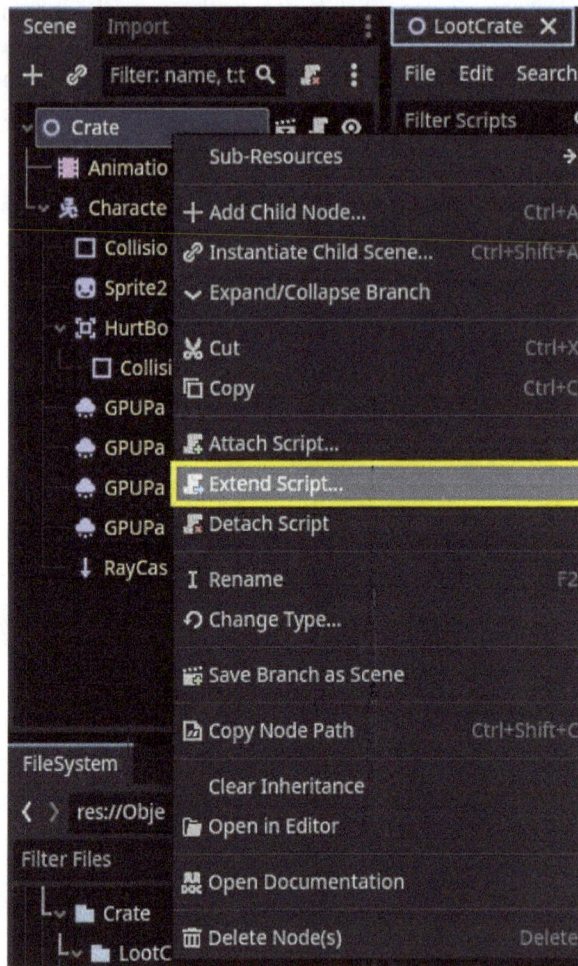

Figure 2.2 – The Extend Script option from the node's drop-down menu

4.   Now, it's time to implement our abstraction. So, let's create an exported variable that represents the scene of the loot item. We will call it `loot_scene`; by default, it will preload the `Diamond` scene:

```
extends "res://Objects/Crate/Crate.gd"

@export var loot_scene := preload("res://Objects/Diamond/
Diamond.tscn")
```

5. We will also export a variable to represent the drop rate. Here, we will use a special version of the `@export` annotation so that we can limit the variable's value range between `0.0` and `1.0`. By default, it will be `0.3`:

```
extends "res://Objects/Crate/Crate.gd"

@export var loot_scene := preload("res://Objects/Diamond/
Diamond.tscn")
@export_range(0.0, 1.0) var drop_rate := 0.3
```

6. Now, it's time to implement its main behavior: to drop loot. Let's implement the `drop()` method we've established in the abstraction stage. The first thing we are going to do inside this method is randomize a number between `0.0` and `1.0` to represent the player's luck with this specific `LootCrate` instance:

```
func drop() -> void:
    var luck := randf()
```

7. Then, we need to check whether the luck is enough to trigger the loot. So, if the player's luck is greater than the `drop_rate` value, we will create an instance of the `Diamond` scene and add it as a child of the level's `Diamond` nodes. Here, we set `global_position` of `Diamond` node to match `global_position` of `LootCrate` node so `Diamond` object looks like it was inside `LootCrate` object:

```
func drop() -> void:
    var luck := randf()

    if luck >= drop_rate:
        var loot: Node2D = loot_scene.instantiate()
        loot.global_position = global_position
        find_parent("Level").find_child("Diamonds")
            .add_child(loot)
```

8. With that, it's done. The final step is to save this script as `res://Objects/Crate/LootCrate/LootCrate.gd`.

    The complete `LootCrate` class' script should look like this by the end of these steps:

```
extends "res://Objects/Crate/Crate.gd"

@export var loot_scene := preload("res://Objects/Diamond/
Diamond.tscn")
@export_range(0.0, 1.0) var drop_rate := 0.3
func drop() -> void:
    var luck := randf()
```

```
    if luck >= drop_rate:
        var loot: Node2D = loot_scene.instantiate()
        loot.global_position = global_position
        find_parent("Level").find_child("Diamonds")
          .add_child(loot)
func shatter():
    drop()
    super()
```

Notice that, at the top of the script, we have the `extends` keyword followed by a string containing the path to the `Crate` object's script file. This is one way that GDScript implements inheritance. You just need to use the `extends` keyword, followed by a string with a path pointing to the file of the class you want this new class to inherit from. An alternative for that is to use the `extends` keyword followed by the class' name. For that, in the referred class, you need to use the `class_name` keyword followed by a unique name. Just as an example, we could do the following in the `Crate` class:

```
class_name Crate
extends Node2D
```

Then, in the `LootCrate` script, we could do the following:

```
extends Crate
```

In this section, we learned that inheritance is another fundamental concept in OOP. It allows subclasses to inherit properties and behaviors from superclasses, promoting code reuse and hierarchy in class relationships. Although there are critics for creating tight coupling between classes using inheritance, inheritance remains fundamental for extending and specializing classes.

With inheritance, subclasses can access and expand on the functionalities of superclasses without explicit object references. However, it can also lead to challenges such as breaking encapsulation, whereby subclasses gain access to superclass implementation details. It's essential to use inheritance wisely, avoiding mirroring real-world hierarchies and focusing on abstraction and specialization. By employing inheritance as a refactoring tool and creating subclasses when needed, we can maintain flexible and self-contained class structures. Additionally, inheritance is integral to design patterns and ensures compatibility with superclass clients.

With that, we have our `LootCrate` class main behavior implemented and ready to be used. Any user class that wants `LootCrate` nodes to drop its loot just needs to call the `drop ()` method. It's a very simple interface. However, there's a small problem. Ideally, `LootCrate` node drops its loot on its own when its shatter behavior occurs. The `LootCrate` node shatters, and then it drops its loot. So, what are we going to do about that? Will there be a user class that will be constantly monitoring `LootCrate` class so that when it shatters, that class will also call its method? That makes no sense, right? The `LootCrate` class inherits the `Crate` class, which is the one that has the `shatter ()` method, so the very `LootCrate` class itself has everything it needs to perform its behavior. However, how are we going to trigger the `drop ()` method together with the `shatter ()` method?

Here comes one of those instances where we need to maintain the superclass' contract with its user classes in the subclass. Every user class of `Crate` class should only call the `shatter()` method in order for `Crate` class to perform its intended behavior. So, the `LootCrate` class should only need its `drop()` method to be called in order for it to also perform its intended behavior to keep its contract with the `Crate` class user classes. Well, this is a typical problem that we can solve with polymorphism!

In the next section, we will explore how we can maintain subclasses' compatibility with their superclass' clients while adding or overriding the superclass' behavior.

Maintaining compatibility with polymorphism

As we saw in the previous section, we need to design subclasses such that they maintain the superclass' contract with its clients. For that, the subclasses must maintain the superclass interface, not only explicitly through the function signature and other technical details but also conceptually. A subclass must specialize its superclass. This means that it should do the same behavior as its superclass but for more specific contexts.

Polymorphism, in that sense, comes as a way to extend and even change superclass behavior while maintaining its interface. We usually do that through method overriding. Method overriding is a trademark of polymorphism. It simply means that the subclass can change the implementation details of its superclass methods. To do that, the subclass just needs to declare the method again, of course, maintaining the method's signature. After that, it needs to change the implementation completely.

We do that all the time in Godot Engine, for instance, overriding the virtual methods and callbacks. Examples include the `_ready()`, `_process()`, and `_input()` callbacks. It's a phenomenal feature if you think about it. The whole engine works using the node's interfaces to process their behavior, feeding them with a delta time, in the case of the `_process()` callback, or with `InputEvents` in the case of the `_input()` callback. All we have to do, as users of this interface, is override these methods and declare what will happen when the engine calls these methods, which it will since it was designed to do so. The engine itself has many user classes interacting with the node's interface and we can plug our own classes into these intricate interactions.

Ideally, we would use polymorphism with subclasses to leverage the superclass behaviors and user classes. However, as a side note, polymorphism is also the core of **duck typing**. Duck typing is a programming technique that avoids looking for specific objects or data types and instead focuses on features. It presumes that as long as an object has the methods and properties required, the program should run without any problems. In other words, "if it quacks like a duck and talks like a duck, then we can treat it like a duck," so to speak. Whether or not it is a duck is not relevant. Duck typing looks for what an object can do, especially in terms of its methods and interface, instead of what the object is in terms of its type or inheritance. This allows us to create objects that are from different types and inheritance hierarchies but still use them interchangeably in client classes. This is fundamental to understand when we start to apply the concepts of composition over inheritance. The idea is that we can dynamically change a component by changing the object's instance reference and make it point to a different component with a similar interface. By doing so, we can completely change an object's behavior at run time by simply mixing and matching new components. It's a programming technique that not many people experiment with, but it's at the core of some design patterns.

Since GDScript is a scripting language that has dynamic typing features at its core, we can do duck typing by using the has_*() methods. For instance, has_method() can be used to pass the name of the method we need. The following code is an example of duck typing:

```
func damage(object):
    if object.has_method("apply_damage")
        object.apply_damage(5)
```

With this approach, it doesn't matter what type the object is. As long as it has a method called apply_damage() that accepts an integer number as an argument, this will work. Another duck typing feature that is especially good to know about is the has_node() method. Since in Godot Engine, we are always composing objects with both built-in and custom nodes, it can be handy to check whether a given node has a specific composition so we can treat it properly. For instance, let's say that you have a menu. Some buttons of the menu emit particles when interacted with, some emit sounds, and some do both:

```
func button_interacted(button):
    if button.has_node("SoundEffect"):
        button.get_node("SoundEffect").play()
    if button.has_node("ParticleEffect"):
        button.get_node("ParticleEffect").emit()
```

Then, you just need to attach these components to the buttons based on what you want them to do.

As you can see, polymorphism essentially allows us to treat a range of objects using the same interface but getting different outcomes. This is especially useful for our LootCrate class since we want it to extend the Crate class behavior while also maintaining its interface. Well, let's see how we can do that. Open res://Objects/Crate/LootCrate/LootCrate.gd and follow these steps:

1. Declare the shatter() method from the Crate class in the LootCrate script:

    ```
    func shatter():
    ```

2. Now, instead of emitting the broke signal and playing the *break* animation, we will just call the drop() method. With that, when user classes call the shatter() method, it will trigger the drop() behavior:

    ```
    func shatter():
        drop()
    ```

3.   However, we don't want to change the `Crate` class shatter behavior. Instead, we want to extend it. So, for that, we need to also perform its procedure. We can implement its behavior manually again, but here, I want to present you with the `super()` keyword. By calling `super()`, we can perform the superclass' implementation of the method being overridden. Keep that in mind because the `super()` keyword is a fundamental polymorphism feature in GDScript:

```
func shatter():
    drop()
    super()
```

With that, we have our `LootCrate` class ready to be put to the test. For that, go to the `res://Levels/Level.tscn` scene and add some `LootCrate` instances as children of the `Crates` node. Then hit the **Run Current Scene** button and hit them with the player avatar's attack.

Figure 2.3 – LootCrate nodes dropping their loot after the player's avatar hits them until they shatter

In this section, we learned that maintaining compatibility with polymorphism is fundamental for subclasses to honor the agreements made by their superclasses with client classes. Polymorphism enables subclasses to adjust or expand superclass behaviors while keeping their interface intact, mainly through method overriding. This ability provides versatility in coding, allowing us to implement distinct behaviors while maintaining a unified interface. Making games with Godot Engine relies heavily on polymorphism, especially when it comes to overriding virtual methods and callbacks.

On top of that, polymorphism intersects with duck typing, whereby an object's suitability is assessed based on its behavior rather than its explicit type or inheritance. Duck typing promotes flexible and adaptable code structures, permitting objects of different types or hierarchies to be treated interchangeably if they fulfill necessary methods or behaviors. This approach aligns with the principles of composition over inheritance, enabling objects to dynamically alter behavior at runtime by swapping components. Through practical examples and code snippets, we saw how polymorphism and duck typing shape the design of classes such as `LootCrate` class, ensuring both compatibility and adaptability in object interactions.

Summary

In this chapter, we explored the four foundational pillars of OOP: abstraction, encapsulation, inheritance, and polymorphism. We illustrated their application through the development of a `LootCrate` class in a game project. Abstraction was highlighted as the essential process of simplifying complex systems, enabling us to focus on the relevant aspects of a class while hiding unnecessary details. By abstracting a new `LootCrate` class, we identified its main features and behaviors, such as the ability to drop items with a specified drop rate. This helps in making the game more engaging for players. This abstraction clarified not only the class's purpose but also how it should interact with other parts of the game, providing a clear roadmap for its implementation.

Following abstraction, we talked about encapsulation, which protects the internal state of objects and ensures that only necessary interfaces are exposed to other parts of the application. This principle was applied to control how the `LootCrate` and `Crate` properties, such as health and drop rate, could be manipulated, enhancing the classes' maintainability and scalability. Inheritance was then explored as a method for extending and reusing existing functionalities, allowing `LootCrate` class to inherit from the base `Crate` class while adding unique behaviors such as dropping loot. Lastly, we examined polymorphism, which permits us to override inherited methods and alter behaviors in subclasses without changing their interface. This concept was vital in enabling `LootCrate` class to perform additional actions, such as dropping loot upon being shattered, while maintaining the established behaviors of its superclass. Through practical examples, this chapter demonstrated how these four pillars support the development of robust and flexible OOP designs, ultimately facilitating the creation of a more dynamic and interactive game environment code base.

In the upcoming chapter, we will talk about one of the most important acronyms in the whole programming and development world: the SOLID principles. People have very polarized opinions about them and sometimes even say that these principles slow down the development process and should be banned. However, we will learn that complying with these principles is pretty natural. We will learn that by following one, you naturally comply with the others and get clean, readable, and maintainable code.

3

Creating SOLID
Design Solutions

In the previous chapters, we discussed the foundations of **Object-Oriented Programming** (**OOP**) and explored its four fundamental pillars: abstraction, encapsulation, inheritance, and polymorphism. These concepts are essential for crafting well-structured, flexible, and maintainable code, particularly within game development projects, where the complexity of systems and the need for extensible architectures are essential. Building upon this foundation, this chapter transitions into an equally important yet more nuanced set of principles that further refine our approach to OOP: the SOLID principles.

The SOLID principles, coined by Robert C. Martin (often referred to as *Uncle Bob*), represent a set of guidelines designed to improve the robustness and scalability of software, and developer productivity. These principles address common design flaws, promote code reusability, and simplify the maintenance process. As we dive into game development, which is a field where projects rapidly evolve, feature sets expand, and code bases can become unwieldy, adhering to these principles becomes not just beneficial, but essential.

This chapter is structured around the five principles of SOLID, with each section dedicated to addressing specific aspects of each principle:

- **Single Responsibility Principle** (**SRP**): We start by dissecting the SRP, emphasizing the importance of creating classes that are focused and unambiguous in their purpose. This principle advocates for a design where a class should have only one reason to change.

- **Open-Closed Principle** (**OCP**): Next, we explore the OCP, which dictates that software entities should be open for extension but closed for modification. This principle encourages us to design components that can grow through the addition of new features without altering existing code, preventing unintended consequences.

- **Liskov Substitution Principle (LSP)**: Then, we look at the LSP, highlighting the importance of ensuring that subclasses can be substituted for their base classes without altering the desirable properties of the program. This principle is crucial for maintaining the integrity of the code base's behavior as it evolves.

- **Interface Segregation Principle (ISP)**: The ISP states that clients should not be forced to depend on interfaces they do not use. By decomposing "bloated" interfaces into smaller, more specific ones, we can ensure that classes only need to concern themselves with the methods that are relevant to them, enhancing modularity and flexibility.

- **Dependency Inversion Principle (DIP)**: Then, we talk about the DIP, which involves inverting the direction of dependencies to reduce coupling between high-level components and low-level components. This principle encourages a design where components remain as independent as possible, facilitating easier testing and modification.

By integrating these SOLID principles into our game development practices, we can create systems that are not only robust and scalable but also easy to understand, extend, and maintain. Throughout this chapter, we are going to see each of these principles and apply them to a new class in our game so you understand that besides being conceptually complex, the SOLID principles are intuitive and almost natural if you know the four fundamental pillars of OOP.

Unbloating objects with the SRP

When we talk about making good code bases, the SRP is the main principle for designing cohesive and focused classes. It helps us create classes that are cleaner but also easier to manage and extend. At its core, the SRP states that a class should have one, and only one reason, to change. This means that when adding or removing functionalities to this class, you should always ask yourself: *Does this deviate from this class' purpose? Does this help it perform its core function?* In that sense, the SRP helps us encapsulate a single responsibility or functionality.

This principle challenges the common inclination to create bloated classes with "jack-of-all-trades" purposes that handle multiple aspects of a game. A bloated class is a class that has become overly large and complex, often containing too many responsibilities, methods, or properties. This can lead to difficult maintenance and testing, and potential bugs, as the class tries to manage too many aspects of the game. You have probably heard of, or even made yourself, a Game Manager, or something like that, right? A class that handles game logic, user interface, mechanics, and player data management, among other functions. By subscribing to the SRP, we can untangle the complex web of dependencies often found in such classes, creating the environment for modular, maintainable architectures.

Note that applying good code principles rarely comes as a consequence of the first implementation of the code. Rather, these principles are applied throughout the process; they are an iterative process of polishing and improving the code base. In that sense, the journey towards unbloating classes begins with identifying and segregating the distinct functionalities embedded within a monolithic class.

Consider, for instance, the `GameManager` class, which may manage player data, handle input, control game state transitions, and manage the **Graphics User Interface (GUI)**. By applying SRP, we can break down this multifunctional class into smaller, purpose-specific classes: `PlayerData`, `Input`, `GameState`, and `UserInterface`. Each of these classes has its own set of methods and performs one specific responsibility, but together they achieve the same functionality as the original monolithic class.

This is incredibly powerful when communicating with the team about a specific feature or issue as well. You can simply point out where the problem or feature is likely to be implemented or fixed, instead of trying to figure out a way to explain that somewhere in the `GameManager` class right above a method that handles input you will fix the issue regarding the player's data. And oh, be careful not to mess with the user interface code!!

This decomposition has immediate and palpable benefits. First, it simplifies understanding the code, as each class now has a clear and narrow focus. Other developers can easily pinpoint where specific functionalities are implemented, reducing the cognitive load and accelerating the development process. On top of that, testing becomes more straightforward. Isolated classes with a single responsibility are easier to test since the test cases are more focused and there are fewer potential interactions to account for. The scalability of the project is enhanced as well. When new features or changes are required, the team can pinpoint the exact class that needs extension or modification without worrying about unintended side effects spilling over into unrelated functionalities tangled into a single class.

But, for me, the main advantage of applying the SRP is how it facilitates code reuse. By isolating functionalities into distinct classes, it's more likely that we can reuse these classes in different parts of the game or even in other projects since they become more generic and modular. This not only saves time but also promotes a more consistent and bug-free implementation across the board.

However, the application of the SRP is not without its challenges, especially in complex game development environments. It demands a thoughtful analysis of the system's architecture and a disciplined approach to class design. Developers must resist the temptation to take shortcuts by lumping together unrelated functionalities for the sake of expediency. This discipline requires a paradigm shift in how classes are conceptualized, emphasizing modularity and responsibility segregation from the outset.

We can find the SRP all over the Godot Engine's API. For instance, we have the `PhysicsBody2D` class, which is a generic abstract class that handles objects that can interact with physical forces. Then we have three subclasses specializing in this responsibility, each with its own responsibility:

- `CharacterBody2D`, which is a specialized class for physics bodies that are meant to be user controlled.

- `RigidBody2D`, which is a specialized class for simulating 2D physics and cannot be directly controlled, but we can apply forces to it and allow the physics engine to simulate its movement.

- `StaticBody2D`, which, as the name implies, can't be moved by external forces and when moved manually, it won't affect other bodies. But there's a specialized `StaticBody2D` class called `AnimatableBody2D` whose sole responsibility is to affect other physical bodies when moved manually, usually through code or animations.

Those were just a few examples of nodes that follow the Single Responsibility Principle, but in fact, most nodes do. It's no coincidence that the Godot Engine's API contains so many nodes.

The SRP is a cornerstone of good game development code bases, offering a path to clearer, more manageable, and scalable code. By ensuring that each class in our project encapsulates a single responsibility, we lay the groundwork for a code base that is easy to understand, extend, and maintain. As we transition to the section on the OCP, we'll build on the foundation laid by the SRP, exploring how we can maintain and extend our now well-organized classes without modifying their source code, thereby preserving their integrity while accommodating new features and behaviors. This progression from one principle to the other is natural as they are complementary to each other, and by adhering to one, you are highly likely to subscribe to the next one as well. The coolest thing is that this usually happens following the SOLID acronym: applying the Single Responsibility leads to Open/Closed, which leads to Liskov Substitution, and so on.

Maintaining and extending objects with the OCP

Building on the groundwork laid by the SRP, we will now dive into the OCP. The OCP advocates that software entities (classes, modules, functions, etc.) should be open for extension but closed for modification.

This principle propels us toward a design where the behavior of a class can be extended without altering its existing code base, thus mitigating the risk of introducing bugs into a stable system. Applying the OCP enables us to add new functionalities or respond to changing requirements with minimal disruption to the existing code, a common necessity in the dynamic environment of game development.

Understanding how to apply the OCP in practice involves recognizing the mechanisms available for extending a class's behavior without modifying its source. Polymorphism stands out as a key strategy in that sense. We do that all the time in Godot Engine by extending nodes' behavior. The code base is already set and, supposedly, stable on each release. Godot Engine developers create the code base using C++ and provide an API so we can extend the classes to use in our games, but we can't directly modify the node's code. This is a perfect example of the OCP.

Another practical application of the OCP is the use of event-driven programming. Events allow dynamic behavior extensions by enabling objects to subscribe to and react to various signals or actions occurring within the game world. This approach aligns with the OCP by allowing new reactions or behaviors to be added as responses to events without modifying the emitting or handling mechanisms. In Godot Engine, we apply this approach by overriding the engine's callbacks, such as the `_ready()`, `_process()`, and `_input()` and callbacks. This way, we inject our game logic in the engine's code base at predetermined places without messing with the engine's internal code base.

The OCP also encourages modularity and reusability, as well-designed modules or classes that adhere to this principle can be easily reused across different parts of a game or even across projects. This not only accelerates development time but also enhances the overall quality and consistency of the game's code base.

However, applying the OCP requires foresight and a deep understanding of the game's architecture and future requirements. Over-abstracting in anticipation of changes that may never come can lead to unnecessary complexity. Thus, striking a balance between flexibility for future extensions and the simplicity of the design is crucial.

The OCP provides a strategic blueprint for developing game systems that are robust against change and evolution. By designing our classes to be extensible through mechanisms such as polymorphism, we can introduce new features and adapt to changing game requirements without the risk of destabilizing our existing code. As we proceed to the next section, we'll explore how to maintain and extend class hierarchies in a manner that ensures interoperability and consistency, further fortifying the flexibility and reliability of our game architecture. This progression from the OCP to the LSP seamlessly integrates the concepts of safe extension and behavioral consistency, ensuring that our game's foundation remains SOLID while it grows and evolves.

Ensuring compatibility with the LSP

The LSP is yet another fundamental aspect of robust object-oriented design. It advocates for the interchangeability of subclasses without affecting the superclass' methods contracts, or, in other words, its interface. This principle, named after computer scientist Barbara Liskov, stipulates that objects of a superclass can be replaced by objects of its subclasses without altering any of the desirable properties of the application.

To implement the LSP effectively, subclasses must maintain the behavioral expectations set by their superclasses. For instance, if a superclass has a method that accepts an input range and guarantees an output, any subclass should honor these operational boundaries. Consider a weapon class in a game that calculates damage based on certain attributes. If a subclass overrides this method but introduces new, unexpected side effects or constraints (such as ignoring input parameters or altering unrelated state), it could lead to runtime errors or logic bugs when the subclass is used in place of the superclass.

One practical approach to adhering to the LSP in game development is through the use of comprehensive unit tests that verify the behavior of subclasses against the expected behavior defined by the superclass. This method ensures that subclasses behave as intended when they replace their superclasses, whether it's in combat systems, AI behaviors, or interactive game elements. These tests can serve as a contract that cements the expected behaviors and interfaces, making the game's components more predictable and reliable.

Another important aspect of the LSP is the design of subclass methods that do not strengthen pre-conditions or weaken post-conditions. This means that a subclass should not require more restrictive input conditions, nor should it produce less precise results than its superclass. By diligently observing these constraints, developers can ensure that their game components are interchangeable and can interact seamlessly, thereby enhancing modularity and flexibility in the game's architecture.

In Godot Engine, the editor prevents us from breaking these contracts. For instance, if you create a subclass and use polymorphism to override one of its methods, you can't request incompatible types as the method's arguments and you can't return an incompatible type as well. Essentially, you can think of the LSP as a two-way checklist for overriding any method:

- Does this method ask for more generic types as arguments?

- Does this method return a more specialized type than the original method's return type?

This makes sense, right? To maintain the contracts of superclass, the subclass needs to be interchangeable with the superclass. So, it can't ask for a more specialized type when overriding a function, because this would prevent its superclass' users from passing the correct types. It should also return the same or more specialized types as the user classes expect to have access to some methods and properties from the returned type. If you return a more generic type, it may not have all the requirements that the user class was asking.

A practical example would be to create a class that has a method called `get_sprite()` which returns a `Sprite2D`. Then, extending this class, the subclass overrides this method but instead, it returns a `Node2D`. Now, every user class that was using this method to change `Sprite2D.texture` will throw an error since `Node2D` nodes don't have such a property.

The LSP is crucial for creating a stable, reliable architecture that supports safe extensions and modifications through subclassing. By ensuring that subclasses fulfill the contracts established by their superclasses, we can prevent a wide range of bugs and maintain system integrity. As we progress to the next section, we will explore how designing lean, targeted classes can enhance component compatibility and maintainability, providing a more focused and efficient way to manage game system interactions. This shift from ensuring behavioral compatibility to optimizing interface design allows more granular and effective control over how components communicate and operate within the game.

Creating components with the ISP

The ISP advocates for creating lean and specialized interfaces rather than general-purpose, bloated ones. This principle ensures that a class should not be forced to implement interfaces it does not use, thereby preventing **code pollution**. The ISP is particularly crucial in game development, where multiple game components might interact differently with the same entity. By segregating interfaces according to the specific needs of different classes, we can create modular and clean architectures, reducing the overhead and potential errors associated with unnecessary dependencies.

Implementing the ISP begins with a careful analysis and understanding of the functionalities required by each component or class. For example, in a game that features both airborne and ground-based enemy types, rather than having a single movement class that includes methods for flying and walking, the ISP would suggest creating two distinct classes: one for flying and another for walking. This way, an airborne enemy would implement the flying interface, and a ground-based enemy would implement the walking interface. Each class would only need to know about the methods pertinent to its specific type of movement, thus adhering to the ISP.

This principle not only simplifies the implementation of classes but also enhances code maintainability. When changes are made to a particular action or behavior, they are confined to the specific interface that governs that behavior, minimizing the impact on other parts of the system. On top of that, testing becomes more focused and easier to manage because each interface has fewer methods and, consequently, fewer test cases to consider, which directly improves the clarity and efficiency of the test documentation and debugging processes.

Moreover, the ISP facilitates the reuse of code. By designing interfaces that are highly specialized, they can be more easily reused across various parts of a game or even in different projects without dragging along unnecessary functionality. This reuse promotes a clean separation of concerns, a fundamental aspect of a maintainable and scalable system architecture.

We can see the ISP principle all over Godot Engine's code base, but, for instance, check out all the `AudioEffect` subclasses. We could, for instance, bloat the `AudioEffect` class with all the alternative effects and simply select from a menu which specific effect this `AudioEffect` should perform. Instead, each effect has its own class with lean and clean code. This allows us to extend specific effect functionalities as well, instead of extending a bloated class just to override a method.

The ISP plays a fundamental role in crafting well-defined, maintainable, and scalable game architectures by advocating for specialized and segregated interfaces. This approach not only streamlines the development process by reducing dependency complexities but also enhances system robustness. Moving forward, we will talk about how these cleanly segregated interfaces tie into the DIP, which focuses on decoupling high-level modules from low-level modules through high-level abstractions.

Making high-level abstractions with the DIP

The DIP is a sophisticated and profoundly impactful principle within the suite of SOLID design principles. It advocates for high-level modules not to depend on low-level modules; instead, both should depend on abstractions, one of the reasons why I emphasize that abstraction is a fundamental skill to develop as a programmer. This principle effectively inverts the typical dependency relationship in programming, shifting the reliance from concrete implementations to abstract interfaces or base classes.

Implementing the DIP typically involves defining an abstraction that encapsulates the high-level logic of a module. This abstraction then becomes the cornerstone of both high-level and low-level modules. For example, in a game scenario where different types of characters might have various weapon behaviors, instead of character classes directly instantiating specific weapon classes, we could introduce a `Weapon` interface. Both the character classes (high-level modules) and weapon classes (low-level modules) would depend on this `Weapon` interface.

Characters would use weapons through this interface, allowing the addition of new weapon types or changing existing ones without altering the character code. This approach has the dual benefit of promoting a system that is both more testable and more maintainable. Since high-level modules depend only on abstractions, testing can be conducted using mock implementations of these abstractions, thereby focusing tests on the behavior of the high-level modules without interference from the details of the low-level modules.

Additionally, it enables the system to adapt more fluidly to new requirements or changes in the game's design, as new modules that implement these interfaces can be introduced without modifying the existing high-level modules.

On top of that, the DIP promotes a scalable system architecture. As games grow in complexity and feature sets, having a flexible system where new functionalities can be added as discrete modules reduces the overall integration overhead. It allows developers to plug and play different functionalities as needed, facilitating a modular approach to game development.

This concept is something we don't see directly when making games with Godot Engine. Usually, we use direct implementations of the API without wrapping it in interface classes. Doing that would allow us to migrate projects to new versions of the engine a bit safer since we would use an interface class that would be under our control throughout the whole code base, so if something changes between versions, we will just need to change the code in the specific implementation of our interface, and no other places.

The DIP is highly dependent on dependency injection, which makes it so that an object's dependencies are provided externally, by an user class, rather than being hardcoded within the object's class. Dependency injection promotes loose coupling and makes the code more modular, testable, and maintainable. Since we couple our classes to abstract interfaces, we should provide the concrete classes we will actually use in the user class. This also helps us keep the code flexible, favoring composition over inheritance, since the user class can tell which concrete class it couples with. With that, we can change the game's system behavior during run time instead of only during compile time. For instance, the same class can couple to two different concrete `Weapon` subclasses depending on the current game context simply injecting a new instance of a different subclass of the `Weapon` interface class. It sounds very abstract, but as you practice, you will notice that this is very intuitive. For instance, whole patterns rely on this principle alone, such as the Mediator and the Facade patterns. The Mediator design pattern, which centralizes communication between objects by using a mediator object, reducing direct dependencies, is usually used when we have two objects from distinct APIs that we want to wire together. The Facade design pattern provides a simple, unified interface to a complex subsystem, making it easy to use and understand while hiding the subsystem's underlying complexity. We won't go into the details of these patterns in this book as they are more relevant to other types of applications. But it is definitely worth your time to research them after you read this book so that you can use them if you find them necessary.

The DIP encourages a resilient, adaptable architecture by ensuring that both high-level and low-level modules depend on shared abstractions rather than concrete implementations.

Summary

In this chapter, we delved into the SOLID design principles, which are fundamental for creating robust, scalable, and maintainable software, especially in game development projects.

We started by exploring the SRP, emphasizing the importance of each class having a singular focus. This approach reduces complexity and enhances modularity by ensuring that a class has only one reason to change, thereby simplifying both maintenance and scaling of the code base.

Following the SRP, we talked about the OCP. This principle teaches us that software entities should be open for extension but closed for modification. It highlights the necessity of designing systems that can evolve without altering existing code, which helps prevent potential issues and enhances the durability of software.

Next, we covered the LSP. This principle underscores the importance of subclass interchangeability without affecting the application's desired properties. Ensuring that subclasses can effectively replace their base classes without side effects is essential for a reliable and robust design.

We then learned that the ISP advocates for creating specific and targeted interfaces, which prevent classes from being burdened by unnecessary methods. By adhering to the ISP, we achieve cleaner, more efficient code that is easier to manage and extend.

Finally, we explored the DIP. We learned that high-level modules should not rely on low-level modules but on abstractions. This principle facilitates a decoupled architecture that is easier to compose and modify, thus promoting flexibility across the software life cycle.

By integrating these SOLID principles into our game development practices, we create systems that are not only easy to understand and extend but also maintainable over time. This chapter provided examples, demonstrating the application of these principles in real-world game development scenarios, particularly in the Godot Engine, helping us understand that these principles are accessible and besides their abstract description, they are all over the place in good software.

In the next chapter, we are going to learn how we can implement the idea of favoring composition over inheritance.

Get This Book's PDF Version and Exclusive Extras

Scan the QR code (or go to `packtpub.com/unlock`). Search for this book by name, confirm the edition, and then follow the steps on the page.

Note: Keep your invoice handy. Purchases made directly from Packt don't require an invoice.

4

Favoring Composition Over Inheritance

Throughout the past chapters, we have seen a recurrent topic: the idea that we should favor composition over inheritance is a fundamental idea to keep in mind when developing a good reusable code base. Weirdly, we have a fundamental **object-oriented programming (OOP)** pillar for inheritance, but we don't have one for composition, right?

In OOP, one effective design strategy is to favor composition over inheritance. This approach suggests building objects using combinations of smaller, reusable components instead of forming rigid class hierarchies through inheritance. Composition offers a range of benefits, such as increased flexibility, simpler code maintenance, and dynamic adaptability during runtime. This chapter will explore why composition often provides a more modular and adaptable framework, especially useful in scenarios where requirements might evolve during production.

Inheritance has been a fundamental aspect of OOP, but it can lead to a brittle architecture as applications expand. It tends to establish fixed relationships that may complicate modifications and extensions in the future. Composition, in contrast, allows for constructing objects with distinct functionalities encapsulated within other objects, promoting reusability and reducing interdependencies. This structure supports a more decentralized and flexible system architecture.

The advantage of composition shines when you need to modify or extend functionalities. In game development, where iterative design and frequent updates are the norm, being able to switch out components easily without extensive refactoring is invaluable. Throughout this chapter, I will use a practical example from game development to show how you can quickly adapt to changes in game mechanics or design elements using composition.

We'll wrap up the chapter by putting theory into practice by turning the loot of the `LootCrate` functionality into a component we can reuse on other objects. Rather than embedding this directly within a class structure, we'll design it as a `Loot2D` component. This method not only eases the integration of `LootCrate` into different areas of the game but also keeps our options open for future updates or changes. Through this implementation, the aim is to highlight the real-world benefits of a compositional approach, underlining how it leads to software that's both scalable and easier to manage.

In this chapter, we will cover the following topics:

- Understanding the composition approach
- Creating complex scenes by composing with nodes
- Making games by composing with scenes

Technical requirements

To follow along with the chapter's instructions, use the project files available inside the `04.favoring-composition-over-inheritance/01.start/` project. You can use the files present in the `04.favoring-composition-over-inheritance/02.final/` folder as a reference in case you feel lost or get errors or bugs through the process of following the instructions.

Download the repository files through the following link: `https://github.com/PacktPublishing/Game-Development-Patterns-with-Godot-4`.

That said, let's start with understanding what it means to favor composition over inheritance, what the composition approach is, and when to apply it.

Understanding the composition approach

The composition approach emphasizes constructing complex objects by assembling simpler, independent components. You will see that composition effectively adheres naturally to all the SOLID principles. This method facilitates development by allowing each piece to be crafted and tested separately, then integrated as needed. This modular setup not only simplifies modifications but also enhances the system's adaptability. Components can be swapped or updated with minimal impact on the overall system, making it particularly useful in environments where requirements can evolve rapidly or where functionality needs to be reused in various parts of an application.

Composition's strength lies in its flexibility and the ease with which developers can extend and adapt application features. Unlike a fixed inheritance structure that might constrain objects to predefined behaviors and relationships, composition empowers developers to dynamically mix and match capabilities in runtime. This flexibility is crucial for managing complex software applications, especially games, that must adapt to changing requirements without extensive rewrites or debugging.

In comparison, inheritance structures objects in a strict hierarchy, which can simplify understanding and implementing relationships in the object model. However, this can lead to a rigid system where changes to base classes cascade through the hierarchy, potentially causing widespread disruptions. Composition offers a more flexible alternative, enabling developers to build systems with interchangeable parts that mitigate such risks. While inheritance has its place, particularly in cases where we extend functionalities already validated, composition often provides a more resilient and adaptable framework for software development.

This method aligns beautifully with how the Godot Engine handles game development through its scene and node architecture, making it a practical example of composition in action.

In Godot, a scene is essentially a composition of various nodes, where each node represents a distinct functional element, such as sprites, sounds, scripts, or collision areas. Think of a scene as a container that organizes and groups these nodes into a coherent unit representing a game entity or environment. This structure allows us to build complex game features from simple, interchangeable parts. The real power of this approach is evident in how easily these components can be modified or reassembled. For instance, if a developer wants to change how a character interacts with its environment, they can simply swap out or adjust the relevant nodes without the need to overhaul the entire character or scene. Out of curiosity, this composition approach that Godot Engine uses is a design pattern called **Composition Tree**.

On top of that, this modular structure extends beyond mere convenience. It promotes a clear organization paradigm where each component maintains its independence, reducing the dependencies commonly seen in inheritance-based architectures. This modularity ensures that changes in one part of a system have minimal impact on others, simplifying both debugging and development processes. In game development, where iterative changes and refinements happen daily, the ability to adjust components without side effects is priceless. Godot's approach also enhances reusability. Nodes developed for one project can be easily reused for another, or even shared with the community, thanks to their self-contained nature. This reusability not only accelerates development cycles but also promotes a more robust and tested code base.

In essence, the composition approach in Godot exemplifies how a flexible and maintainable game architecture can be achieved. By treating scenes as compositions of nodes, developers gain the ability to construct, experiment, and iterate with efficiency and clarity. This methodology not only streamlines game development but also empowers developers to explore creative solutions without the constraints typically imposed by more rigid programming structures. In the next section, we will understand how this applies to how we make games with Godot Engine.

Creating complex scenes by composing with nodes

Godot Engine almost equally emphasizes the importance of both approaches, inheritance and composition. By default, you need to compose your scenes using the available default nodes. Then, you specialize, in other words, extend or inherit, them. For example, let's understand how the player's avatar scene was built up by a mix of these techniques. Usually, it all starts by laying down the general features using a composition of nodes, and then you extend their behaviors with scripts:

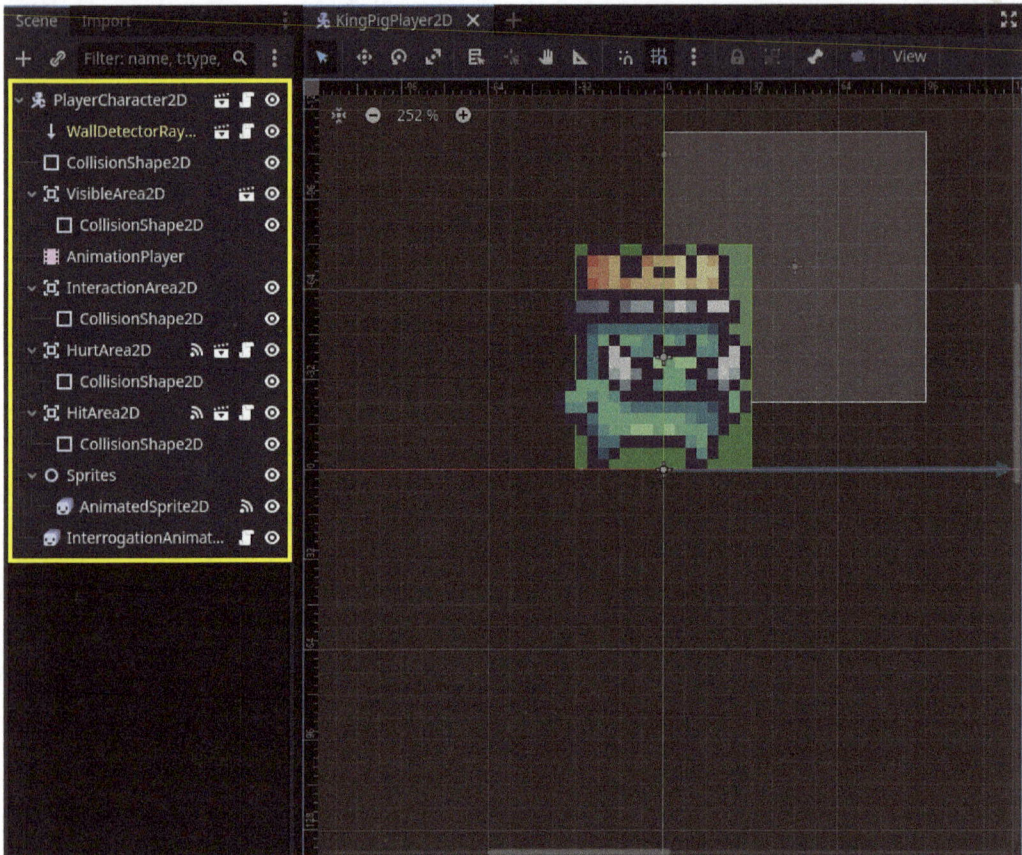

Figure 4.1 – The KingPigPlayer2D scene's hierarchy composed of fifteen nodes

Notice that there are certain nodes and compositions that may not make sense at first glance, even the default ones. For instance, why don't the Area2D nodes allow us to set a Shape2D directly? Why do we need to make a composition together with the CollisionShape2D node? The simple answer is that this way the CollisionObject2D nodes, such as CharacterBody2D, StaticBody2D, and Area2D, can focus on handling their collision and overlapping logic instead of having shape logic polluting their code.

On top of that, with a specialized class to handle shapes, we can make changes to collision logic and shape logic without these changes impacting each other. Also, with this composition approach, every class that needs to calculate shapes to handle their collision or overlapping logic can rely on the `CollisionShape2D` node as a component instead of having to inherit a general class that implements the `CollisionShape2D` logic and making these classes unnecessarily coupled to each other. With a component, we decouple them and make their code comply with the single responsibility principle, which in turn makes their code more maintainable and reusable.

Also, as we saw in *Chapter 3*, as you comply with one of the SOLID principles, you naturally comply with the others if you manage to do it right. In good APIs, it's common to see classes that are similar with slightly different changes that could be merged into a single class with an option to set the desired behavior. For instance, we have `CharacterBody2D`, `RigidBody2D`, `StaticBody2D`, `PhysicalBone2D`, `AnimatableBody2D`, and `Area2D`, which are all `CollisionBody2D` nodes, and except for the `Area2D` nodes; they are all `PhysicalBody2D` nodes as well.

Godot Engine developers could have done what Unity developers did with their `RigidBody2D`, where a single class has three distinct physical behaviors and you need to choose which one you want at any given time: dynamic, kinematic, and static. As for the equivalent of `Area2D`, they use `Collider2D`, which is equivalent to `CollisionShape2D`. But Unity's `Collider2D` is where the actual collision is handled; so, if you want an object to simulate physics behaviors and collide, you compose it using `RigidBody2D` and `Collider2D`. `Collider2D` has a property called Is Trigger, which allows the `Collider2D` to detect overlapping objects without physically interacting with them; in other words, without colliding with them and changing their movement and other physical properties.

Well, we don't have access to the code that implements these classes in the Unity core code base, but I think is safe to imagine that it is tricky to maintain these two classes in opposition to Godot Engine's approach where we naturally have compliance with the **interface segregation principle**, having multiple classes each with its distinct responsibility. So, if we ever need to find a bug related to physics-simulated motion, the first stop would be on the `RigiBody2D` node. If we have an issue regarding custom movement, we can look at `CharacterBody2D`, and so on and so forward. With Unity's approach, everything is in the same place and we would need to pray to God to pinpoint the issue.

Now that you have a grasp of the importance of favoring composition, it's time to fix a small error we committed! In the next section, we will take the `LootCrate` loot logic and turn it into a `Loot` node!

Turning a behavior into a component

The importance of understanding the concepts we've been through since *Chapter 1* is that we can make good design decisions from the beginning and prevent future problems and reworks. For instance, the designer who asked us to make `LootCrate` now wants to add looting to enemies as well so that players have the incentive to face and defeat the enemies. He realized that players were mostly avoiding enemies and came out with this as a solution.

Now, a novice programmer would think that since the LootCrate and BumpingPig classes will share common behavior, it would be necessary to create a superclass, maybe called LootObject, and make both Crate and BumpingPig inherit from this class. But apart from that, these classes have nothing else in common and it makes no sense to couple them to the same common superclass just to implement this behavior. Instead, we can extract the loot behavior from LootCrate into a Loot class and use it as a component in both the Crate and the BumpingPig classes. We also have the extra advantage that we can use this with any other thing in our game if we want to implement loot to them. To achieve this, let's follow these steps:

1. Open the project inside the 04.favoring-composition-over-inheritance/ start/ folder.

2. With the project opened in Godot Engine, open the res://Objects/Crate/LootCrate/ LootCrate.tscn scene and let's start the surgery to extract this loot behavior!

3. First of all, we will cut everything from *line 4* to *line 14* and keep it in our Pastebin.

4. Then, create a new scene. Use Marker2D as the root node, rename it Loot2D, and save it as res://Objects/Loot2D/Loot2D.tscn.

5. Attach a script to Loot2D and paste the extracted code. It should look like this at this point:

```
extends Marker2D

@export varloot_scene :=
    preload("res://Objects/Diamond/Diamond.tscn")
@export_range(0.0, 1.0) var drop_rate := 0.3

func drop() -> void:
    var luck := randf()

    if luck >= drop_rate:
        var loot: Node2D = loot_scene.instantiate()
        loot.global_position = global_position
        find_parent("Level").find_child("Diamonds")
            .add_child(loot)
```

6. Save the Loot2D scene and switch to the LootCrate2D scene instead. Inside the LootCrate2D scene, add an instance of the Loot2D scene as CharacterBody2D of the Crate child, as shown in the following figure:

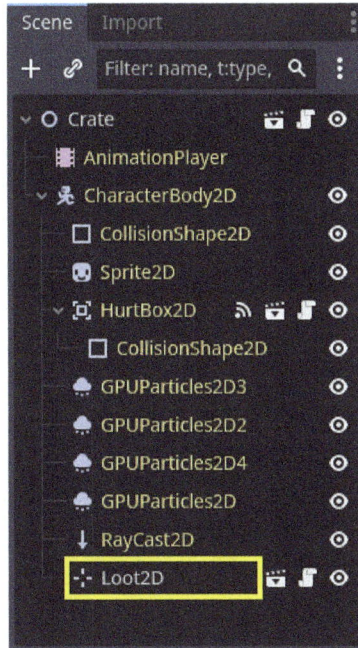

Figure 4.2 – The LootCrate scene node hierarchy showcasing the Loot2D scene instance

7. Open the `res://Objects/Crate/LootCrate/LootCrate.gd` again and let's start
    by making a reference to the `Loot2D` node:

    ```
    extends "res://Objects/Crate/Crate.gd"

    @onready var loot = $CharacterBody2D/Loot2D
    ```

8. Then, inside the `shatter()` method, we will remove the `direct drop()` call, since
    this class doesn't have this method anymore, and instead, we will make a call to the `loot.`
    `drop()` method:

    ```
    extends "res://Objects/Crate/Crate.gd"

    @onready var loot = $CharacterBody2D/Loot2D

    func shatter():
        loot.drop()
        super()
    ```

With that, if you test the res://Levels/Level.tscn scene and destroy the crates, we will get the same behavior as we had before! In the following figure, you can see two crates being shattered and one of them dropped a diamond:

Figure 4.3 – The crates on the level scene shattered and one of them dropped a diamond

Our loot component is working as it should and now we can use it with the BumpingPig class to create LootBumpingPig as requested by the designer. Throughout this section, we've seen how we use composition to create scenes by combining nodes and creating complex hierarchies of nodes. I really wish Godot Engine could call them compositions instead of scenes; it would make way more sense. In the next section, we will take this concept even further and make complex compositions of scenes!

Making games by composing with scenes

Godot Engine in its very core is an implementation of the **Composition Tree design pattern**. Composition Tree is a structural design pattern that lets you compose objects with other objects and then work with these compositions as if they were also objects; in other words, compositing with compositions as well. This is exactly how the node and scene system works. You create a scene (i.e., a composition) using nodes, and then you can use scenes to compose other scenes as if they were nodes as well.

Note that when you instantiate a scene into another scene, Godot Engine ensures that the details of its implementation are hidden; in other words, it encapsulates the scene's node composition. This makes it so that the scene behaves exactly like a node, with the addition that you can toggle the **Editable Children** option to get access to the implementation details. The following image showcases the PlayerCharacter2D instance before and after toggling on the **Editable Children** option.

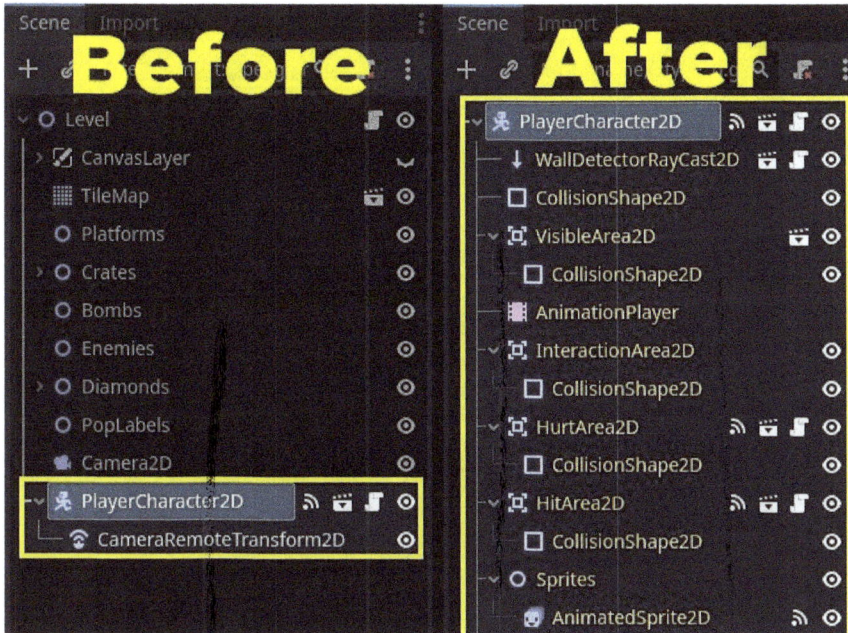

Figure 4.4 – The PlayerCharacter2D before and after toggling the Editable Children option

The Editable Children option exposes the implementation details of this specific instance of the scene, allowing you to change the children's properties, but effectively breaking its encapsulation.

Well, now that we understand how Godot Engine naturally allows us to use the composition approach when making our games, it's time to implement the requested looting feature to BumpingPig and use it in our testing level scene to create more complex compositions and ultimately compose our whole game! In the next section, we will use the Loot2D component together with the BumpingPig scene and then use these in the level scene to compose a scene where we can play with these basic game features and get a feel of our design.

Creating the LootBumpingPig

Now that we have the Loot2D component, we can use it anywhere we like. So, let's follow the designer's request and create the LootBumpingPig enemy so players can drop some diamonds by fighting enemies in the game. For that, follow these steps:

1. Use the **FileSystem** dock to search for the BumpingPig scene; right-click it and from the drop-down menu, choose the **New Inherited Scene** option, as shown in the following figure:

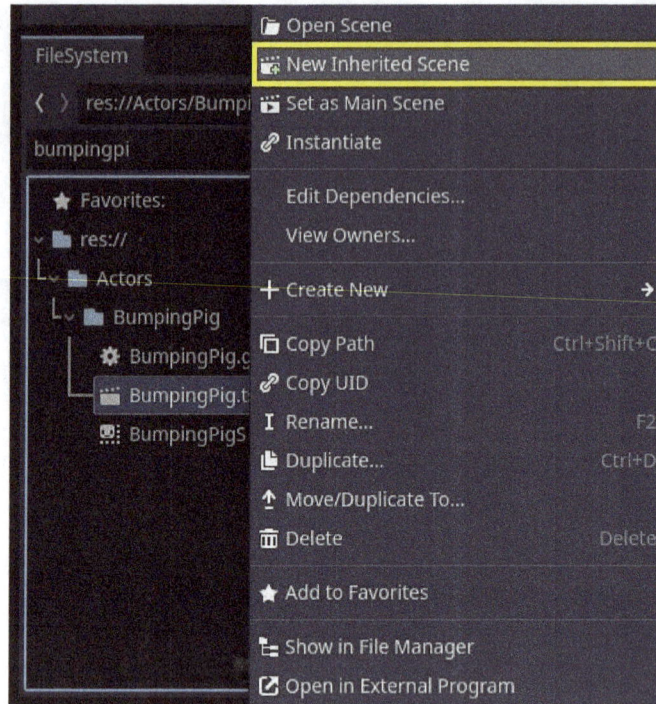

Figure 4.5 – Creating a new inherited scene using the FileSystem dock drop-down menu

Note that we are following the SOLID principles here as well, since the `BumpingPig` scene is, technically, on production, following the open-closed principle, we will extend it to add the new behavior, also complying with the interface segregation principle by having both classes segregated but with the same interface. See how things naturally flow without us realizing it? Usually, when people struggle to follow SOLID principles, it is because their design has some fundamental flaws from the beginning.

2. With the new scene opened, select the `BumpingEnemy2D` node and use the **FileSystem** dock to search for the `Loot2D.tscn` file.

3. From there, right-click it and from the drop-down menu, select **Instantiate** to create an instance of this scene as a direct child of the `BumpingEnemy2D` node.

4. Next, let's extend the script of the `BumpingPig` node by right-clicking on it and from the drop-down menu, picking the **Extend Script…** option, as shown in the following figure:

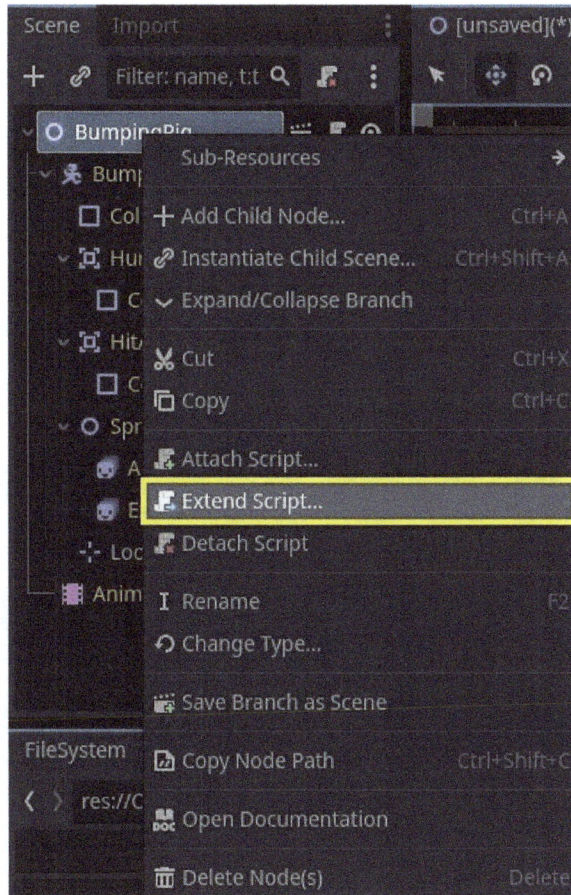

Figure 4.6 – Extending the BumpingPig script using the Scene dock drop-down menu

5. You can save the script as res://Actors/BumpingPig/LootBumpingPig.gd and do the same with the scene, saving it as res://Actors/BumpingPig/LootBumpingPig. tscn.

6. With the script open, let's do the same thing we did with the LootCrate script, but instead of overriding the shatter() method, we will override the die() method. The script should look like this at the end of the process:

```
extends "res://Actors/BumpingPig/BumpingPig.gd"

@onready var loot = $BumpingEnemy2D/Loot2D

func die():
    loot.drop()
    super()
```

7. Now, open the `res://Levels/Level.tscn` scene, add an instance of the `LootBumpingPig` scene as a child of the `Enemies` node, and position it somewhere in the level so we can test it and see if it is working.

Remember that there's a chance that defeating the enemy won't drop anything as well, so we may either play with the Loot's Drop Rate property or test it multiple times. But if everything goes well, at some point, we will get a diamond drop by defeating the enemy, as shown in the following figure:

Figure 4.7 – The Bumping Pig dropping a diamond after being defeated by the player

Note that, with this approach, we also complied with the single responsibility principle, since the new class maintains a single responsibility of dropping loot when the Bumping Pig dies, the Liskov substitution principle, as we kept the contracts from all the functions in the parent class of `LootBumpingPig`. As I said, complying with the SOLID principles flows naturally. You don't need a checklist to try to force compliance on your classes. If you understand the principle fundamentally, you apply it without forcing it into your code.

Summary

Throughout this chapter, we learned that favoring composition over inheritance is a powerful strategy in OOP to create more flexible, maintainable, and adaptable code. Inheritance, while fundamental to OOP, can lead to rigid and brittle architectures as applications grow. Composition, on the other hand, promotes the construction of objects using smaller, reusable components, allowing for easier modifications and dynamic adaptability.

We explored the technical requirements and advantages of the composition approach, which adheres to the SOLID principles. This method allows for each component to be developed and tested independently, enhancing the system's adaptability and making it easier to swap or update parts without significant impact on the overall system.

The chapter detailed how Godot Engine naturally implements composition through its scene and node architecture. Scenes in Godot are compositions of various nodes, each representing a distinct functional element. This modular structure promotes clear organization and reusability, simplifying both development and debugging processes.

Inheritance, although a fundamental aspect of OOP, often leads to brittle architectures that complicate modifications and extensions. In contrast, composition allows us to construct objects with distinct functionalities encapsulated within other objects. This promotes reusability and reduces interdependencies, promoting a decentralized and flexible system architecture. In this chapter, we explored how composition can be more modular and adaptable, using practical examples from our game project.

One of the main advantages of composition is the ease with which functionalities can be modified or extended. Iterative changes are what usually happens in game development projects and being able to switch out components without extensive refactoring is invaluable. We saw how composition allows for rapid adaptation to changes in game mechanics or design elements, highlighting its practical application.

Practical steps were provided for transforming behaviors into components. For example, we converted the loot functionality from the `LootCrate` class into a separate `Loot2D` component, demonstrating how this can be reused across different objects in the game as we did by adding loot functionality to the `BumpingPig` class. This not only makes the code more maintainable but also aligns with the single responsibility principle, ensuring each class has a single responsibility.

Finally, the chapter covered how to create complex scenes by composing with nodes, further exemplifying Godot's strength in using the Composition Tree design pattern. We implemented the `LootBumpingPig` enemy by inheriting from the `BumpingPig` scene and adding the `Loot` component, showcasing how composition allows for easy extensions and modifications.

As we move forward, we will dive deeper into implementing design patterns in the Godot Engine. In the next chapter, specifically, we will learn how to maintain game states using the singleton pattern.

Get This Book's PDF Version and Exclusive Extras

UNLOCK NOW

Scan the QR code (or go to packtpub.com/unlock). Search for this book by name, confirm the edition, and then follow the steps on the page.

Note: Keep your invoice handy. Purchases made directly from Packt don't require an invoice.

Part 2:
Basic Design Patterns

After getting introduced to the programming paradigm that we will use throughout the book, it's time to understand what design patterns are, when we should use them, why we use patterns, and how to implement them in our project.

We will start with patterns that are used the most and we can implement them to achieve basic functionalities in our game projects. These design patterns will help us get used to refactoring bad code and implementing scalable solutions in the form of design patterns.

This part includes the following chapters:

- *Chapter 5, Maintaining Global States with the Singleton Pattern*
- *Chapter 6, Decoupling Objects with the Observer Pattern*
- *Chapter 7, Spawning Game Objects with the Factory Pattern*
- *Chapter 8, Changing Object Behavior with the State Pattern*
- *Chapter 9, Designing Actors with the Command Pattern*

5
Maintaining Global States with the Singleton Pattern

Games are complex dynamic systems with an infinite amount of different internal states and it is common to lose track of data when we do clean-ups from one major state to another. For instance, in most game engines, it's a common practice, built into the engine, to get rid of all objects before adding new ones when we load a new level – in Godot's case, a new scene. This causes some issues when we need to maintain some data or even the object itself processing.

If you played with background music in Godot, it's likely that you noticed that it suddenly stops playing when you switch to another scene using `get_tree().change_scene_to_file()` or `get_tree().change_scene_to_packed()`. This is because Godot frees the current scene's node hierarchy from the `SceneTree` before adding the new scene's node hierarchy. If you don't manage to have your node outside of the current scene's hierarchy, you will lose it during the scene dump. But, there's a way around this. Godot offers us the powerful Autoload feature, which allows us to have nodes being processed parallel to the current scene. Autoload nodes also allow us to have a global reference to said nodes if we want. Ultimately, this gives us the necessary features to implement the Singleton pattern, allowing us to maintain a global reference to a single instance of a node throughout the whole game run.

In this chapter, we will learn what the Singleton pattern is, its advantages, and when we should use it. Then, we will implement it in our game to create a node that will carry the player's score throughout the whole game run so that the player feels that they are making cumulative progress, instead of progress that is lost when they move on to the next level.

In this chapter, we are going to cover the following topics:

- Understanding the Singleton pattern
- Spotting use cases of singletons in games
- Implementing the Singleton pattern in Godot

Technical requirements

To follow the instructions in this chapter, utilize the project files located in the 05.maintaining-global-states-with-the-singleton-pattern/01.start/ directory. If you encounter any confusion, errors, or bugs while following the instructions, refer to the files in the 05.maintaining-global-states-with-the-singleton-pattern/02.final/ folder, and don't forget to report them to our support team!

If you haven't downloaded the repository yet, you can get it from the following link: https://github.com/PacktPublishing/Game-Development-Patterns-with-Godot-4. With that said, we will start by exploring the Singleton pattern, its core functionalities, and what it fundamentally solves.

Understanding the Singleton pattern

The Singleton pattern is a creational pattern that allows developers to ensure that there will only be a single instance of a class throughout the application and this class is globally accessible to all other classes. The way that developers usually implement the Singleton pattern is by making the constructor method private. They then provide an alternative static method that will act as a constructor method. Instead of returning a new instance of the class every time, this method always returns the same instance, ultimately allowing the existence of only one instance.

Well, this is the technical approach in which most programming languages implement the Singleton pattern, but something that I want you to keep in mind is that there is no unique way to implement design patterns. They are solutions to problems and, ultimately, when we implement them, we are looking more into getting their benefits than being strictly technical and rigid regarding the way to implement them. If you find yourself needing a single instance of a class that every class can access, you are talking about implementing a singleton. On the other hand, if you manage to implement a class that only has one instance running and that every class can access, you have a singleton. The way you implement it is not absolutely relevant.

I know you are smart and, at this point, you already understand that using the **Autoload** feature doesn't necessarily implement a singleton. First of all, nothing is preventing us from creating new instances of a class that is also being used as an Autoload object. According to the Godot documentation itself,

> *"The Singleton pattern is a useful tool for solving the common use case where you need to store persistent information between scenes. In our case, it's possible to reuse the same scene or class for multiple singletons as long as they have different names."*

I highly recommend you read the complete Autoload documentation so you understand its little caveats. To do that, check out the following link: https://docs.godotengine.org/en/stable/tutorials/scripting/singletons_autoload.html.

This is how Godot deals with this specific issue. You can have multiple instances of a scene or class but the global reference will be unique for each one of these instances. This ultimately means that all classes will be accessing the same cached instance when they use any given Autoload object name.

Most of the time, when we use Autoload objects, the very nature of the class itself doesn't need more than one instance. So, we naturally, but without any rigid constraint, keep only one instance running. We don't have to, but with that, we comply with the usual Singleton implementation by keeping only one instance running and globally accessible to all classes.

In the next section, we will spot some use cases for the Singleton pattern in games, and for that, we will research some real-world case problems that we can solve using the Singleton pattern and understand why it became a pattern.

Spotting use cases of singletons in games

Now that you understand what a singleton is, let's research some real-world use cases that are very likely to happen in any game project. In these use cases, we will note that they will present a problem that we can solve by applying the Singleton pattern. As we saw, the problem that the Singleton pattern solves is that you require all classes to access the same instance of a given class. We do that by turning this instance globally accessible and ensuring that its reference will always point out to the same instance.

I want to make sure that you understand this; the Singleton pattern is not about having a `static` method that returns an instance of a class and prevents the creation of other instances. This is how programmers typically implement it.

However, the goal of the Singleton pattern itself is to provide a globally accessible instance of a class that all other classes can access. The reason why we typically prevent other instances from existing is so that we don't get confused by multiple instances' states. Instead, we maintain a single coherent state within a single instance.

In the next section, we will talk about the usefulness of the Singleton pattern to allow us to maintain the player's data when we need to clear the current game state, but we want to maintain the player's data so we can use it in future states and convey the feeling that the player is living within a continuous world.

Maintaining players' data throughout the game states

One of the main challenges game developers face is that a game can't be expressed as a single screen or a single state. So, when transitioning from one state to the next, they lack a strategy to maintain the player's data between these states, hindering the sense of continuity and progress.

A less efficient way to achieve that is by serializing the data and outputting it into a file. Then, you load the file, deserialize it, and use the data again. Although this is a good way to maintain this data, especially between play sessions (in other words, when the application closes and opens again), this method is usually slow and the fact that you have to serialize and deserialize adds a layer of complexity that you shouldn't be wasting time and process power with on every change of the game state.

Instead, an effective way to achieve this is by implementing a singleton that can be used to store and provide this data whenever necessary. And since the Singleton pattern maintains a single instance of the class alive and available, we are safe to clear the game state knowing we will be able to access it again on the next clean state.

One concrete example of this use case is the player's score. Since many entities will need to access this data, it needs to be globally accessible to them, and since the score is a convergence of all the player's actions, both positive and negative, it needs to be a single instance. All these entities and actions must culminate in the same expression of the player's performance.

In most game engines, when we switch from one scene to the next, the engine performs a state cleanse, getting rid of everything that is in the current scene and loading the next. For instance, this is what happens in Godot Engine when we call the `SceneTree.change_scene_to_*()` methods: the engine removes the current scene node and all its children nodes and then loads the next scene and its nodes hierarchy. But when you use an Autoload node, Godot will add it as a sibling of the current scene. So, when Godot performs the cleanse to load the next scene, the Autoload nodes are not removed and we maintain their current state. In the following figure, you can see the `Score` node as a direct child of the `root` node alongside the `Level` node, which is the current scene's node.

Figure 5.1 – The Remote SceneTree showcasing the root node's hierarchy
with the Score node as a sibling of the Level node

By doing that, we prevent losing the relevant data when we need to change the scene. This allows us to carry on this data throughout the whole game run and use it whenever we need it—for instance, if we want to make a high-score leaderboard. In the next section, we will see another useful application of the Singleton pattern in games: background music.

Playing background music without interruptions

Another issue that usually happens due to the scene cleanse that most game engines do when we change between scenes is that if the object responsible for playing the music is part of the current scene's hierarchy, it will be removed during the cleanse. This makes it so that the music will stop playing, ending up in a bad player experience.

Since singleton objects keep their instance always available, this means that they don't get affected by these cleanses. So, it's a common practice to apply the Singleton pattern to take care of the background music, especially if you want to implement some kind of dynamic background music that can be affected by various objects in the game. An example is when you want a piece of stealth music when your character enters into sneaky mode or a piece of high-beat music when your character enters into combat. These would need different objects to access and alter the current playing music, and with the Singleton pattern, they would have global access to the same object instance responsible for playing the music.

Just imagine the chaos of having multiple objects playing different music! It's a clear use case for the Singleton pattern. In the next section, we will see yet another, among many others, use case for the Singleton pattern: when we implement third-party plugins.

Using third-party APIs and plugins

One of the most common ways that developers and companies make their APIs available is by creating a class that exposes relevant methods and communicates with lower-level classes. These classes usually take quite some space in memory because they serve as mediators, or rather, interfaces, between our current project code base and their services' code base. In most cases, there's no need to have multiple instances of these classes running, and since most of these services include generic features that can be useful for various classes in a game, they also need to be globally available. Well, you already guessed, right? Another perfect use case for the Singleton pattern.

Still in the same idea of using third-party services, when developers create plugins that their peers can tweak through code, it's a common practice to turn the main plugin's class into a singleton object so that it behaves as an interface as well, allowing us to use the plugin's features easier. Since there's usually no need to have multiple instances of a plugin's interface class, the Singleton pattern comes as a good solution. In the next section, we will talk about another use case for the Singleton pattern, the last example in this chapter, but you will notice that there are many more that we can think of.

Accessing the engine's built-in features

It's common to have singleton objects in the engine's API itself as well. Since game engines provide a framework to create games with a common premade code base, most of the time, the game engines also implement the Singleton pattern, especially to objects that naturally don't need more than one instance running and must be globally available.

One example of this kind of object in the Godot Engine's API is the OS singleton, which provides access to common functionalities directly related to the operating system, such as getting the processor's name, memory usage, executing commands, and opening files, among other features. Another example is the `Input` singleton, which is responsible for handling inputs such as the accelerometer, mouse, keyboard, gyroscope, and others. As a final example, we also have the `Engine` singleton, which provides access to the very engine properties such as time scale, frames per second, and even a list of available singletons! It's a meta singleton! It's through the Engine singleton that we can easily implement slow motion, for instance.

Well, with all these examples giving us context about the usefulness of the Singleton pattern, it's time to put this knowledge to work! In the next section, we will implement a score system and a door system in our game. Yet another request from the game designer!

Implementing the Singleton pattern in Godot

As you can see from the previous examples, the use cases for the Singleton pattern are many. With this new power in your hands, you must be careful and use it responsibly. As we know: with great power comes great responsibility. It's time to put our knowledge into practice.

In this section, we will assess two use cases for the Singleton pattern and implement solutions for them. You will see the process of pointing out accurately whether the Singleton pattern fits the presented requests properly and will understand when to implement it and when to use alternatives. Remember, as a design pattern, the usage of singletons should come naturally as a solution for specific issues. You shouldn't just jump right into it as soon as you note that some data should be globally accessible or as soon as you want to mediate various classes through a global central hub. That said, in the next section, we will see our designer's request and assess it to understand how to solve the issue presented.

Understanding the designer's request

Throughout the book, we are working on our problem-solving skills, specifically, using programming tools. In our practical studies, we will receive requests from a fictional designer. We are working on a game project together and our job is to understand and create the desired outcome presented by the designer. In this section, we will understand the request and break it down into problems that we can solve. Then, we will note whether any specific pattern emerges from this assessment.

Now, let's begin. The designer of our team came to us with some features that they think will help improve the game as a whole. They noticed that players currently can't add up the score they are making by collecting the diamonds. Players also don't understand when and where these points will be useful and don't even know whether their score is per level, per play session, or kept until the end of the game. So, the designer presents you with the following request:

I made an interface to express the internal state of the player's current score. Since players pick up diamonds and a score pops, I want them to be aware of how many points they made. But we don't have this score stored and available anywhere. So, I need something that I can easily access from this interface to access the player's current score.

I also want to provide more positive incentives to players to reward them for other actions than picking up diamonds. For that, I need the ability to quickly turn any object into something that the player can score. For instance, I want to reward players with some points for punching enemies.

Now that we have multiple levels in our game, I need to be able to keep the player score when we change from one level to another. This will help players have a sense of progress and understand that they carry the impact of their actions throughout the whole game. For instance, players who explore more will have higher scores as they progress through the game and will be able to compare their high-scores with their peers, which will help players engage more in the game and spend more time playing it.

Talking about levels, I need an upgrade to the door system. Currently, our door system only leads to the next level door. But I'm thinking about having some hidden rooms that can only be accessed through other levels' doors. This will give players a sense that the world is interconnected and not as linear as it seems. So, I need the ability to discriminate which door the player will be led to by entering any other door.

Alright, we have some interesting requirements here. First of all, we need an interface to visually express the current internal state of the player's score. The problem is that we don't have a class that maintains such a state, and we will need to create one for that—we can call it `Score`. Note that `Score` must be easily accessible to the interface, but since we also have other objects that will modify the state of `Score`, this class must be easily available for all of these classes. Maybe we even create a leaderboard, or a high-score screen in the future, so `Score` must be a hub that all these classes can access and modify as they need.

Now, the other request is about being able to add the ability to any object to increase the player's score. This sounds more like an instance where we will implement a composition approach. We can extract the scoring logic from the `Diamond` class into a new class that will be responsible for handling scores. We can call this class `ScorePoints`, and it will have a property for the number of points it should increase and it will also pop `ScoreLabel`.

As you can see, the designer wants to maintain the player's score throughout multiple game state cleanses, so the `Score` object should remain in memory and maintain its state. This means that it's not viable to create multiple instances of the `Score` class. This is a perfect use case for the implementation of the Singleton pattern since there's no need for multiple objects storing the player's score. We met all conditions for a singleton.

Finally, the designer also wants to be able to maintain the target door in which the player's avatar should appear at any given level. This means that both the Door class and the Level class should communicate somehow. But they can't communicate directly, since Level node itself is subject to the game state cleanses when we load the next level. This means that if we manage to send the target door from Door node to Level node, this data will be lost when we load the next level, ultimately having no effect. Since there's no reason for having multiple object instances with different values for the target door, it's safe to assume we only need one instance of a class to maintain this data throughout the game state cleanse.

And since both the Level and Door classes need to have access to it, it's a good opportunity to implement the Singleton pattern as well. We can call this new class TeleportData as it will carry on the data related to the player's *teleport* position.

Enough abstraction! It's time to make some concrete work and see how this will turn out. In the next sections, we will implement these abstractions into the project, starting with the Score singleton.

Creating the score system

As the designer pointed out, the game needs a score system. Currently, we just display a bunch of numbers on the screen, but they don't mean anything since we are not storing them anywhere. So, our first task is to create a class that will handle the storing of the player's score. For that, open the project located in the 05.maintaining-global-states-with-the-singleton-pattern/01. start/ folder and follow these steps:

1. Create a new scene, use a Node node as the scene's root node, and rename it Score.

2. Save the scene as res://Game/Score/Score.tscn. The res://Game/ folder represents all the meta classes in our code base that represent the actual game itself. Here, we are talking about the systems and incentives related to the game, which includes the score system.

3. Attach a new script to the ScorePoint node, save it as res://Game/Score/Score. gd, and open it.

4. Let's start by creating a variable to store the current player's score. Let's call it current, which has a default value of 0:

    ```
    extends Node2D

    var current = 0
    ```

5. Next up, let's create a variable to store the player's high score in case we need to use this later. Let's call this variable `high` and its default value will also be `0`:

```
extends Node2D

var current = 0

var high = 0
```

6. Then, we will encapsulate a setter procedure so that every time the `current` score changes, this class will compare it with the `high` score, and if it's greater, the `high` score will update its value:

```
extends Node2D

var current = 0:

    set(value):
        current = value
        if value > high:
            high = value

var high = 0
```

7. Finally, we will add a method to reset the score to zero in case we have a hard game-over condition that resets the player's score. This is how the complete `Score` class should look:

```
extends Node2D

var current = 0:
    set(value):
        current = value
        if value > high:
            high = value

var high = 0

func reset():
    current = 0
```

8. After finishing the script, we need to turn it into an Autoload object to use it as a singleton in Godot. For that, from the **Project Settings** menu, choose the **Autoload** tab. You will see the following menu:

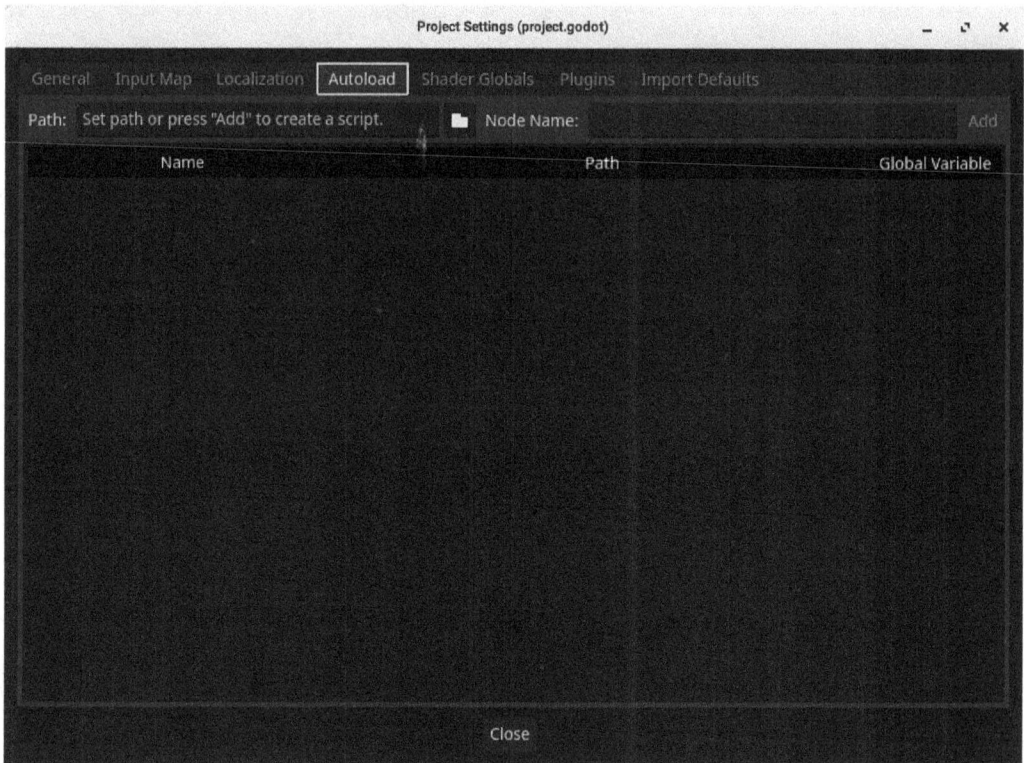

Figure 5.2 – The Project Settings' Autoload menu

9. From there, click on the small folder icon to the left of the **Node Name** field and select the `Score.tscn` file:

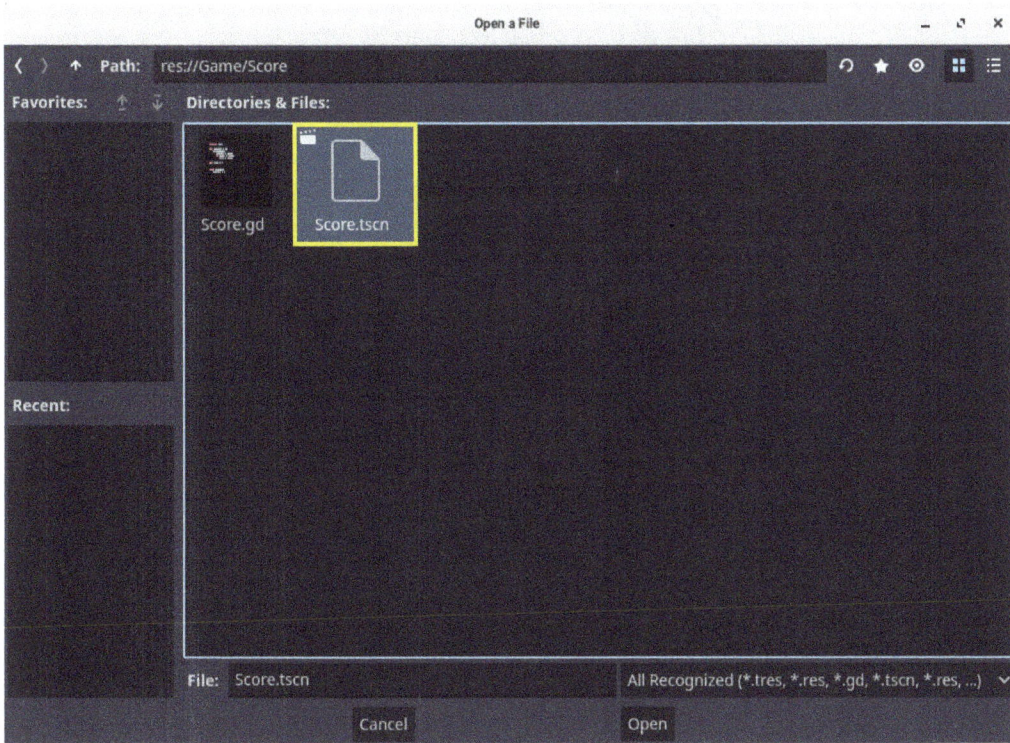

Figure 5.3 – Selecting the Score.tscn file from the Open (a file) menu

10. After that, you will be prompted to choose a name for the node. This is how you will refer to this Autoload instance globally. Usually, we keep the original class's name, which is `Score` in this case:

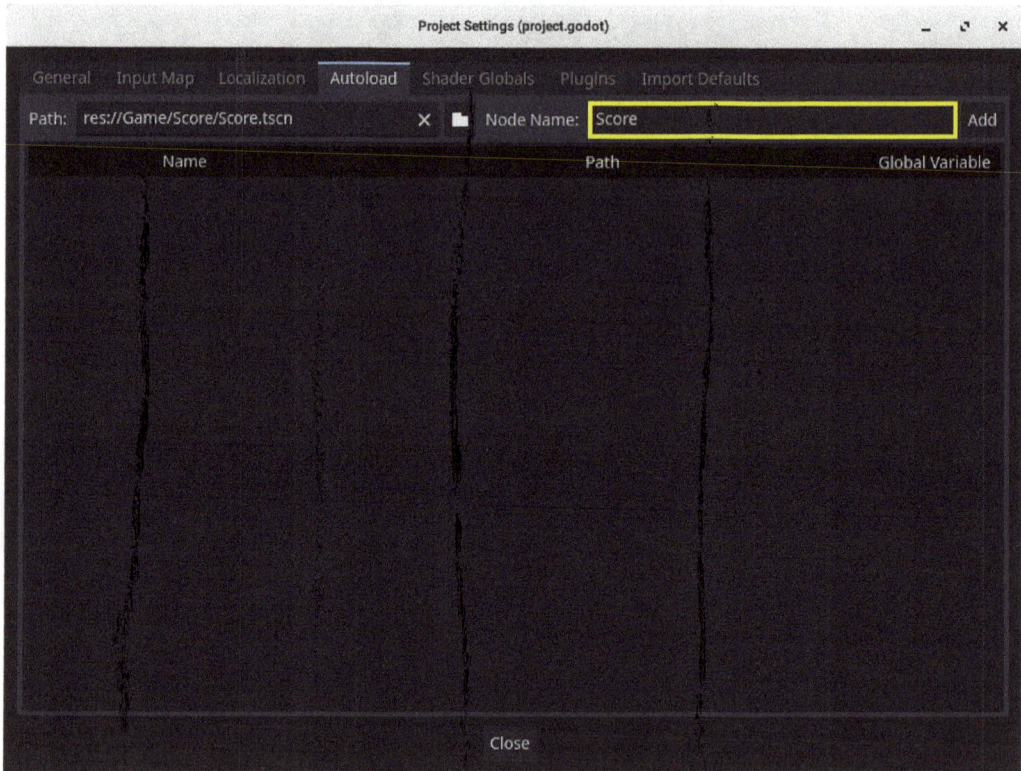

Figure 5.4 – Naming the Autoload node after selecting its file

11. With that, you can click on the **Add** button and you will see it now appears on the list of currently available Autoload nodes.

Note that there are some options to enable or disable its **Global Variable**. This can be useful if you just want to keep it running in the background and maintain it through game cleanses, but you don't want it to be globally available. Turning this off effectively breaks one of the Singleton pattern's core features, so we couldn't call it a singleton any more. This is just a jargon technicality, so don't bother with that too much. It's just so you can express yourself accurately if you need to talk about an Autoload object that is or isn't globally accessible.

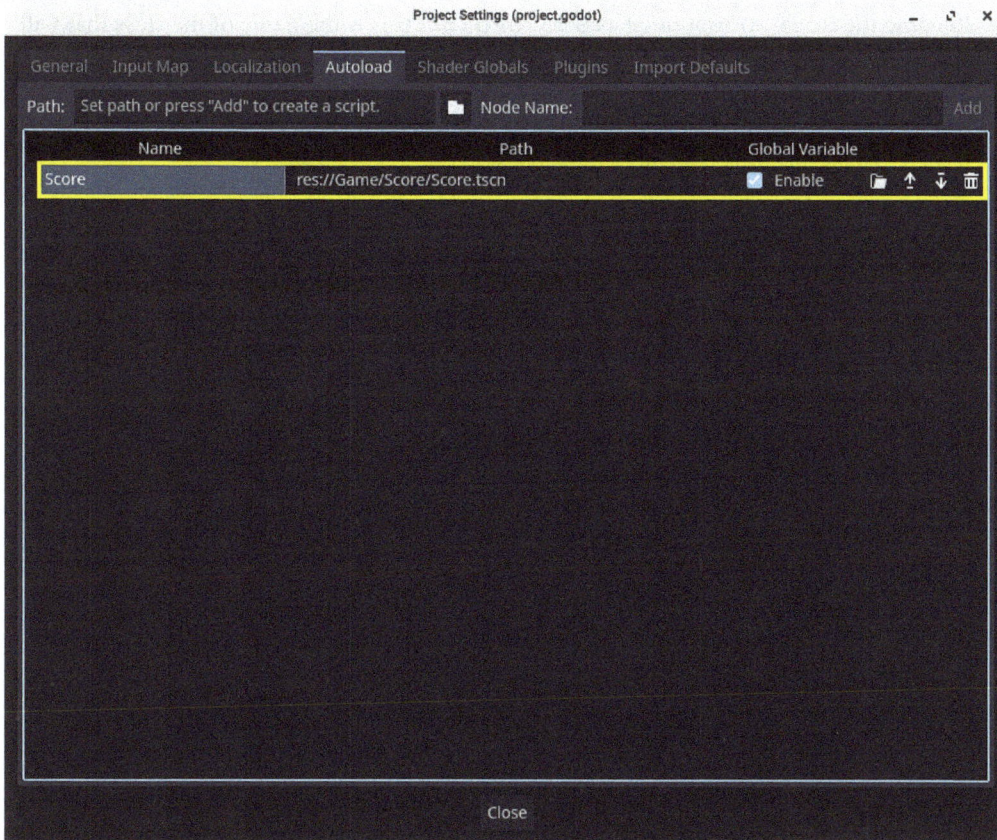

Figure 5.5 – The Score node appearing in the Autoload list

Following these steps, we have successfully implemented our first singleton on Godot! It wasn't hard, was it? Technically, you don't even need a single line of code. Now, let's move on to the next feature of the scoring system: scoring!

Removing the diamond's scoring responsibility

To implement the ability to score, we will need to tweak the Diamond class. It currently has the responsibility of handling scoring. However, the designer wants the ability to reward the player with various items in ways other than just the diamonds. This means this capability needs to be a separate responsibility from the Diamond class itself. This is a good signal to turn this responsibility into a reusable component. So, this is our next task. Follow these steps:

1. Create a new scene and use a Node2D node as the scene's root node. This is because we will need a position in the game space to instantiate PopLabels and, since this will become a responsibility of this new class, it is the one that will need such a position.

2. Rename the `Node2D` root node as `ScorePoint`; this is the name of the class that will represent scoring in our game. Save the scene as `res://Game/Score/ScorePoint/ScorePoint.tscn`. The `res://Game/` folder represents all the meta classes in our code base that represent the actual game itself. Here, we are talking about the systems and incentives related to the game, which includes the score system.

3. Attach a new script to the `ScorePoint` node, save it as `res://Game/Score/ScorePoint/ScorePoint.gd`, and open it.

4. Let's start by exporting a variable that will represent the number of points that the player will score; we can call it `amount`. The designer will use this to change the number of points each object or action will provide to the player:

    ```
    extends Node2D

    @export var amount = 100
    ```

5. Then, since this class will also handle the instancing of `PopLabel`, let's export a variable so we can point out to the scene file of `PopLabel`:

    ```
    extends Node2D

    @export var amount = 100
    @export var pop_label_scene = preload("res://Interface/PopLabel/
    PopLabel.tscn")
    ```

6. After that, create a new function that will be responsible for increasing the player's score. For that, it will receive two optional arguments—one for the amount it should increase in the player's current score points and another to tell whether it should or shouldn't pop `PopLabel`. By default, it will increase `Score.current` by the same amount as its `amount` property and it will instance a `PopLabel`:

    ```
    func increase_score(_score = amount, _pop_score = true):
    ```

7. Here's where the magic happens. We will access the `Score` singleton and increase its `current` property without having to create any class reference to its instance!

    ```
    func increase_score(_score = amount, _pop_score = true):
        Score.current += _score
    ```

8. Then, we will find the Game node and tell it to update the score label the designer created. The Game node could become a singleton as well to facilitate access to it, but in this case, we want it to be affected by game cleanses:

```
func increase_score(_score = amount, _pop_score = true):
    Score.current += _score
    var game = find_parent("Game")
    if game:
        game.update_score_label()
```

9. The next thing to do is to check whether the class needs to instance a PopLabel and, if it does, instance it. For that, we will call a method that we will create in the next step:

```
func increase_score(_score = amount, _pop_score = true):
    Score.current += _score
    var game = find_parent("Game")
    if game:
        game.update_score_label()
    if _pop_score:
        pop_label()
```

10. Finally, let's create the pop_label() method. Here, we will extract the logic directly from the Diamond class's script, but use the amount property instead of the Diamond score property. It should look like this:

```
func pop_label():
    var pop_label = pop_label_scene.instantiate()
    find_parent("Level").find_child("PopLabels")
        .add_child
    pop_label.pop(str(amount), global_position)
```

11. Before we call this task done, let's open the res://Game/Game.gd script and, in the update_score_label() method, we will format the placeholder string to display the Score.current value, like so:

```
func update_score_label():
    score_label.text = "%s" % Score.current
```

With that, we completed our ScorePoint component and the designer can make anything give points to the player. All they have to do is to instance ScorePoint in the scene and call the ScorePoint. increase_score() method. After implementing all the preceding steps, the ScorePoint script should look like the following script:

```
extends Node2D


@export var amount = 100
@export var pop_label_scene = preload("res://Interface/PopLabel/
PopLabel.tscn")

func increase_score(_score = amount, _pop_score = true):
    Score.current += _score
    var game = find_parent("Game")
    if game:
        game.update_score_label()
    if _pop_score:
            pop_label()



func pop_label():
    var pop_label = pop_label_scene.instantiate()
    find_parent("Level").find_child("PopLabels")
      .add_child(pop_label)
    pop_label.pop(str(amount), global_position)
```

To test whether this component is working, let's fix the Diamond class so it maintains its previous behavior. Open the res://Objects/Diamond/Diamond.tscn scene and follow these steps:

1. Add a new instance of the ScorePoint scene as a child of the Diamond node.

2. Open the res://Objects/Diamond/Diamond.tscn script and implement the following changes. Here, I'm presuming you extracted the code from the class, meaning the lines in the ScorePoint class were removed from the Diamond class:

    I.   Create a reference for the ScorePoint node; we can call it score_points:

    ```
    extends RigidBody2D


    @onready var score_points = $ScorePoint
    ```

II.   In the _on_interactive_area_2d_interaction_available() method, before calling the queue_free() method, call increase_score() on the score_points node. The whole Diamond class script should look like this:

```
extends RigidBody2D

@onready var score_points = $ScorePoint

func _on_interactive_area_2d_interaction_available():
    score_points.increase_score()
    queue_free()
```

With that, the Diamond class is able to increase the player's score! You can test res://Game/Game.tscn, collect some diamonds, and see the score increasing in the top-right corner of the screen.

You can also play a bit with this system by adding the ScorePoint component to other classes as well. For instance, in the 05.maintaining-global-states-with-the-singleton-pattern/02.finished/ project, I added the ability for Crate Pig and Bumping Pig nodes to increase the player's score upon getting hit or defeated.

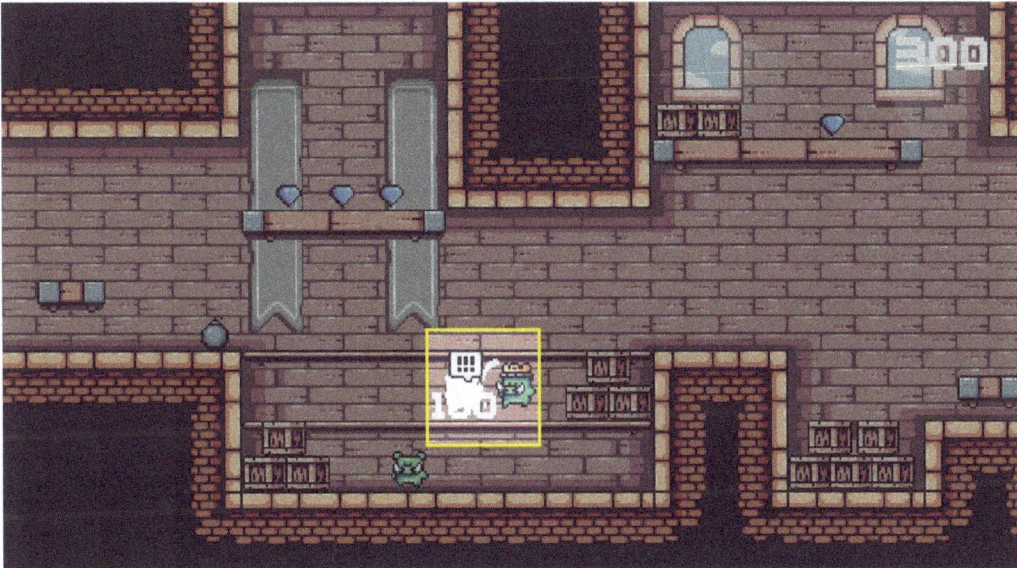

Figure 5.6 – The player hits a Bumping Pig, which increases the player's score and instances Pop Label

With the score system in place, there's another request from the designer that we must take care of. The door system currently only moves the player to the next level's initial door, but the designer wants to have multiple doors and be able to tell where each door leads. In the next section, we will see how we can implement such a system, taking into account that there is some data that we need to preserve and must be accessible for multiple classes from the same source.

Implementing the multi-door teleporting system

The next system that the designer requested an upgrade to is the door system. This is a fairly simple system that currently ensures that once the player interacts with the door, the `Level` node will fade out the current scene. Then, the door tells the `SceneTree` to change the current scene to the next one, and once the new scene loads, the `Level` node will position the `PlayerCharacter2D` node at the `Door` node's position.

This gives the idea that the player entered through the door to the next level. But our designer wants to improve the game world by allowing players to explore multiple doors that will lead to secret rooms or other entrances in the next level.

The major issue is that, as it is, the system doesn't support that by itself. Since the `Door` and the `Level` nodes are removed from memory once we change the scene, we need to maintain this data throughout game cleanses so that we know which `Door` node should be used in the next level to reposition the player's avatar. This system has two, or potentially more, classes involved. The `Door` class is the one that will define its target door, in other words, where the player should appear in the next level. But it's the `Level` class that repositions the player. So, this data must be available for both to access and modify. Due to that, it is safe to say that there's no need to have multiple instances of a class that will hold this data; it's the very opposite of that: the `Level` node must have access to the same object the `Door` node mutated. So, this is a good case for the implementation of another singleton class! For that, let's follow these steps:

1. Create a new scene using a `Node` node as the scene's root.

2. Rename it `TeleportData` and save it as `res://Objects/Door/TeleportData/TeleportData.tscn`.

3. Attach a new GDScript to it and save it as `res://Objects/Door/TeleportData/TeleportData.gd`.

4. Inside the script, we will just create a new variable to store the target portal name. The script should look like this:

    ```
    extends Node2D

    var target_portal_name = "Door"
    ```

5. Then, we will turn this scene into an `Autoload` node. Go to **Project | Project Settings | Autoload** and repeat the process we did in the previous section to add the `Score` scene as an `Autoload` node. Your **Autoload** list should look like this at this point:

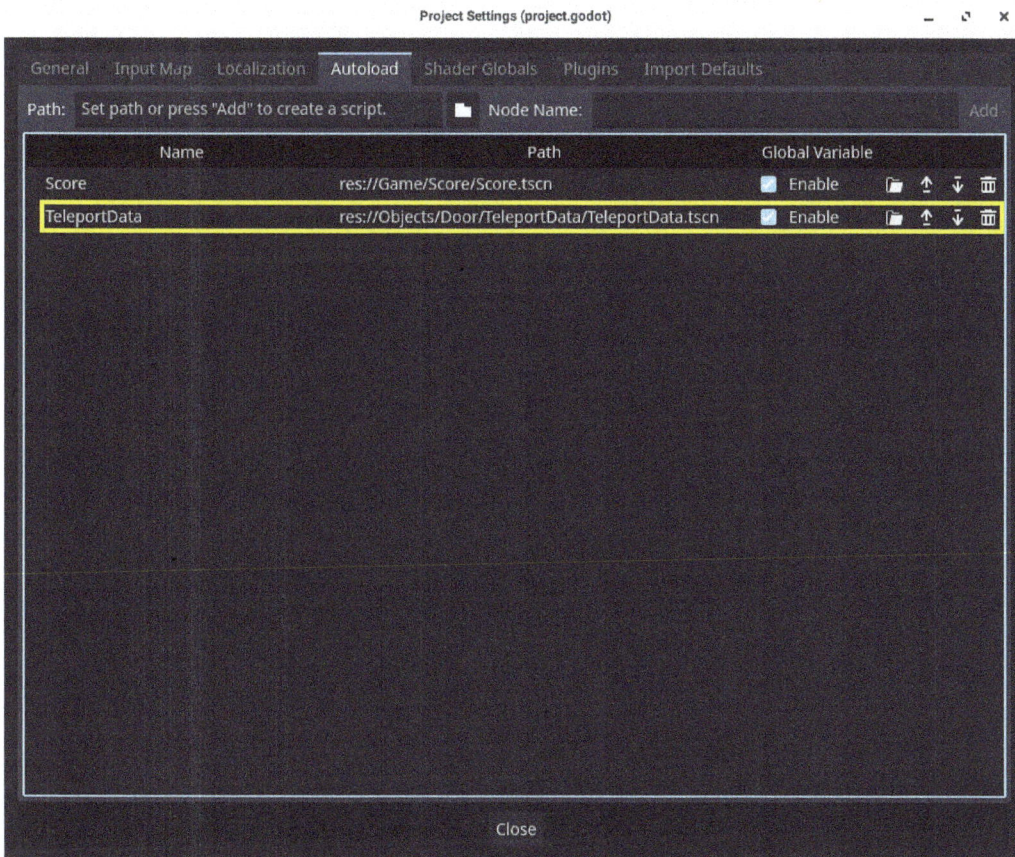

Figure 5.7 – The Autoload list is updated and now displays the TeleportData node as an Autoload

6. Now, let's make some updates to the user classes so they take advantage of these new features. We will start with the `Door` class. Open the `res://Objects/Door/Door.gd` script and do the following:

    I. Right below the line declaring `target_scene`, create an exported variable to hold the name of the target door as well. We can call it `target_door`:

```
extends Node2D

signal opened
signal closed
```

```
@export_file("*.tscn") var target_scene = "res://Levels/Level.
tscn"
@export var target_door = "Door"
```

II. Then, at the beginning of the `load_next_scene()` method, we will set the `TeleportData.target_portal_name` value to be the same as `target_door`:

```
func load_next_scene(next_scene = target_scene):
  TeleportData.target_portal_name = target_door
```

Note that the terminology here is slightly different. This is because I'm using one of my own game programming design patterns called Portal2D. You can find more about it, along with 13 other recipes, in my book, *Platformer Essentials Cookbook*.

7. With that, we made the necessary adjustments to the `Door` class. Now, let's move on to the `Level` class. Open the `res://Levels/Level.gd` script and follow these steps:

I. Inside the `_ready()` callback, let's change the player's target position in the `player.global_position = door.global_position` line. Instead of accessing the `door` variable, we will use the `find_child()` method passing `TeleportData.target_portal_name` instead:

```
func _ready():
    player.global_position = find_child(TeleportData.target_
portal_name)
        .global_position
    player.fade_in()
    fade.play("fade_in")
```

II. Then, to prevent confusion, let's remove the `door` variable declaration since we don't use it anywhere in the class anymore. This will keep the class clean. It should look like this at the end:

```
class_name Level
extends Node2D

@onready var player = $PlayerCharacter2D
@onready var fade = $CanvasLayer/ColorRect/AnimationPlayer

func _ready():
    player.global_position = find_child(TeleportData.target_
portal_name)
        .global_position
    player.fade_in()
```

```
        fade.play("fade_in")


func _on_player_character_2d_died():
    get_tree().reload_current_scene()

func _on_door_opened() -> void:
    player.fade_out()
    fade.play("fade_out")
```

This is all we need to do to achieve the designer's requirements! Go ahead and play a bit with this new ability. Add multiple doors to your levels and see how you can connect one to the other. For instance, in the 05.maintaining-global-states-with-the-singleton-pattern/02. finished/project, we have a secret door on the first level that leads the player to a secret room in the second level, and vice versa:

Figure 5.8 – The Level 1 and Level 2 secret doors

With this, we finished up our tasks and I'm sure the designer will be more than happy with the additions we implemented. Now, let's see a summary of what we learned throughout this chapter!

Summary

In this chapter, we explored how to maintain global states in a game using the Singleton pattern. We began by discussing the importance of preserving essential data and object states across different levels or scenes, addressing the problem that such data can be lost during transitions. The Singleton pattern provides an effective solution for keeping this data accessible and persistent throughout the game.

Our game designer tasked us with creating a global scoring system and enhancing the door system to allow teleportation between multiple doors across levels. To achieve this, we implemented a `Score` class designed as a singleton, ensuring that a single instance manages the player's score. This class included features such as storing both the current score and a high score. We made the `Score` class globally accessible by setting it as an `Autoload` node in Godot and updated the relevant classes, especially when we turned the diamond scoring behavior into the `ScorePoint` class, which allowed us to use it as a component in other classes.

To facilitate teleportation between different doors, we introduced the `TeleportData` class as another singleton. This class manages target door information, ensuring the player's position is accurately maintained across scenes. We modified the `Door` and `Level` classes to utilize `TeleportData`, enabling the multi-door teleportation feature.

Throughout the chapter, we implemented these features step by step, starting with the setup of the `Score` singleton and then integrating the door teleportation logic. We tested the new features by updating the `Diamond` class to interact with the scoring system and ensured the `Level` class handles player positioning correctly.

By the end of this chapter, we had successfully created a robust system for maintaining global states using the Singleton pattern with the Godot Autoload feature. This approach ensures that critical game data remains persistent and accessible within a single instance, thereby, subscribing to the Singleton pattern!

In the next chapter, we will keep on improving our project together with our team's designer. This time around, we will talk about one of the most flexible patterns, the Observer pattern. With this one, we are capable of easily decoupling classes and orchestrating event-driven systems for our game!

6

Decoupling Objects with the Observer Pattern

In this chapter, we will explore the Observer pattern, a powerful design pattern used to decouple objects. This pattern is especially useful for creating flexible and maintainable code, allowing objects to communicate without being tightly coupled. By the end of this chapter, you will understand the Observer pattern, identify its use cases in game projects, and learn how to implement it using Godot Engine 4.0's built-in signal system.

The idea behind the Observer pattern is that objects can have a loose reference if they manage to create a common interface with a method that they can call to get updated about state changes from another object. This helps us decouple direct (or hard) references between user classes and user classes. Imagine that a co-worker reaches out to you in the morning and asks you to let them know when you'll leave for lunch. It doesn't matter what they will do with this information.

They ask you to send a message on their phone when you leave saying "Going to lunch." You agree to that, and as soon as you get up from your chair to go for lunch, you send them the message; they receive it and do what they planned with this information.

This is how the Observer pattern works: an object subscribes to another object's events through a common interface. The subscribing object is called the observer and the other object is called the subject. When the subject's event happens, it calls a method on all its observers, triggering their behavior.

We will see some interesting use cases for this pattern and, after that, we will take our project and improve upon previous features by using Godot Engine's signals system, which is a built-in implementation of the Observer pattern. By using signals, we can rely on Godot's editor interface to subscribe nodes to other nodes' events, or rather, signals. In this chapter, we will cover the following topics:

- Understanding the Observer pattern
- Spotting use cases for the Observer pattern
- Implementing the Observer pattern in Godot

Without further ado, let's get started!

Technical requirements

To follow the instructions in this chapter, use the project located in the `06.decoupling-objects-with-the-observer-pattern/01.start/` directory. If you encounter any confusion, errors, or bugs while following the instructions, refer to the files in the `06.decoupling-objects-with-the-observer-pattern/02.finished/` folder. Don't forget to report any issues on the repository's issue tracker through this link: `https://github.com/PacktPublishing/Game-Development-Patterns-with-Godot-4/issues`.

If you haven't downloaded the repository yet, you can get it from the following link: `https://github.com/PacktPublishing/Game-Development-Patterns-with-Godot-4`.

With that said, let's start exploring the Observer pattern, its core functionalities, what it fundamentally solves, and how people usually implement it. It's important to understand its usual implementation so that we understand what's happening behind Godot's built-in implementation as well.

Understanding the Observer pattern

The Observer pattern is a behavioral pattern that allows us to subscribe to multiple objects to define a one-to-many relationship between observer objects and a subject. It allows one object, known as the subject, to notify multiple observer objects about state changes without knowing who or what those observers are.

Imagine that there are a multitude of enemies in a top-down shooter and they all need to know whether the player entered an invulnerable state, so they flee from the player instead of trying to fight them. They can access the player's object state every single frame to determine whether the player is in an invulnerable state or not. But this would be costly performance-wise. Not only that but now these enemies will also be hard-coupled to the player's object, so maintaining them means we need to keep the enemies' class up with changes in the player's class. What if we decide to change the state-changing logic? What if it doesn't have a clear invulnerable state anymore? What if we decide to use an enumerator approach to have more control over the available states? What if we decide to implement the State pattern at some point? How will the enemies' class adapt to these? And how many other classes will be impacted by these changes? How will the enemies even know about the existence of the player's object if they don't have any direct relationship?

Well, the Observer pattern comes as an excellent solution for this kind of hard coupling, especially when there's no direct relationship between the classes. The subject object maintains a list of observer objects and the method the subject calls when the desired event occurs. This allows the subject to remain unaware of the observers' specific implementation details.

The way this is typically implemented is through a subscription system that both the subject and the observer implement, so they share the same interface and don't need to be aware of any implementation details from other classes. For instance, in Godot Engine, we have the base `Object` class. It provides several methods regarding the implementation of an Observer pattern: mainly, `Object.add_user_signal()` (which allows us to create new signals in runtime for `Object`), `Object.connect()` (which allows us to connect a signal to a method, or rather, a **Callable** object). Note that `Callable` is a class that represents an `Object` method or a standalone function. `Object.connect()` is effectively the subscription mechanism of Godot's Observer pattern implementation. Since signals are also first-class citizens in Godot Engine 4.0, we can also directly subscribe `Callable` objects to them by using `Signal.connect()`. Just to make it clear, a `Callable` object can be a reference to an object's method, this allows us to bind a signal to an object's method directly. Previously, in Godot Engine 3.x, we needed to pass the object instance followed by the function's name as a String. Another interesting method in Godot's Observer pattern implementation is `Object.emit_signal()`, where we can use a String to tell which signal we want to emit. This fundamentally updates observers about changes in the state of the subject, in other words, effectively updates observers about an event in the subject. Talking about observers, `Object.get_signal_connection_list()` allows us to access all the `Callable` objects subscribed to the Object's signals. Again, note that since signals are first-class citizens in Godot Engine 4.0, there are equivalent methods to allow us to access signals more specifically. Using the `Signal.emit()` method, we can trigger a signal, and using `Signal.get_connections()`, we can get a list of `Callable` objects bonded to this signal. There are other interesting methods, such as `Object.disconnect()` and `Signal.disconnect()`, that make Godot's signals feature an excellent implementation of the Observer pattern. Note that, as stated by Godot Engine's documentation, the `Object` class is the class from where all classes in the engine inherit from:

> *"An advanced Variant type. All classes in the engine inherit from Object. Each class may define new properties, methods or signals, which are available to all inheriting classes."*

This makes it so that they all share these signal-related methods. In other words, they all share the interface where the Observer pattern is implemented. This ultimately gives us some safe ground to use these methods knowing that, since our classes will inherit the same superclass, they all share this interface already, allowing us to move forward without being concerned about unnecessary coupling. A small note on that is that the classes are already coupled to the `Object` class through inheritance, so there's coupling at some level. The advantage is that they are not coupled with each other but with a class provided by the framework we are working with. Because of this, the built-in classes are unlikely to change once we get into production. That's why is important to choose a version and stick to it during the game's production cycle.

After all this abstract explanation about what the Observer pattern is, what it solves, how it's typically implemented, and how Godot implements it, in the next section, let's see some common use cases to help us understand where we can find problems that can be solved by this pattern.

Spotting use cases for the Observer pattern

The Observer pattern is a versatile behavioral pattern. Since its core intent is to promote loose coupling, or total decoupling, of classes, we can implement it in a variety of systems in our games. In this section, we will see some applications of this pattern, but they are not the only places where we can use the Observer pattern. Keep in mind its core features and you can see that it can be used in different cases, especially when you want to communicate between two indirectly related objects or if you want objects to be notified about changes in the state of another object.

A good use case for the Observer pattern is the **Graphical User Interface** (**GUI**) and especially **Heads-Up Display** (**HUD**) elements. Usually, when we create games, the HUD elements are implemented separately from the game world's elements. For instance, in Godot Engine, it's common to have a `CanvasLayer` node holding the HUD and other GUI elements as its children, as shown in the following figure:

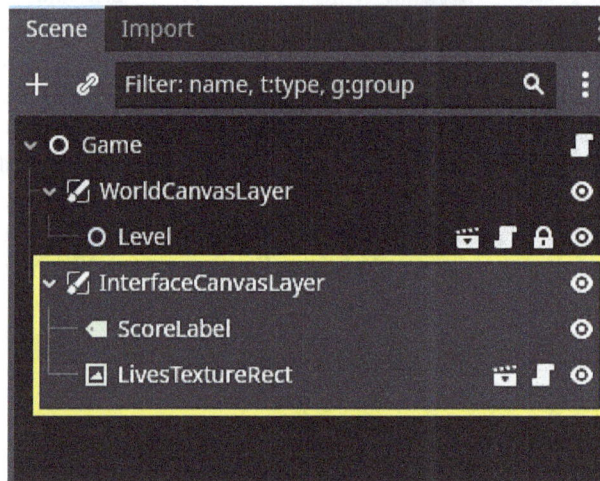

Figure 6.1 – A node hierarchy with a CanvasLayer node dedicated to the interface elements

In that sense, score systems, health, energy, and other resource systems typically benefit from implementing the Observer pattern. Let's say you want to display the player's health on the HUD. You can implement a signal on the player's object that emits a `health_changed` signal passing the new value argument for its subscribed `Callable` objects. Then, you can use a common ancestor object (in other words, a node that can be found in both node hierarchies) to connect them. The way I usually approach this is by using the `Game` node itself, which usually is the parent node of `InterfaceCanvasLayer` and `WorldCanvasLayer`, so it mediates the interactions between the game world and the game interface.

Another good use case for the implementation of the Observer pattern is an inventory system, especially when you have some database representing the player's inventory. In games such as *Ragnarök Online* where monsters drop some items and the player has to manually pick them, the object that represents the loot in the game world is likely just a data container with the item's ID. So, when the player picks the item, it emits a signal to the player's inventory passing the item's ID, and using this item ID, the inventory adds the item to the player's inventory.

Enemies with AI is another good example of implementing the Observer pattern. One common mistake people make when trying to integrate enemy behavior with the player's object internal state is that they add a reference to the player's object instance in the `enemy` class, hard-coupling these classes. In some cases, it's inevitable to hard-couple these classes; for instance, if you need to access the player's position every frame, it's better to just have a direct reference to the object and check it every frame than emit a signal every frame updating enemies about the player's current position. Remember, the Observer pattern itself is meant to only update interested objects (namely, subscribers) about relevant changes in the observed object. So, whenever you have data that needs constant updates or is not directly interpreted as an event, it's likely not a good use case for the Observer pattern.

On the other hand, let's say you want an object to know when the player's life reaches a critical amount, for instance, 10%, so they can perform a risky attack that will kill the enemy. We could connect a player's `health_changed` signal to the enemy once the player entered the enemy's sight area; we can use an `Area2D` node for that and connect the `Area2D.body_entered` signal to the enemy's node responsible for decision-making. Then, when the player's health changes, the enemy will be notified and can make the proper movement. When the player leaves the enemy's sight area, we can disconnect its `health_changed` signal to prevent the enemy from taking any action if it can't reach the player anymore. For that, we can use the `Area2D.body_exited` signal and then we can call `health_changed.disconnect()` to disconnect the signal from the `Callable` object we connected it to the enemy's object. Well, now that you get some concrete examples of how to use the Observer pattern to improve the interactions of the objects in your game while maintaining them loosely coupled, it's time to do some practice! In the next section, we will get another brief from our game designer asking us to improve our project's GUI. And for that, we will use the Observer pattern, of course!

Implementing the Observer pattern in Godot

As we saw in the *Understanding the Observer pattern* section, Godot Engine has its own built-in implementation of the Observer pattern called signals, which is a core functionality of the `Object` class, the base class for Godot's framework.

Ever since signals became first-class citizens in GDScript, we also have the `Signal` class offering the functionalities in a standalone manner. This allows us to implement the Observer pattern in classes that don't inherit from `Object`; usually, these are custom classes we create. But it's very rare that we need to do that.

Nonetheless, in this section, we will use the standalone implementation instead of the `Object` class implementation.

Well, our game designer has yet another demand for us. Let's see the request and assess it so we can elaborate a good solution for the issue:

Hey there, game designer here.

I figured that we needed more interface elements for the game. The player is playing it blindly without having any cues about the game's internal states. So, I decided to make a HUD element to display how many lives the player has. I called it LivesTextureRect because we are using a TextureRect as the root node. I also made some nice animated hearts that animate when they disappear. Everything is set up already, but I can't manage to find a good way to access the player's health, so it's currently useless.

I need this object to be aware of changes in the player's health, both if it increases so it plays an animation restoring a heart, and decreases when the player takes damage. Keep in mind that this is an interface element, so it's currently outside of the player's node hierarchy since we use a CanvasLayer node to draw the interface on top of the game world's elements.

Let's assess this request. First of all, it's good that the designer took the initiative to make some implementations on their own. It seems like they made a simple object with two main functions, `hit_hearts()` and `recover_hearts()`, which remove and add hearts to the HUD element that represents the player's current lives. There's also a class named `HeartTextureRect`, which is the HUD element that represents each heart individually. It has two methods, `hit()` and `recover()`, which basically play animations. Apart from that, there's nothing really connecting this to the in-game element that it represents, namely, the player's health points.

Based on the designer's request, we will need to call the `hit_hearts()` method every time the player loses a health point. Thinking about it for a second, if the player loses two or more points in an enemy hit, the interface will need to know so it calls the `hit_hearts()` method accordingly. Let's keep that in mind.

Now, the other requirement is that the interface is not supposed to know about the player. This means they are supposed to be completely decoupled from each other. In other words, they should not hold a reference to an instance of each other. This means we will need to use another object that is aware of the existence of both of them so it can behave as a mediator in their communication.

Note that we have all the requirements to implement the Observer pattern in this case. We have an object that needs to react to changes in another object's state but must not be coupled to this object. In this case, `LivesTextureRect` is the observer class while `KingPigPlayer2D` is the subject class. In that sense, we will need to implement signals in `KingPigPlayer2D` and connect them to `Callable` objects in `LivesTextureRect`. But these `Callable` objects can't be the current methods, since they lack an argument to tell the amount of hearts to be hit or recovered. We will need to create two callback methods to wrap up an argument telling how many lives were lost or recovered. In the next section, we will put this into practice by implementing the requirements for this task!

Integrating the player's health interface

Our game needs a HUD element to display the player's current health points, and for that, the designer implemented some basic methods to perform the desired behavior. But the major issue is that it currently can't communicate with the player object so it gathers the data it needs to express the current amount of lives in the player visually. To solve that, we will implement the Observer pattern and integrate the HUD element and the player's object.

Now that we understand the game designer's request, it's time to work. Open the project inside the `06.decoupling-objects-with-the-observer-pattern/01.start/` folder and let's follow these steps:

1. The first thing we will need to do is to create and properly emit the necessary signals in the `KingPigPlayer2D` class. Open the `res://Actors/KingPig/KingPigPlayer2D.gd` file and create two signals right below the dead signal, `lives_increased` and `lives_decreased`. Both of them will pass an argument communicating the number of lives that were increased or decreased:

    ```
    extends Player2D

    signal died
    signal lives_increased(amount)
    signal lives_decreased(amount)

    @export var lives = 3
    ```

2. Then, in the `_on_hurt_area_2d_hurt()` method, right below the line where we decrease `current_lives`, let's emit the `lives_decreased` signal passing the `damage` variable as the number of lives decreased:

    ```
    func _on_hurt_area_2d_hurt(damage):
        set_physics_process(false)
        set_process_unhandled_input(false)
        direction = 0
        current_lives -= damage
        lives_decreased.emit(damage)
    ```

The next step is to create the callback methods that we will use as `Callable` objects to connect these signals.

3. For that, open res://Interface/LivesBar/LivesTextureRect.gd, the class our designer prepared for us. At the bottom of the class, create two methods that receive an argument for the lives lost or recovered. Let's call these methods _on_player_lives_increased() and _on_player_lives_decreased(). It's a common practice to use the _on_[object_name]_[signal_name]() structure for functions that work as signal callbacks so we know that they are meant to react to a specific event from a specific object:

    ```
    func _on_player_lives_increased(amount):
        pass
    func _on_player_lives_decreased(amount):
        pass
    ```

4. Then, inside the _on_player_lives_increased() and _on_player_lives_decreased() methods, we will call the respective LivesTextureRect methods based on the amount argument received:

    ```
    func _on_player_lives_increased(amount):
        for i in amount:
            recover_hearts()

    func _on_player_lives_decreased(amount):
        for i in amount:
            hit_hearts()
    ```

With that we have our in-points, the callback methods that will trigger the LivesTextureRect behavior, and the out-points, the signals on the KingPigPlayer2D class. But they are currently completely unrelated and unaware of the existence of one another, which is ideal. This is how we keep them decoupled. Now, we need to find a common ancestor to connect them. In our case, this common ancestor is the Game class. If you open the res://Game/Game.tscn scene, you will notice that Level, the parent of the PlayerCharacter2D node, is a child of WorldCanvasLayer, whereas LivesTextureRect is a child of the InterfaceCanvasLayer node.

Both these CanvasLayer nodes are children of the Game node, so the Game node is the common ancestor between the LivesTextureRect and PlayerCharacter2D nodes. This is important to keep in mind because this helps us create good abstractions for our high-level game logic. Since the Game node is the one aware of required classes, it is already coupled to them, so we are not adding any layer of coupling by using this class to mediate the communication. That said, let's open the res://Game/Game.gd script and follow these steps:

1. First of all, we need to create references for the nodes we will use, namely, PlayerCharacter2D and the LivesTextureRect, so, right below the score_label variable declaration. For that, we need to penetrate the Level node hierarchy to access the PlayerCharacter2D node.

    ```
    extends Node
    @onready var score_label = $InterfaceCanvasLayer/ScoreLabel
    ```

```
@onready var player = $WorldCanvasLayer/Level/PlayerCharacter
@onready var lives_interface = $InterfaceCanvasLayer/LivesTex
```

Note that this breaks the encapsulation principle. And here is where we develop some maturity in programming. Principles are guidelines to achieve better code, but they are not mandatory. As long as we are aware of this approach, we will be able to develop strategies to compensate for this violation if it causes any issues.

2. The next step is to create a method to mediate the signal connections. Something interesting that I want to highlight here is that the SOLID principles don't necessarily apply only to classes, so a note you should take is that methods and variables should subscribe to these principles. In this case, this method has the single responsibility of connecting the player's lives to the respective lives HUD element. So, let's call it `setup_lives_interface()`:

```
func setup_lives_interface():
```

3. Inside this method, we will connect `player.lives_decreased` and `player.lives_increased` to their respective callbacks in `lives_interface`:

```
func setup_lives_interface():
    player.lives_decreased.connect(lives_interface
    ._on_player
    player.lives_increased.connect(lives_interface
    ._on_player
```

4. Now, in the `_ready()` callback, we will call the `setup_lives_interface()` method right below the `update_score_label()` method call. This will effectively glue the `PlayerCharacter2D` class with the `LivesTextureRect` class without coupling them:

```
func _ready():
    update_score_label()
    setup_lives_interface()
```

With that, we implemented custom signals in our player class, allowing the player class to communicate to the interface class its internal state only when it changes. We effectively used Godot's implementation of the Observer pattern to solve an issue properly. I want to keep reminding you that design patterns are solutions to specific, but common, problems. In this case, the Observer pattern was a perfect match for the problem we needed to solve. But don't get stuck trying to build code bases based on design patterns. Evaluate the issue and try to assess whether there's a known solution that can provide a predictable result. This is what design patterns are. That said, if you test `res://Game/Game.tscn`, you can play-test the game and take some damage to see whether the solution works. In the following figure, we have the interface before and after the player takes some damage. This effectively validates our solution!

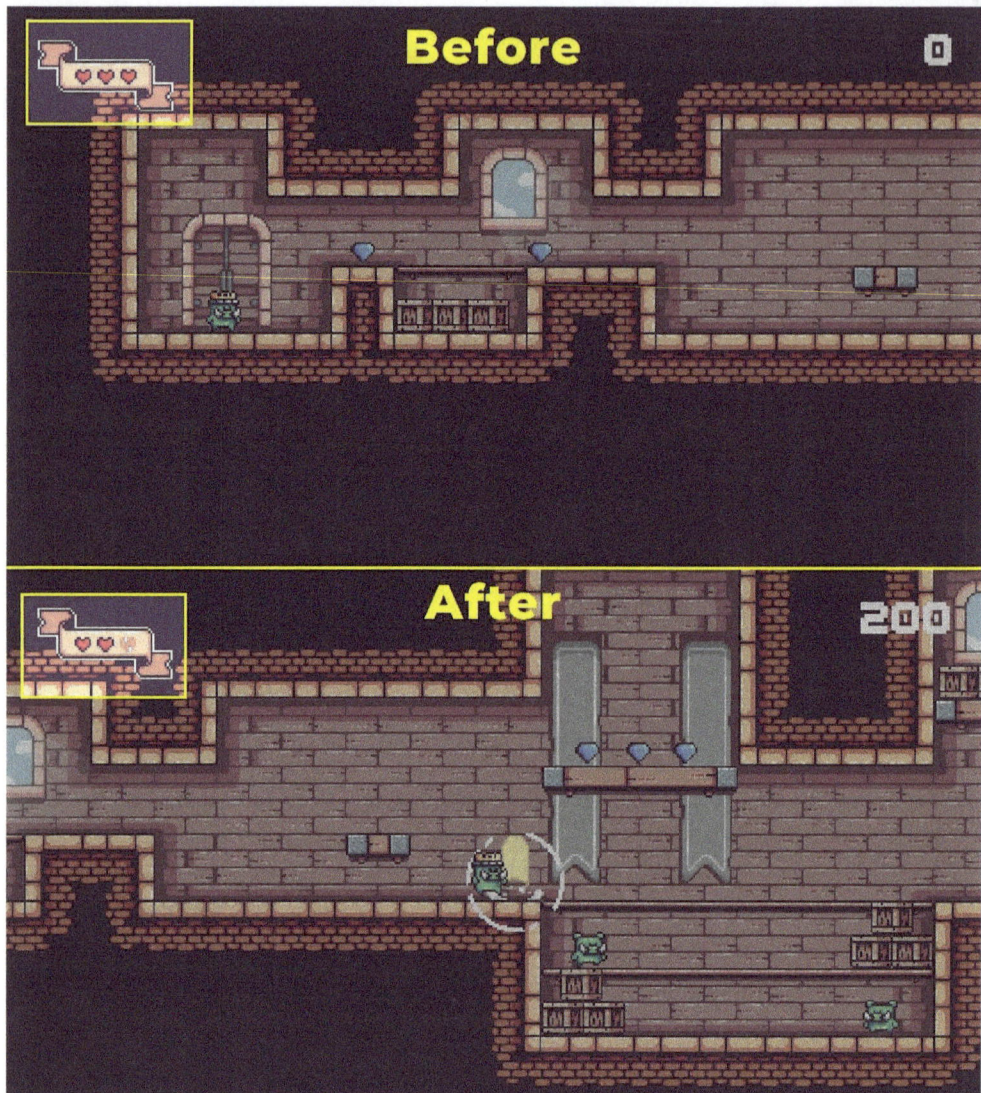

Figure 6.2 – The lives bar before and after the player took damage

You can go on and test the implementation on other use cases. For instance, try to increase the bomb damage and see whether `LivesTextureRect` properly sets the hearts displayed. With this in place, we can safely call it a day and move on to the next task!

Summary

In this chapter, we saw the usefulness of the Observer pattern, a fundamental design pattern for decoupling objects and enhancing the flexibility and maintainability of code. We began by exploring the core concept of the Observer pattern, which allows objects, referred to as observers, to be notified and updated automatically when the state of another object, known as the subject, changes. This pattern is particularly useful in scenarios where multiple objects need to be aware of state changes without being tightly coupled to the subject. This allows us to create a more modular and loosely coupled design.

We then examined a practical implementation of the Observer pattern in the context of game development using Godot Engine. By implementing this pattern, we created a system where various game elements, such as UI components and game entities, can react to changes in the game state seamlessly. This decoupling ensures that modifications to one part of the game do not necessitate changes in other parts, thus adhering to the Open/Closed principle and making the code base more robust and easier to maintain.

Next, we looked into the specific roles of the subject and observer interfaces in our implementation. The subject interface manages a list of observers and provides methods to add, remove, and notify them of state changes. The observer interface defines the update method, which is called by the subject to notify observers of any changes. This separation of concerns allows each class to focus on its specific responsibilities, further enhancing code clarity and reusability.

We also discussed the advantages and potential drawbacks of the Observer pattern. On the positive side, it significantly reduces the dependencies between subjects and observers, making the system more modular and flexible. However, we also acknowledged that improper use of this pattern could lead to performance issues, especially if the number of observers grows significantly or if the update process becomes too frequent, for instance, updating observers in the `_process()` callback. Therefore, it's essential to carefully design and optimize the observer notification process to avoid potential bottlenecks.

In the end, we used Godot Engine's signals, a built-in implementation of the Observer pattern, to connect the GUI element that displays the player's health points to the player object, allowing it to properly display the game's internal state to the player.

Throughout this chapter, we saw a comprehensive understanding of the Observer pattern and its practical application in games using Godot Engine. We learned how to implement this pattern to create a more decoupled and maintainable code base, especially regarding the user interface.

In the next chapter, we will explore the Factory pattern, which will help us create a robust system for spawning objects dynamically and efficiently!

Get This Book's PDF Version and Exclusive Extras

UNLOCK NOW

Scan the QR code (or go to packtpub.com/unlock). Search for this book by name, confirm the edition, and then follow the steps on the page.

Note: Keep your invoice handy. Purchases made directly from Packt don't require an invoice.

7

Spawning Game Objects with the Factory Pattern

In this chapter, we will explore the **Factory pattern**, a creational design pattern that allows us to establish a default interface in a superclass, which will allow it to create new objects. Subclasses can then change the type or the way these objects are created, allowing us to use a common interface to create a range of different objects.

By using the Factory pattern, we can decouple an object's creational responsibility and delegate it to the factory object, which will take care of all the procedures necessary to create this object in the application. Generally speaking, the Factory pattern can create any type of object. Keep in mind our definition of an object: the concrete instance of a class. This means that it does not necessarily create game objects, in other words, objects that are part of the game world. In this chapter, we will create a specialization of the Factory pattern known as Spawner, which is specifically designed for creating objects in the game world.

We already saw in *Chapter 1* how we can create instances of scenes using the `PackedScene.instantiate()` method. Throughout this chapter, we will see that this may not be enough to insert an object into the game world properly and we may need to do some procedures in the object so it appears in the right place. At the end of the chapter, we will turn the diamond-dropping behavior from the `LootCrate` class into a component that we can attach to other objects and allow them to drop `Diamond` objects and other items.

In this chapter, we will cover the following topics:

- Understanding the Factory pattern
- Spotting use cases for the Factory pattern
- Implementing the Factory pattern in Godot

Are you curious about how this will unfold? Well, let's get started!

Technical requirements

To follow along in this chapter, use the project files in the `07.spawning-game-objects-with-factory/01.start/` folder. If you encounter any confusion, errors, or bugs while following the instructions in the *Implementing the Factory pattern in Godot* section, refer to the files in the `07.spawning-game-objects-with-factory/02.finished/` folder. Report any issues you find to Packt's support team so we can address them! To report any issues you've found, use the following link: `https://github.com/PacktPublishing/Game-Development-Patterns-with-Godot-4/issues`.

If you don't have the repository files yet, you can get them from the following link: `https://github.com/PacktPublishing/Game-Development-Patterns-with-Godot-4`.

With that said, let's start with understanding the fundamental principles of the Factory pattern. Understanding the pattern's function, features, the problem it solves, and how it is usually implemented will help us find good use cases for it and implement it in Godot, taking the best out of Godot's built-in features and avoiding getting into technicality traps.

Understanding the Factory pattern

The **Factory pattern** is a creational design pattern. This means that it solves a particular problem related to how we will create objects in our application, or in our case, in our games. The singleton pattern is another creational design pattern, for reference, as it addresses how to create a given object. In the Singleton pattern's case, it ensures that a given variable always points to only one instance of the same object. This variable is made static, allowing any object to access it. In the case of the Factory pattern, it allows us to instance a family of objects without specifying their types, and these objects are known as products. It does it so that we can centralize common procedures and prevent duplication of these procedures in multiple classes; instead, these classes become user classes of the Factory classes.

One of the most fundamental aspects of the Factory pattern is that it is not supposed to be a single class that handles all types of object instancing. Instead, it provides a generic interface so that user classes can communicate with all subclasses of the Factory. A good example so you can envision this is to think about a class that represents a firearm. It can shoot a range of different bullets, for instance, an explosive bullet, a piercing bullet, and an impact bullet. We can create a `BulletFactory` class and make the `FireArm` class a user class of it. `BulletFactory` has a method called `create()`, which returns the product. Now, let's say we create three subclasses based on `BulletFactory`: `ExplosiveBulletFactory`, `PiercingBulletFactory`, and `ImpactBulletFactory`. In the `FireArm` class, we only need a variable to hold a reference to the current `BulletFactory` instance and we can mutate it when the player changes the bullet type. The code will look something like this:

```
var bullet_factory: BulletFactory = BulletFactory.new()
func shoot() -> void:
    var bullet: Bullet = bullet_factory.create()
```

```
func change_ammo(new_bullet_factory: BulletFactory) ->
  void:
    # Plays an animation changing the ammo

    bullet_factory = new_bullet_factory
```

One usual approach to implementing the Factory pattern is to have multiple methods, or a method with multiple arguments, to indicate what type of products the Factory should create. This allows the Factory to execute the right procedures for the product depending on its type. On top of that, by providing information about the product, the Factory can adjust it accordingly, changing the necessary properties to make the desired product.

In Godot Engine, we can embed all these aspects by serializing this data into a `PackedScene` resource, which makes the implementation of the Factory pattern way simpler since we can essentially use `PackedScene` resources as a reference for our products. The products themselves will be the nodes created based on the `PackedScene` resource, so we should take care of the type of nodes we are instantiating in the process. According to the Godot Engine's official documentation (`https://docs.godotengine.org/en/stable/classes/class_packedscene.html`) about `PackedScene`:

> *PackedScene, one of the most common Objects in a Godot project, is also a resource, uniquely capable of storing and instantiating the Nodes it contains as many times as desired.*

With that, we have the perfect data structure to provide as an argument for the creation of a Factory pattern creation method in order to produce any product we need. Keep in mind that, depending on the type of node we are creating through the Factory, it may require different procedures to handle it and achieve the desired result. For instance, `Node2D` is likely to need some procedures to properly position it in the game.

Now that we have a sense of what is the Factory pattern, in the next section, we will see some common use cases that can benefit from this design pattern, especially in the realm of games.

Spotting use cases for the Factory pattern

Due to the dynamic nature of games, creating objects is very common. I'd risk saying that understanding how to properly create and delete objects together with the ability to make them interact with each other is the bread and butter of game development. In that sense, mastering the Factory pattern can help you implement the features you want in your game. In this section, we will see some use cases that can benefit from the implementation of the Factory pattern so we can understand when to use it in our game's code base.

A common use case for the Factory pattern is regarding monster spawners. **Spawners** are objects that create instances of monsters around a given area. This term comes from **role-playing games (RPGs)**, where we have an invisible or visible object whose main responsibility is to maintain a flow of monsters in a map or area. In that sense, spawners are a clear implementation of a Factory pattern, as we can create a generic interface for instancing monsters and simply change the type of monster that the spawner should create. We can also extend the behavior to implement more specialized instancing. For instance, we can create a timed spawner that creates monsters based on a time tic.

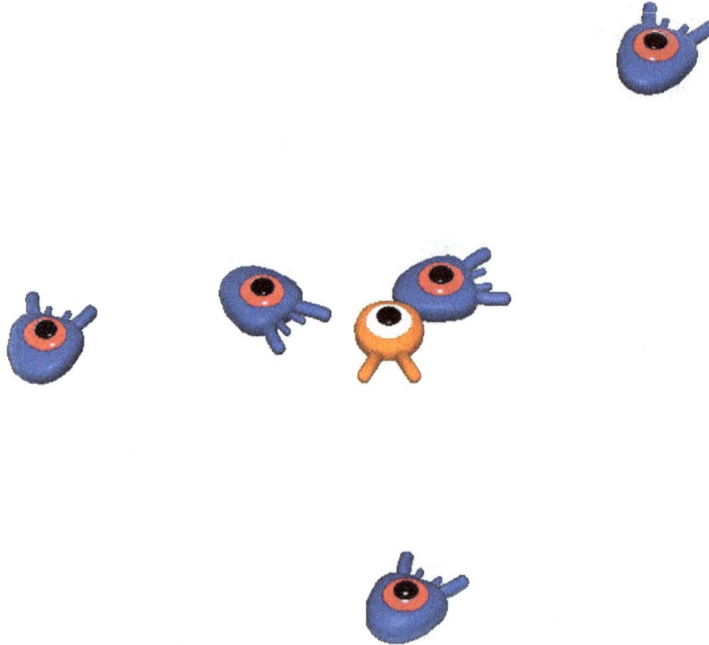

Figure 7.1 – Creeps dynamically spawned around an area in the game. Image taken from the
Official Godot Engine. "CC-BY 3.0 Juan Linietsky, Ariel Manzur, and the Godot community"

Another good use case for the Factory pattern is the creation of magic spells. We can create a class in which products are magic spells that will be created in the game world, such as fireballs, ice bolts, and earth spikes. We can implement an interface that allows the player to select a target area or enemy and use a `SpellFactory` class to create the instances of the magic spell upon confirmation of a valid target.

As mentioned earlier in the previous section, instancing bullets is another use case for the Factory pattern as well. In a sense, firearms can be abstracted as factories of bullets that can create a limited amount of products at a time to represent the magazine size. Then, changing the firearm is essentially changing the bullet factory subclass to create different products, in other words, different bullets:

Figure 7.2 – The player casting fireballs in the GDQuest's 2D Gunner
project. "CC-BY 4.0 - GDQuest and contributors"

Finally, and this is where we will connect it to our game, another good use case for the Factory pattern in games is when we need to create items, especially as loot from enemies or other objects in the game. In the next section, we will see how we can implement the Factory pattern as a component in our game to allow us to create loot in the game.

Implementing the Factory pattern in Godot

Alright, now that we have an idea of what the Factory pattern is, it's time to put it into practice. In this section, we will have another round of role-playing with our fictional studio's game designer. This time around, we will create a class in which we can set PackedScene and a container node found in the Level node hierarchy and it will create the object in the game world.

So, our game designer implemented a cool new object called Heart, which recovers one life of the player, but they want to be able to make this object appear in the game as a drop from the LootCrate objects. They also want to be able to make Diamond objects drop from the Bumping Pig enemy as well as the Heart objects. Here's their briefing:

Hello there,

I noticed that the game is currently lacking some incentives to make the players more aggressive toward the enemies. If we don't give anything in return for defeating an enemy, the player will just avoid them as much as they can. This makes the combat system pointless.

So, I want to come up with a way to allow the enemies to also drop diamonds. Now that the players are going to take more risks to defeat the enemies, I also thought about balancing this out by creating an item to recover the player's health points, so I created the Heart node. I already made the proper adjustments on the player's class using a setter method to emit the signals you've created to update the LivesTextureRect I made; thank you for that.

Now, I want you to create a class that will allow me to create and insert objects in the game world, so it should create the objects at its own position. This will allow me to design some specific points where some things will appear. On top of that, since I also want to place some heart objects manually, I created a container class for them in the Level scene. It would be good if the class that creates and inserts objects in the game used this container as the parent of its creations. This way, we can keep things organized, so I would appreciate it if I could indicate the parent's name in a field in that class.

Thank you in advance.

Game Designer.

Our designer is getting clever! Thanks to the way we implemented our signals in the previous chapter, the designer managed to create a new item that recovers the player's health points and updates the life bar interface. This is the power of making a good, simple, and elegant code base. This time around, the designer needs us to create an object that creates objects in the game world. Note that since these objects need to appear directly on screen, in other words, in the game world, they will have a position, so they will likely be instances of Node2D or subclasses of the Node2D class.

Whenever we talk about an object that creates objects, it's very likely that we are talking about a Factory. In this specific case, a Factory of Node2D objects, or using the right terminology, a Factory with Node2D products. Since we will need the Factory to also have a position so the designer can place it according to where they want the objects to appear, the Factory will also need to be Node2D. For visual reference, we can use Marker2D for the Factory node as this will allow the designer to have a visual cue about the position, rotation, and scale of the Factory node.

Another thing the designer asked for is the ability to indicate the name of a parent node to which the products will be parented. Essentially, what we are going to do is extract the LootCrate class' diamond creation behavior into a new class. But instead of instantiating Diamond nodes, it will accept any Node2D object in the form of a PackedScene object. Well, let's get it started. In the next section, we will create the Factory class responsible for creating and inserting objects in the game world.

Creating the Node2DFactory class

With our abstraction of the problem done and potential solutions in place, we can get our hands dirty. Open the 07.spawning-game-objects-with-factory/01.start/project.godot file using Godot Engine and let's follow these steps to implement our Factory class of Node2D nodes:

1. Create a new scene and use Marker2D as the root node.
2. Rename it as Node2DFactory to make it clear through its name what it does.

3. Save the scene as `res://Objects/Node2DFactory/Node2DFactory.tscn`.

4. Attach a new GDScript to the `Node2DFactory` node and save it along the scene file using the same name. Its full path should be `res://Objects/Node2DFactory/Node2DFactory.gd`.

5. In the script, we will start by creating a new signal that will be emitted when the Factory class creates a new product. This signal will pass the product as an argument so that other classes access it and perform further procedures on it:

```
extends Marker2D
class_name Node2DFactory

signal created(product)
```

6. Then, declare a new exported variable to hold a reference to `PackedScene`, which will be used by the Factory to create its product.

```
extends Marker2D
class_name Node2DFactory

signal created(product)

@export var product_packed_scene: PackedScene
```

7. After that, we will export yet another variable. This time around, it will hold a reference to the name of the node that will be used as a container for the products created by the Factory:

```
extends Marker2D
class_name Node2DFactory

signal created(product)

@export var product_packed_scene: PackedScene
@export var target_container_name: StringName
```

8. Now, it's time for what is known as the **Factory Method** ; this is yet another design pattern and it's the core of our Factory Method. Note that our Factory is very similar to the Abstract Factory pattern but different from the Abstract Factory. It is a concrete implementation instead of an abstract interface that subclasses need to implement the concrete logic for its Factory method. Anyway, our method will be called `create()` and it will receive an optional argument that by default will be the `product_packed_scene`. We do that in case we want to use `Node2DFactory` to create other products without losing reference to its original product. This method will also return its product in case the user class needs to do further procedures on it.

```
func create(_product_packed_scene :=
   product_packed_scene) ->
```

9. Inside the `create()` method, we will declare a variable that must be of a `Node2D` type. Its value will be the returning value of calling the `instantiate()` method on the `_product_packed_scene` argument. This will effectively deserialize `PackedScene` and turn it into an actual node, ideally `Node2D`:

```
func create(_product_packed_scene :=
    product_packed_scene) ->
        var product: Node2D =
            _product_packed_scene.instantiate()
```

10. Now that we have the reference to the recently instantiated product, we will now treat it as necessary. This is the whole point of making a Factory; it's not just the instantiation of an object, but encapsulating all the necessary procedures to achieve the desired concrete instance of the product. In this case, we will first position the instance relative to the `Node2DFactory.global_position` variable:

```
func create(_product_packed_scene :=
    product_packed_scene) ->
        var product: Node2D =
            _product_packed_scene.instantiate()
        product.global_position = global_position
```

11. Another necessary procedure concerning these specific products is adding them as children of a container node. For that, we will first need to find this node. So, let's create a variable called `container`, which will be the returning value of using the `find_parent()` method, looking for the `Level` node, and then finding `target_container_name` in its children:

```
func create(_product_packed_scene :=
    product_packed_scene) ->
        var product: Node2D =
            _product_packed_scene.instantiate()
        product.global_position = global_position

        var container = find_parent("Level")
            .find_child(target_cotainer_name)
```

12. After finding the proper container, we need to call the `add_child()` method deferred because we will instance the scene after the physics processing cycle, and calling it deferred will prevent Godot from throwing errors:

```
func create(_product_packed_scene :=
    product_packed_scene) ->
        var product: Node2D =
            _product_packed_scene.instantiate()
        product.global_position = global_position
```

```
        var container = find_parent("Level")
          .find_child(target_cotainer_name)
        container.call_deferred("add_child", product)
```

13. Finally, after properly treating the product, we need to emit the created signal and return it so that any interested class can do any fine-tuning procedure on it:

```
func create(_product_packed_scene :=
  product_packed_scene) ->
    var product: Node2D =
      _product_packed_scene.instantiate()
    product.global_position = global_position

    var container = find_parent("Level")
      .find_child(target_cotainer_name)
    container.call_deferred("add_child", product)

    created.emit(product)
    return product
```

Congratulations! We just finished one of the most useful and powerful classes someone can have in their game code base. By having a Factory that creates products in the game world, we just achieved = the bread and butter of any game, which is to dynamically create objects. I sometimes play with my students and clients saying that game development is about mastering the three I's: **instancing**, **inputs**, and **interactions**. By implementing this Factory class, we just checked instancing off of this list. After all the preceding steps, the Node2DFactory class should look like this:

```
extends Marker2D
class_name Node2DFactory

signal created(product)

@export var product_packed_scene: PackedScene
@export var target_container_name: StringName

func create(_product_packed_scene :=
  product_packed_scene)
  -> No
    var product: Node2D = _product_packed_scene
      .instantiate()
    product.global_position = global_position

    var container = find_parent("Level")
      .find_child(target_conta
```

```
container.call_deferred("add_child", product)

created.emit(product)
return product
```

With this new power in our hands, it's time to use it responsibly. In the next section, we will create some inherited scenes and use `Node2DFactory` to create instances of `Diamond`, `Heart`, and `PopLabel` nodes! Let's go!

Using Node2DFactory in our game

The `Node2DFactory` class allows us to centralize the responsibility of inserting new objects in the game world. We have two main cases in which this happens already and we need to adapt them to this new approach before we move on to the actual game designer's request. So, get yourself ready for some refactoring work! In the following steps, we will start by refactoring the `ScorePoint` class to use the `Node2DFactory` class to create new `PopLabel` nodes as its products. So, open `res://Game/Score/ScorePoint/ScorePoint.tscn` scene and let's get started:

1. Start by adding a new instance of the `Node2DFactory` scene as a child of the `ScorePoint` class.

2. Drag and drop the `PopLabel` scene file to the `Node2DFactory`'s **Product Packed Scene** property:

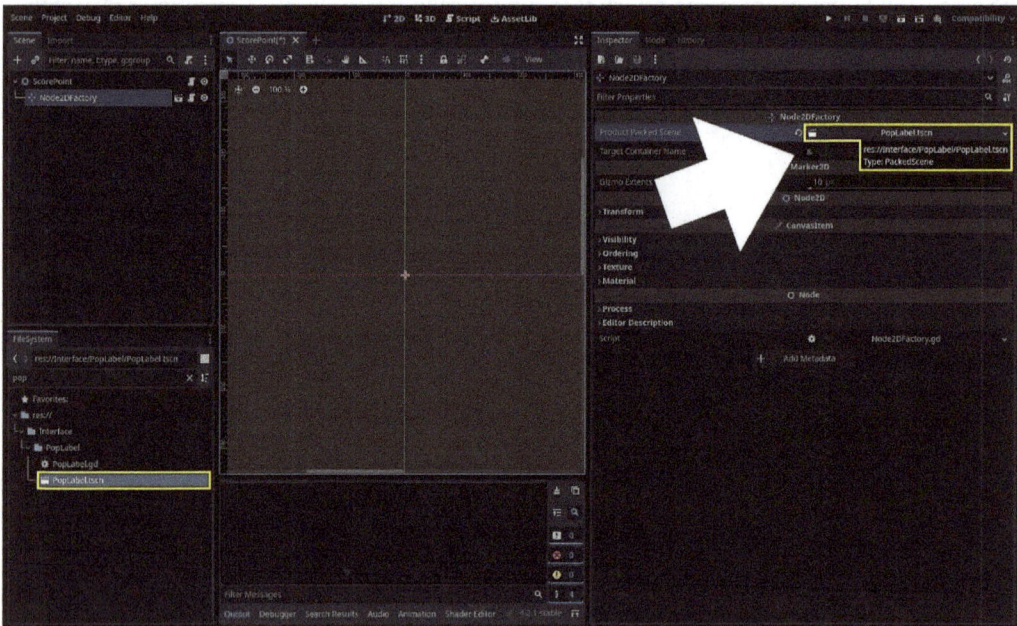

Figure 7.3 – The PopLabel scene set in the Node2DFactory's Product
Packed Scene property in the Inspector window

3. The `Node2DFactory` class also asks for the container's name, and for this one, we will use an already existent container node in the `Level` scene and the `PopLabel` nodes, which is the one we are using in the `ScorePoint` script. So, in the **Target Container Name** property, write `PopLabels`.

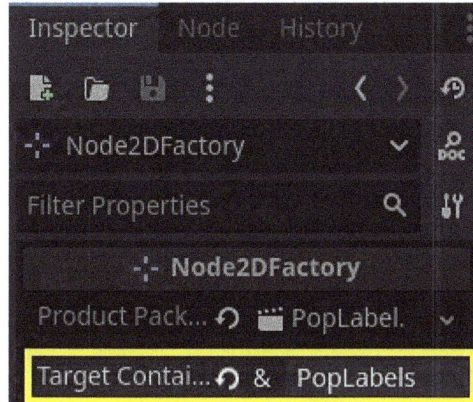

Figure 7.4 – The Target Container Name property set to PopLabels

Now, open the `ScorePoint` script and let's start the refactoring work.

4. Since the`Node2DFactory` class is the one responsible for instancing the `PopLabel` scene now, we can remove the `pop_label_scene` exported variable declaration. Instead, we will create a new `@onready` variable to store a reference to `Node2Dfactory`; let's call it `factory`:

```
extends Node2D

@export var amount = 100

@onready var factory = $Node2DFactory
```

5. Then, in the`pop_label()` method, instead of using the returning value of `PackedScene.instantiate()`, we will use the returning value of the `Node2DFactory.create()` method:

```
func pop_label():
    var pop_label = factory.create()
```

6. Since the `Node2DFactory` class already positions the `PopLabel` instance and inserts it in `SceneTree` by adding it as a child of its container node, we can remove the next line entirely. The complete implementation of the `pop_label()` method is as follows:

```
func pop_label():
    var pop_label = factory.create()
    pop_label.pop(str(amount), global_position)
```

That's pretty much all we need to do in the ScorePoint scene. Note that the ScorePoint class does some extra treatment to the PopLabel instance after theNode2DFactory class creates it. This is the power of having a Factory; it does the repeated work, and the user class can do the specifics. This is yet another excellent example of favoring composition over inheritance. Imagine if the ScorePoint class inherited from Node2DFactory just to implement the creation behavior; what a mess our codebase would become.

Now, with the same composition mindset, we will create a new class that will use Node2DFactory together with the looting logic from the LootCrate class to create a loot behavior, where it processes the drop rate of a given item and the player's luck, and depending on the player's luck, it will tell Node2DFactory to create a new instance of the item. With the following steps, we will implement this behavior:

1. Create a new scene and use a Marker2D as the root node.

2. Rename it as Loot and save the scene as res://Objects/Loot/Loot.tscn.

3. Add an instance of Node2DFactory as its child.

4. Attach a new GDScript to the Loot node and save it as res://Objects/Loot/Loot.gd.

5. Open the script and follow these steps:

    I.   Using @export_range(0.0, 1.0), create a variable to represent the drop rate of this loot's item. Let's call this variable drop_rate:

    ```
    extends Marker2D
    class_name Loot


    @export_range(0.0, 1.0) var drop_rate = 0.3
    ```

    II. Then, declare a new variable to hold a reference to Node2DFactory, again. Let's call it factory:

    ```
    extends Marker2D
    class_name Loot


    @export_range(0.0, 1.0) var drop_rate = 0.3


    @onready var factory = $Node2DFactory
    ```

    III. After that, we will create a new method called drop(). This method will calculate the player's luck and create the product if the player obtains success:

    ```
    extends Marker2D
    class_name Loot


    @export_range(0.0, 1.0) var drop_rate = 0.3
    ```

```
@onready var factory = $Node2DFactory


func drop():
```

IV. Inside the `drop()` method, create a variable, let's call it `luck`, that represents the player's luck. It will store the result of a random number generated between `0.0` and `1.0` using the `randf_range()` method:

```
func drop():
    var luck = randf_range(0.0, 1.0)
```

V. Then, we will check if the luck is within the drop rate threshold. If this is the case, we will call the `factory.create()` method, effectively creating the new item and inserting it in the game world:

```
func drop():
    var luck = randf_range(0.0, 1.0)
    if luck <= drop_rate:
        factory.create()
```

That is pretty much it. With that, we have a scene we can use to represent items that can drop based on a chance. The complete `Loot` class' script implementation should look something like this:

```
extends Marker2D
class_name Loot

@export_range(0.0, 1.0) var drop_rate = 0.3

@onready var factory = $Node2DFactory


func drop():
    var luck = randf_range(0.0, 1.0)
    if luck <= drop_rate:
        factory.create()
```

It's simple and elegant, don't you think? Note that the way we are creating new classes in our game implements the SOLID principles naturally. For instance, small and simple scripts, such as the ones we've been creating, reflect the principles of the interface segregation principle, on top of the single responsibility principle, and so on and so forth. As mentioned in *Chapter 3*, implementing one of the SOLID principles usually leads you to implement all other four naturally.

Now that we have this basic `Loot` scene, we can create new inherited scenes to define which items it will drop. Currently, we only have two possible droppable items: the `Diamond` and the `Heart` objects created by our game designer. So, to create the looting behavior for these items, let's follow these steps:

1. Right-click on the `res://Objects/Loot/Loot.tscn` file in the **FileSystem** dock and from the drop-down menu, click on the **New Inherited Scene** option:

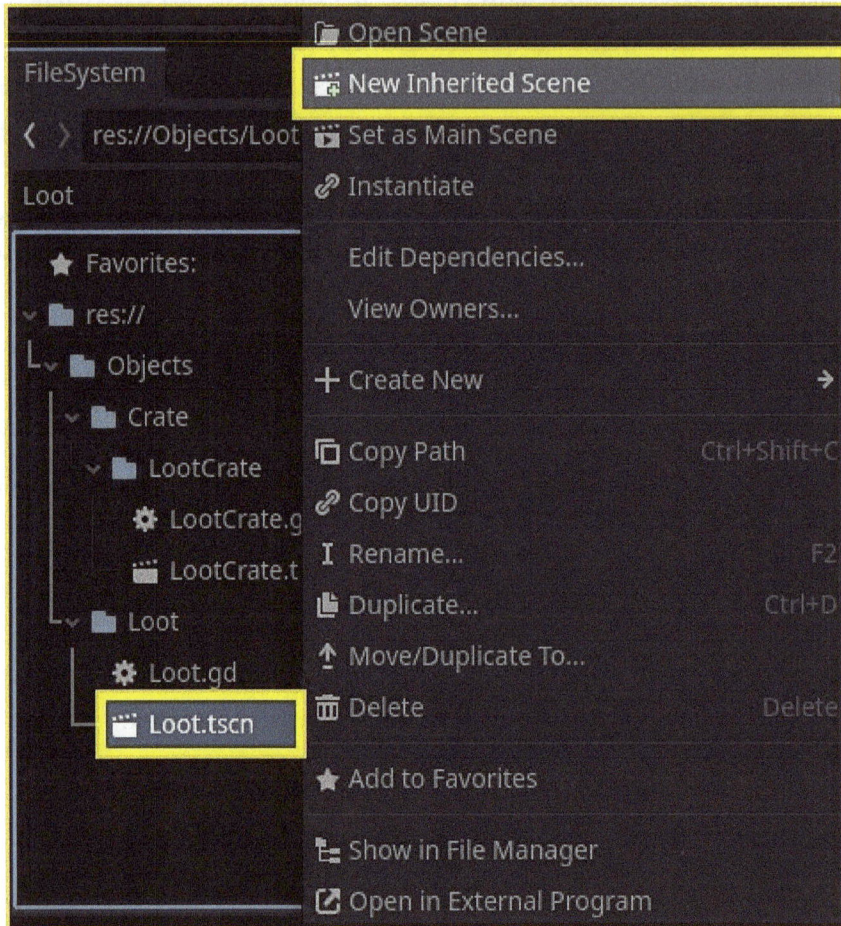

Figure 7.5 – The FileSystem dock New Inherited Scene option from in the drop-down menu that appears after right-clicking the Loot.tscn file

2. In the new scene created, rename the root node as `DiamondLoot`.

3. Then, drag and drop the `res://Objects/Diamond/Diamond.tscn` file on `Node2DFactory`'s **Product Packet Scene** property. You can also approach this by clicking on the **Product Packet Scene** slot on the **Inspector** window and from the drop-down menu,

click on the **Load** option and select the `res://Objects/Diamond/Diamond.tscn` scene from the popup file explorer menu.

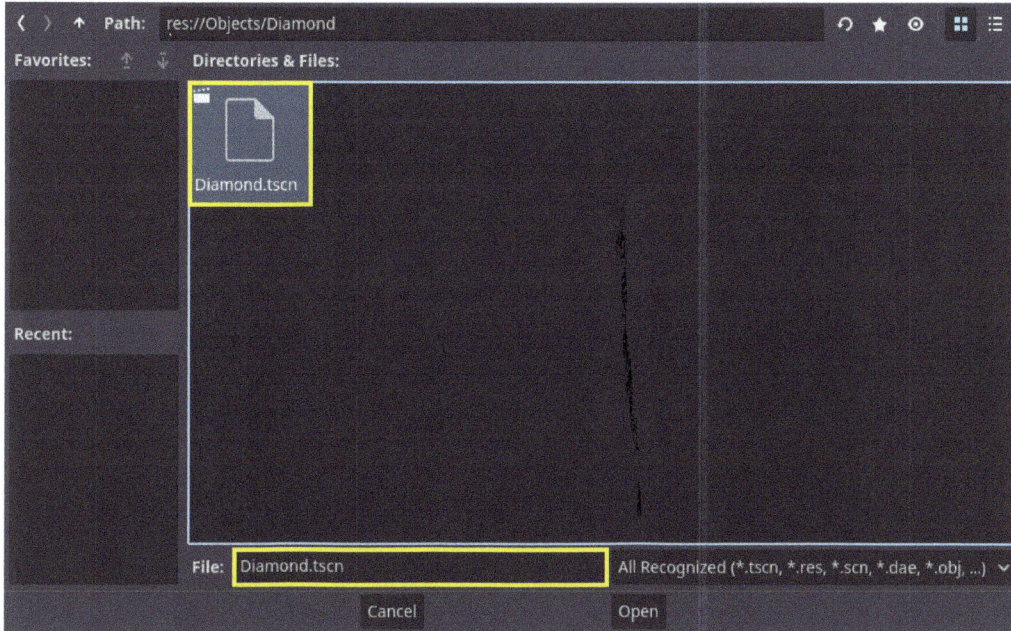

Figure 7.6 – Selecting the Diamond.tscn scene file from the file explorer popup menu

4. In the **Target Container Name** property, write `Diamonds`.

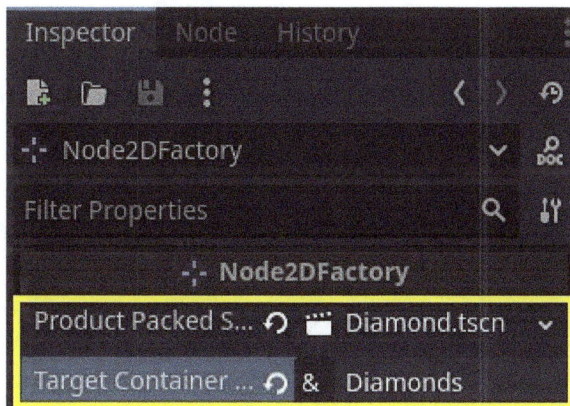

Figure 7.7 – The DiamondLoot's Node2DFactory settings in the Inspector window

After that, you can save the scene. This is all we need to do in order to create new versions of the `Loot` scene with specific details about what they will create. You can consider that the `Loot` scene itself is an abstract scene while the `DiamondLoot` scene is a concrete implementation. We can repeat these steps to create the `HeartLoot` scene, adjusting the necessary variables. `HeartLoot`'s `Node2DFactory` node settings should look like this:

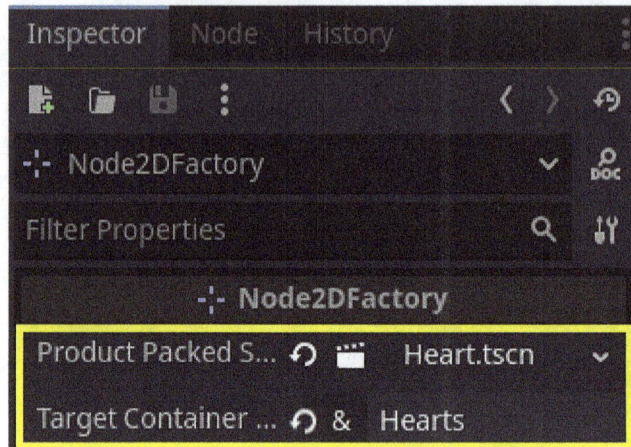

Figure 7.8 – HeartLoot's Node2DFactory settings in the Inspector window

Now, with these in place, we can implement and reimplement the `LootCrate` class's original behavior using the `Loot` components instead. This will allow us to have multiple item drops, each with its own drop rate. Open `res://Objects/Crate/LootCrate/LootCrate.tscn` and follow along with me:

1. First of all, add a new `Node2D` as a child of the `Crate` node and call it `Loots`.

2. As children of the `Loots` node, we will create one instance of the `DiamondLoot` scene and another one for the `HeartLoot` scene.

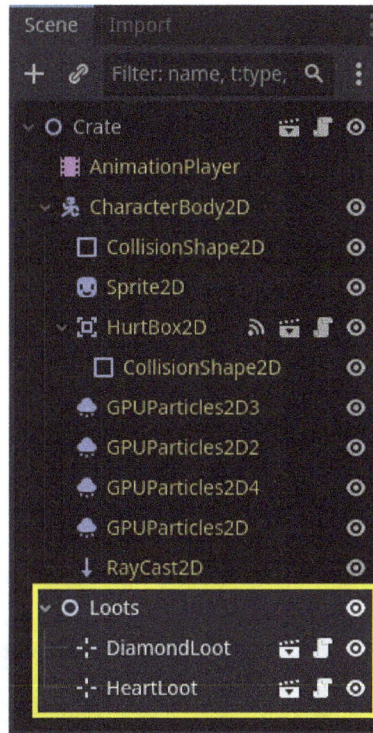

Figure 7.9 – Crate's DiamondLoot and HeartLoot scene instances

3. Open the `res://Objects/Crate/LootCrate/LootCrate.gd` script and remove the variable declared in the class. These are in the `Loot` class now, so there is no reason to have them here.

4. Remove the `drop()` method as well, since the item-dropping logic is now on the `Loot` class and we don't need this method anymore.

    Note that this is by far not advised if this class was part of a consolidated code base, as this would break the open-closed principle, changing the class's interface. But since we are still in production in this role-playing, we are safe to make these kinds of adjustments as this will improve the class's interface by applying the interface segregation principle, removing unnecessary methods from the class, and moving them to other classes' interfaces.

5. Then, in the `shatter()` method before calling `super()`, we will make a `for` loop running through all the children in the `Loots` node:

    ```
    func shatter() -> void:
        for loot in $Loots.get_children():

        super()
    ```

6. Finally, we will call the `loot.drop()` method on them, effectively checking for the possibility of dropping the items when the `LootCrate` objects shatter. The complete `LootCrate` class script follows:

```
extends Crate


func shatter():
    for loot in $Loots.get_children():
        loot.drop()
    super()
```

Now, our game designer can rest assured that he can play with looting and item drops as much as they want to. This is the power of having components that do small tasks. We can just add them to our game and create new interesting behaviors without getting stuck with new bloated classes that would only cause issues further in production. Go ahead and play a bit with this new power. For instance, in the project available in `07.spawning-game-objects-with-factory/02.finished`, the Bumping Pig enemy has a chance to drop `Diamond` and `Heart` objects when defeated. The structure is essentially the same as used in the `LootCrate` scene:

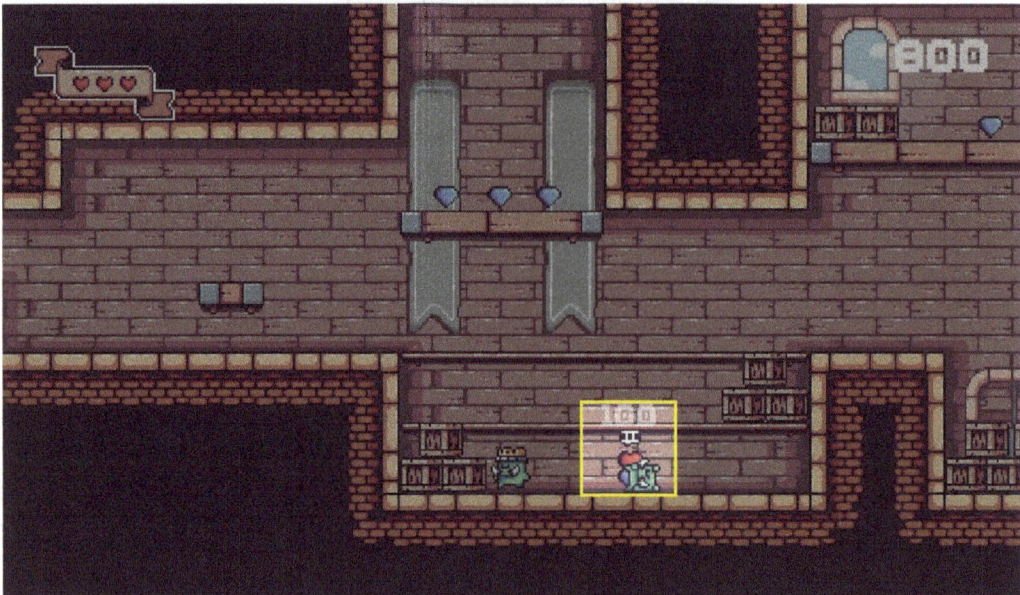

Figure 7.10 – The Bumping Pig enemy dying and creating PopLabel,
Diamond, and Heart nodes in the process

With that, we finished up this fundamental chapter and we are one step closer to a nicer, reusable, and scalable code base for our game. Before we move on to the next chapter, let's recap the fundamental concepts we learned about throughout this chapter.

Summary

In this chapter, we learned about the fundamental concepts and practical applications of the Factory pattern in game development using Godot Engine. The Factory pattern allows for the creation of objects through a common interface, which can be especially useful in dynamically generating game elements such as monsters, items, bullets, or magic spells. This approach enhances the modularity and scalability of game projects, enabling us to easily manage and instantiate different types of game objects.

We can implement the Factory pattern in Godot using the `PackedScene` resource, which can store and instantiate nodes as needed. By serializing the data into `PackedScene` resources, the process of creating objects becomes streamlined and efficient. This method allows us to adjust and fine-tune the properties of the objects being created, ensuring they meet the specific requirements of the game.

We also explored some use cases where the Factory pattern can be beneficial. For example, monster spawners in RPGs can utilize the Factory pattern to maintain a continuous flow of enemies in a map or area. Similarly, the creation of magic spells or different types of bullets can be managed through specialized factories, allowing for easy customization and extension of game mechanics.

In addition to these use cases, we saw a practical implementation of the Factory pattern in Godot. By using methods such as `Node2DFactory.create()` to instantiate objects and adjust their properties, we can ensure that the game elements are correctly positioned and integrated into the game world. This encapsulation of object creation procedures not only simplifies the development process but also enhances code maintainability and readability.

As we conclude this chapter, we can see that mastering the Factory pattern is crucial for efficient game development. In the next chapter, we will talk about the state pattern, exploring how state management can help us optimize the creation and dynamically change object behavior in run time.

8
Changing Object Behavior with the State Pattern

The State pattern is usually associated with the idea of **Finite State Machines** (**FSMs**), a mathematical model of computation, but these are two different terms. While the FSM is a set of abstractions that help us create models for possible states in which a given machine can be, the State pattern is an **Object-Oriented Programming** (**OOP**) approach to abstract object states as objects. After these abstractions, you can implement an FSM to integrate these states and add transitions between one another. But just take note that the State pattern, besides being closely related to the FSM, is just the idea of encapsulating an object's state into a new class and, with that, being able to change the object's behavior in runtime.

Remember, an object's state is just the set of values of the object's properties, and by applying the State pattern, we explicitly give name and meaning to specific states in which an object can be. This allows us to immediately change one object's state to another by making a single mutation instead of a sequence of mutations that may be hard to keep track of.

In this chapter, we will use Godot Engine's `AnimationPlayer` and `AnimationTree` nodes to implement some possible states in which we want our `Bumping Pig` enemy to be. Before we jump into action, I want to state my caveats about the State pattern. Personally, I am not a huge fan of this pattern as it is widely misused as a tool to limit state overlapping of game entities. Games are intrinsically emergent systems and, usually, it is not a good idea to apply an FSM in game entities. This will lead you to many classes with duplicated code to maintain some overlapping behaviors and tend to not scale well. For instance, if you have a platformer character that has three features (idle, move, and attack), it may have some directly correlated states:

- Idling
- Moving
- Attacking

Everything is fine and you can perform maintainable transitions of these states and scale the game knowing how the character will behave in each of these states, what triggers transitions between them, and distinct code between each state. For instance, while attacking, the character doesn't move; while moving, the character can't attack; and while idling, the character is not moving. But if we add one simple feature to our character, this all scales badly. For instance, if the character is supposed to jump, now we have some overlapping:

- Jumping without moving, or Idle Jumping

- Jumping and moving horizontally, or Move Jumping

- Jumping and attacking, or Attack Jumping

- Idling

- Moving

- Attacking

- Jumping in the middle of an attack, or Jump Attacking

- Jumping while moving, or Jump Moving

- Jumping while idling, or Jump Idling

And if we add the ability to perform a dash and an airdash, you can see how things will scale up badly, but just for the sake of exposing this issue, here is a brief list of potential states:

- Idle Jumping

- Move Jumping

- Attack Jumping

- Dash Idle Jumping

- Dash Move Jumping

- Dash Attack Jumping

- Jump Dashing

- Jump Attack Dashing

- Jump Idle Dashing

- Jump Move Dashing

- Idle Dashing

- Move Dashing

- Attack Dashing

- Dash Idling

- Dash Moving

- Dash Attacking

- Idling

- Moving

- Attacking

Now, let's say that when the character gets hurt, it enters a hurt state where it can't perform any actions for a brief moment and is immune to enemies' attacks. Well, we won't spend any more precious space here, but you can imagine this doesn't scale nicely.

Note that this is an absurd implementation of an FSM, but this is what we would have to do if we took it seriously as it is usually implemented in other programming fields, for instance, on traffic lights where there are minimal possible states, or document writing statuses where they can go from draft to review to approved to published and so on.

My point with this is to take this design pattern with a bit of care and not use it in places where you may need more freedom to expand the scope, especially during production. Take note that you don't have to implement the State pattern for all the possible object states; ideally, as we are going to do in this chapter, you can pick one aspect of your object and turn the related properties into individual states and allow other properties and behaviors to be open for overlapping with those strict states we will create. Properties that are usually necessary for the intrinsic emergence of your game, such as position, health, and animation frames, are typically not interesting to be abstracted as states. But you can abstract animations instead of individual animation frames, for instance, as we typically don't want to have overlapping animations in our object, unless we want to apply blending and other animation techniques.

Well, after this ramble, let's try to understand the State pattern better so we can identify good use cases for it and how to integrate it with FSMs.

In this chapter, we are going to cover the following topics:

- Understanding the State pattern

- Spotting use cases of the State pattern in games

- Implementing the State pattern

Technical requirements

To follow along with this chapter, use the project files located in the `08.changing-object-behavior-with-states/01.start/` folder. If you encounter any confusion, errors, or bugs while working through the *Implementing the State pattern in Godot* section, refer to the files placed in the `08.changing-object-behavior-with-states/02.finished/` folder. Report any issues to our support team for prompt resolution.

If you do not have the repository files yet, download them from the following link: `https://github.com/PacktPublishing/Game-Development-Patterns-with-Godot-4/tree/main`.

Now, let's delve into the State pattern to understand its description, technical aspects, the problems it addresses, and how it provides solutions for said problems. With this knowledge in our hands, we will be able to make more informed decisions and implement this solution when it fits.

Understanding the State pattern

The State pattern is a behavioral pattern, which means it solves problems related to an object's behaviors. It aims to provide a reliable way to alter an object's behavior in run-time based on changes in the object's internal state.

The main idea is that, given a finite number of possible states, the object will behave differently in each unique state and will be able to switch between states instantaneously. Depending on each state, the object may or may not switch to certain other states. For instance, if our character has three states to describe where it currently stands (landing, jumping, and falling), then our character can't switch from jumping to landing without falling first. There may be any given set of rules to define how these states mutate from one to another. These rules are called transitions, which must also be finite and pre-determined.

Even if you never heard about state machines, you are likely to have already implemented one. This is the beauty of design patterns: they were not normalized, they were noticed and documented. Typically, when we implement state machines, we use `switch` statements or sequences of `if` and `elif` statements. Inside each one of these, we implement a different behavior that the object should perform depending on the values tested in the statements. The idea of implementing the State pattern is to turn these blocks of conditionals into transitions and the behaviors in `State` objects.

By turning an object's state into a `State` object, we are able to store it into a variable and instantaneously mutate it to another `State` object as soon as a transition is triggered. This helps us have a clear scope of possible states we want a given object to be in and limit our range of issues, bugs, and even features. For instance, let's say we want an object to either emit a red, blue, or green light. We may have an `emission_color` variable. Well, last time I checked, there were 4,294,967,296 colors in the RGBA system. Technically, this object could be in 4,294,967,296 possible states accounting only for the possible colors; if we add other parameters such as visible or invisible, which could be represented by a Boolean variable, then we multiply this by 2. Of course, we are going into extremes here, and unless you give the user the ability to pick a color, the amount of possible colors is limited. One way to limit these possibilities by design is to create three distinct State classes to represent these states (we could call them `RedState`, `GreenState`, and `BlueState`) and create the transitions to dictate how exactly one transitions to the other. This would help us debug better and have more maintainable code.

We do this "objectification" by transforming all the possible states we want an object to be into distinct classes and extracting the state-specific behaviors into these classes. By the way, "objectification" is what most OOP design patterns do. They take programming concepts (such as methods, algorithms, and even data structures such as arrays and dictionaries) and encapsulate them into objects. We do that because this allows us to store these objects in memory and perform further procedures with them in real time. We will see this clearly happening in *Chapter 9*, where we will essentially turn objects' methods into classes that we can instantiate as objects. This will allow us to store them into variables and change an object's behavior in real time. In the specific case of the Command pattern, this will also allow us to store these objects in a chronological list and go back and forward undoing or redoing these behaviors. This is how programs typically implement undo/redo features, by the way.

But notice that, in this case, we are turning an object's state into a class, also called State. By the way, the object in which we are implementing the State pattern, turning its states into classes, is called context. Keep this in mind as we are going to use these terms moving forward: context, state, and transition.

By applying the State pattern to the context object, we now can store it into a variable and delegate state-specific behaviors to the object in this variable. Since all states of a context object share the same interface, we are able to mutate this variable during run-time while keeping the context's code intact. This is one of the advantages of encapsulating these state-specific behaviors. Since the state-specific behavior can change throughout production, this could impact the whole context's class code, breaking the Open-Closed principle. By isolating this code into a State class, we prevent changes in one state-specific code spills into other classes. This is another general principle to follow in OOP: encapsulate what changes. The states of an object change, so we encapsulate it into other classes so we can minimize the impacts of the changes that we may need to do in each individual state.

As I have stated throughout previous chapters, abstraction is the most important skill a programmer can develop, right? After all this abstract talking, I think is time to see some real-world examples of implementations of the State pattern. In the next section, we will spot some use cases for the State pattern in games. This will help us have a better understanding of how all these abstract concepts turn out as practical solutions.

Spotting use cases of the State pattern in games

Now that we have a gist of what the State pattern is, the problems it solves, and how it typically solves them, in this section, we will talk about some potential use cases that we can find in games where game developers usually apply the State pattern.

One common use case for the State pattern is when we are abstracting character movement. In these cases, we usually create one class for each movement state we want the context object to be in. Note that this doesn't necessarily need to be player actions. For instance, it's common to have a `FallingState` class, especially if you want your character to have falling-specific behaviors, such as increased gravity to make the jump mechanic feel snappier. We could abstract this with an FSM that looks like the following:

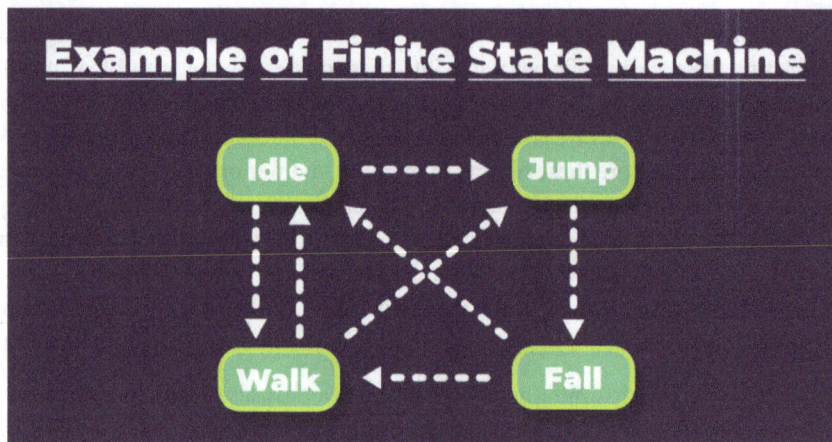

Figure 8.1 – A set of possible states and their transitions as an FSM

Note that the State pattern is not exclusive to in-game objects, so another common use case is to manage abstract game states, such as *playing*, *paused*, and *game over*. For instance, if you don't want your objects just to stop altogether while a Pause Menu pops, maybe you want them to just stop processing physics and some gameplay behaviors, but you want to keep animations running and allow them to talk and say meta-game things such as *Am I supposed to wait here forever?* or *Ohh dang, I can't move!*. You can create a `PausedGameState` state that will stop processing certain aspects of your game. In Godot Engine, you can use `SceneTree.call_group("characters", "set_physics_process", false)`, where `"characters"` is the name of the group that includes all characters that should stop processing physics during `PausedGameState`. This approach is preferable to using `SceneTree.paused = true`, which would stop everything altogether based on the nodes' `process_mode` property.

As mentioned earlier, ideally, the State pattern is applied to specific parts of the game. For instance, weapons are an excellent example of how applying the State pattern can be of good use, especially if you are making games that lean more toward war simulation. We can abstract weapons as being in distinct states such as idling, aiming, firing, reloading, recoiling, overheating, and cooling down. Depending on how detailed you want your weapon system to be, you can go into more or less specific approaches.

Fighting stances are another good example of a mechanic that can benefit from being abstracted into states. Depending on your combat system, players may be slower in a defensive stance but take less damage, faster in an aggressive stance but take way more damage, and balanced in a neutral stance, moving at a medium pace and taking medium damage.

All of those can be turned into independent State classes, with each one making its own calculation of damage and movement speed. Then, you can apply yet another distinct and exclusive State pattern abstraction to manage the animations of each of those stances. I say that because people usually mix responsibilities when they abstract the context object's states but all the SOLID principles should still apply.

We could even go as far as having one `State` family of classes for managing the movement states, another one to manage the damage states, and one to manage the animations states. I say that because, for instance, we may want to implement a power-up that makes the player invulnerable, so this would be a new state. If we isolate it as a new state in the `DamageState` family, we would only need to create one new class. But if we make an abstraction that bundles the movement and the damage together, now we would have to create `SlowPacedInvulnerableState`, `MediumPacedInvulnerableState`, and `FastPacedInvulnerableState`. So this doesn't scale well, and this is why I suggest keeping up with the Single Responsibility Principle and the *composition over inheritance* approach. With distinct State class families, we can compose these superpositions of states way more easily.

Another good example of the implementation of the State pattern is regarding enemies' AI and behaviors. This is what we are going to do in our next section where we will take the current implementation of the `BumpingPig` scene, which already has an implementation of an FSM, but use an enumerator and match statements to manage state changes. In the next section, we will turn this implementation into a family of `State` classes, effectively implementing the State pattern in the `BumpingPig` scene.

Implementing the State pattern in Godot

One of the things that I want to convey through this book's approach to technical topics such as OOP and design patterns is that we should understand their underlying principles instead of strict technical implementations. In other words, by understanding the philosophy behind these concepts, we will be able to abstract them in ways that allow us to make the most of the tools we have available. In that sense, in this section, we will see how we can use animations and the `AnimationTree` node as states and an FSM, respectively. We will also implement the State pattern using GDScript and nodes so you can understand in practice how to implement this pattern. Let's get it started!

Understanding the designer's requirements

The designer of our game is planning to make the Bumping Pig a character with a bit more intelligence. For that, the designer decided that this entity of the game would need a code that provides more control over its behavior and more predictability regarding when it must perform certain behaviors. Well, let's see the designer's request itself:

Hello,

I'm reaching out because I noticed the game doesn't have a compelling enemy. Currently, the enemy, the Bumping Pig, just wanders around and, honestly, doesn't provide any real challenge. I created some animations and introduced an attack behavior when the player enters the sight of the enemy. But it got messy to handle the behaviors, especially because some of them overlap. Sometimes, the enemy is taking a hit and walking, or walking and attacking at the same time!

I need to be able to control these behaviors and prevent them from overlapping with each other. I already have the necessary conditions and I managed to put the behaviors within animations and method calls, but I'm struggling to manage the transitions between these behaviors and to ensure that they are mutually exclusive.

Another issue is that the Bumping Pig doesn't remember what it should do after it gets hit or after attacking. For instance, if it is moving and the player hits it, it plays the animation and goes back to running, but what if it was idling or attacking before getting hit? The same thing happens when it attacks. I need it to go back to the previous behavior after performing these one-time animations.

Can you help me with that?

One important thing to note in this request is that the `BumpingPig` class already has a mechanism to handle states. It isn't a State pattern, but if you look at the code itself, you will note a `STATES` enumerator and a `state` variable. Also, in `_physics_process()`, we have a `match` statement discriminating some behaviors that should only happen within certain state values, for example, `state == STATES.RUN`. You will also note that the designer took the time to create methods to encapsulate each of these behaviors, which is excellent because this will help us understand what should happen within each of these states. But there's a small issue: we don't have any way to ensure a clean slate when the `state` value changes, meaning we may have residual changes that are carried on from one state to another, and this can cause some issues.

Note that having states and state management isn't necessarily an implementation of the State pattern. You can pretty much have states, state management, and state machines without implementing the State pattern. The State pattern itself necessarily turns these states into classes and allows us to treat them as objects.

The designer displays a deep concern about having control over how the enemy is currently behaving. More specifically, there are behaviors that are overlapping and the designer doesn't want that; each behavior should be mutually exclusive with all other behaviors. This is a very good indicator that we are dealing with a state-related problem.

Another problem presented by the designer is that there's no clear or manageable way to control the transitions between one behavior and another, meaning there might be an unpredictable change from one state to another, which is yet another good indicator to implement the State pattern, as it will encapsulate transitions within the state classes and prevent them from flowing freely. By implementing this pattern, we will ensure that one state can only change to a predictable and previously set of other states.

Well, it seems like the presented issues can be solved by implementing a State pattern. Again, I want to remind you of this process: first, face the issue and try to match it to a pattern. Don't go out there implementing design patterns unnecessarily without any good reason. If you face a problem that already has a widely tested solution, then you implement such a solution. This is what a design pattern is.

That said, in the next section, we will use animations and the `AnimationTree` node to create an FSM to handle the transitions between each animation, ensuring that they only play at their respective state.

Implementing an FSM with animations

Before we dive into the practical aspect of this section, I want to make a statement about being abstract with programming concepts. You can program without coding—coding is just a way to formalize the programming of a solution to a given problem. But you can program through many other ways. One of these ways, especially in Godot Engine, is to use animations.

At its core, programming is nothing but mutations, in other words, the alteration of data values. A program then interprets this data accordingly and, ultimately, generates an output. Using animations, we are doing exactly that: mutating data, with the advantage that we can bind these mutations with time, which is excellent.

That said, since each animation bundles mutations on objects' properties, they can be interpreted abstractly as being objects' states. Remember, when we talk about an object's state, we are just referring to the current values of its properties. In that sense, by using animations, we can rely on an excellent interface to manage object states. Now, let's understand how we can create an FSM using animations.

Well, since this book presumes you already have some experience with Godot Engine, it's fair to assume that you already know the `AnimationPlayer` node, right? It is through this node that we create and manage animations within a scene.

Without going into too much detail, it offers an interface to create, delete, and rename animations and their keys. Keys in this context are properties' values bonded to a specific time or frame of the animation. If you open the `res://Actors/BumpingPig/BumpingPig.tscn` scene and select the `AnimationPlayer` node, you can click on the **Animation** tab at the bottom of the editor to display the **Animation** Menu. Select the **attack** animation. The animation should look like the one in the following figure:

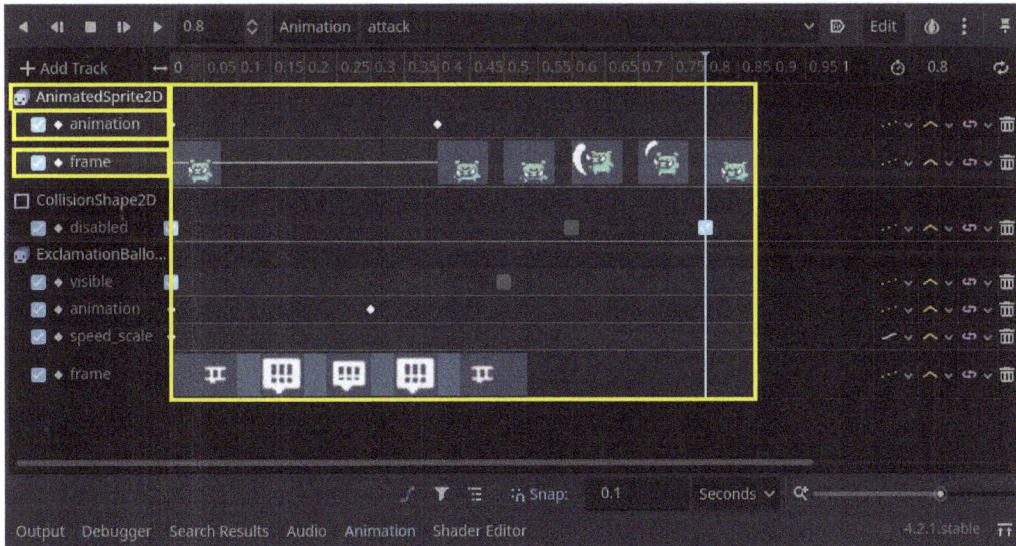

Figure 8.2 – The Animation interface displaying the attack animation's keys

You can see in the figure that we have the node's name, the properties being animated, and the keys in the timeline. With an abstract interpretation, we can say that this bundles the properties' values that compose the `attack` state. That said, it's time to introduce you to intermediate-level animation in Godot Engine!

Don't get me wrong, understanding how to use the `AnimationPlayer` node and create animations is extremely powerful already and absolutely necessary to get the most out of Godot Engine's power. The animation system is by far my favorite feature in Godot, especially when you manage to mix Call Function Tracks and Tweens all together. But when you learn how to use `AnimationTree` node and its `AnimationNode` nodes, you understand how powerful you can get. Coding becomes a secondary tool, almost, as it serves the purpose of allowing your animations to flow. But, unfortunately, we can't get into the intricacies of this system in just one chapter. It would need a whole book dedicated to animations to get the most out of this system, but let's give it a brief introduction.

The `AnimationTree` node allows us to add a layer of logic on an `AnimationPlayer` node. They are meant to work together, where `AnimationPlayer` establishes the animations and `AnimationTree` controls their transitions and blending.

> *According to Godot Engine's official documentation, the `AnimationTree` node is "a node used for advanced animation transitions in an AnimationPlayer."*

The key concept we should pay attention to in this description is the ability of the `AnimationTree` node to make advanced transitions. When we use `AnimationNodeStateMachine` node in the `AnimationTree` node, we are able to create transitions between animation nodes. These transitions have three main properties that are relevant to us:

- **Switch Mode** allows us to choose whether the transition happens immediately when a condition is fulfilled, at the end of the animation once the condition is fulfilled, or synchronized with the current animation's playback position. The last one means it will change immediately and seek the playback time of the previous animation in the new one.

- **Condition** allows us to create a Boolean variable that we can control through the Inspector and through GDScript that, once set to `true`, will trigger the transition.

- **Expression** is an advanced condition. It accepts a logical expression that, if it returns `true`, will trigger the transition. Note that it uses the `AnimationTree` node's **Advance Expression Base Node** property to access properties and use them in the expressions. The **Advance Expression Base Node** can be interpreted as the context object from the lens of the State pattern. For example, we can use the following expression to trigger the attack animation transition: `vision_area.get_overlapping_areas().size() > 0`. Since `vision_area` is a property of the `BumpingPig` node, which is set as the **Advance Expression Base Node**, this expression would be able to access this method and dynamically check this condition.

There's a whole page on the official documentation dedicated to teaching how to use the `AnimationTree` node's features. If you want to master this node, which I highly recommend you do, take a look at the *Using AnimationTree* tutorial on the official documentation website at https://docs.godotengine.org/en/stable/tutorials/animation/animation_tree.html.

Here, we are going to focus on one specific feature: the `AnimationTree` node's `AnimationNodeStateMachine` node, as this is a good visual way to understand how to implement the State pattern using Godot Engine's built-in features. Well, it's time to get our hands dirty. In the next section, we will set up our `AnimationTree` node so it has access to the animations we will use.

Setting up the AnimationTree node

By itself, the `AnimationTree` node doesn't make anything. It needs at least an `AnimationPlayer` node and `AnimationNode` to work and do its magic. So, in this section, we will set up these properties to get `AnimationTree` ready for the heavy work it will do. Open the `res://Actors/BumpingPig/BumpingPig.tscn` scene and follow these steps:

1. Add a new `AnimationTree` node as a child of the `BumpingPig` node.

2. In the **Anim Player** property of **AnimationTree**, select **AnimationPlayer**:

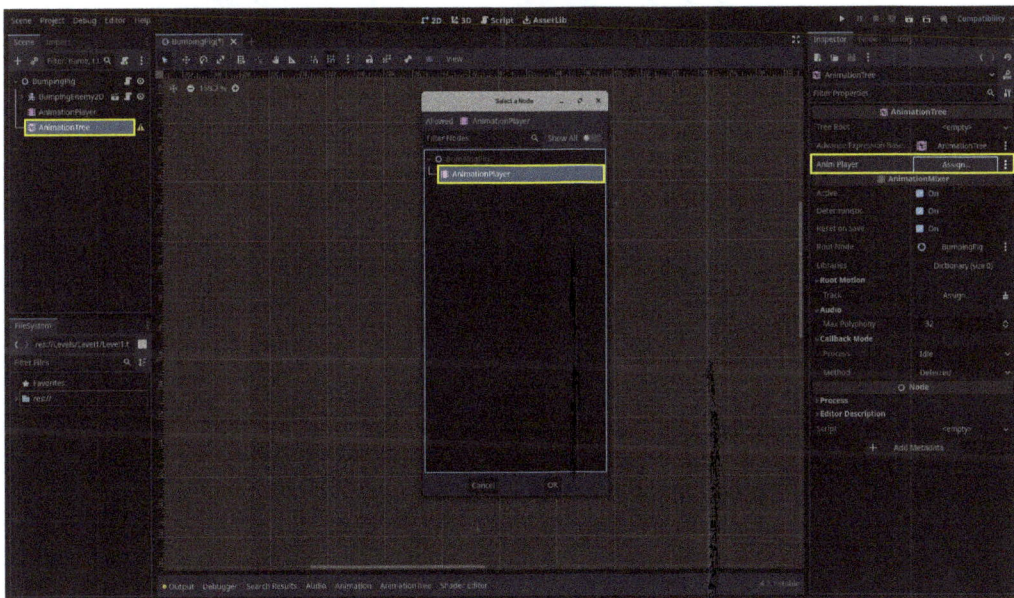

Figure 8.3 – Selecting the AnimationPlayer node from the menu popped
by pressing the Assign button on the Anim Player property

3. Then, let's also set our context object. Change the **Advance Expression Base Node** property of **AnimationTree** from **AnimationTree** to the **BumpingPig** node:

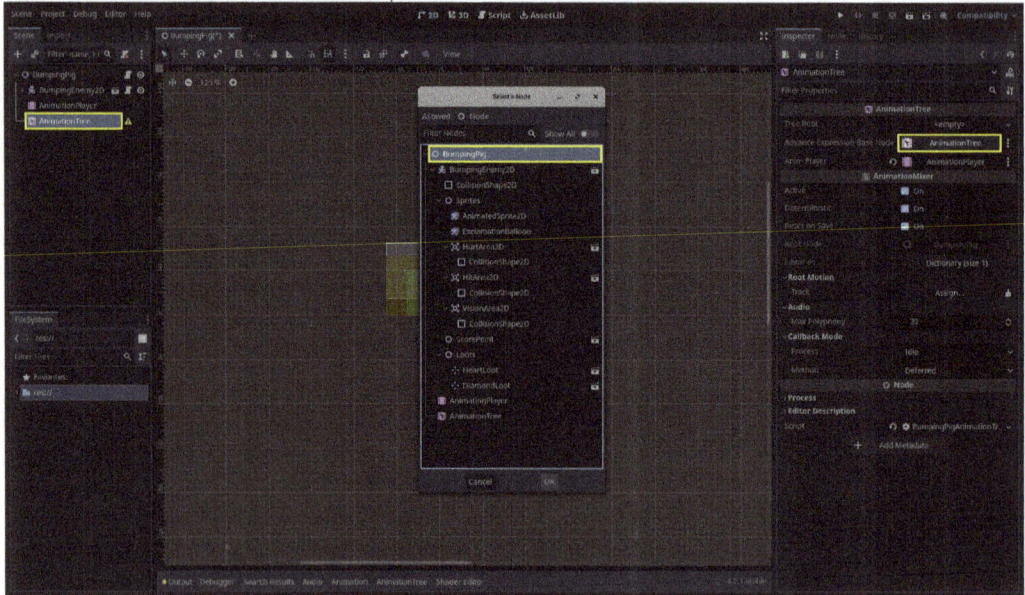

Figure 8.4 – Changing the Advance Expression Base Node property's value
to be the BumpingPig node instead of the default value

4.   Now, it's time for the star of the show. In the **Tree Root** property of **AnimationTree**, click where it says **<empty>**, and from the drop-down menu, select **New AnimationNodeStateMachine**:

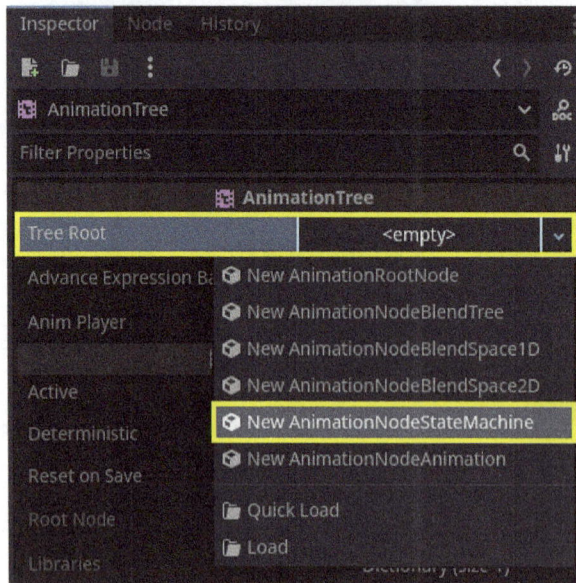

Figure 8.5 – Creating a new AnimationNodeStateMachine as the
value of the AnimationTree node's Tree Root property

As soon as you execute the previous step, the following interface will appear in your editor. This is the `AnimationTree` graph. Here is where the magic happens. This graph displays different elements depending on the current `AnimationNode`. In this specific case, it displays the graph elements of `AnimationNodeStateMachine` node

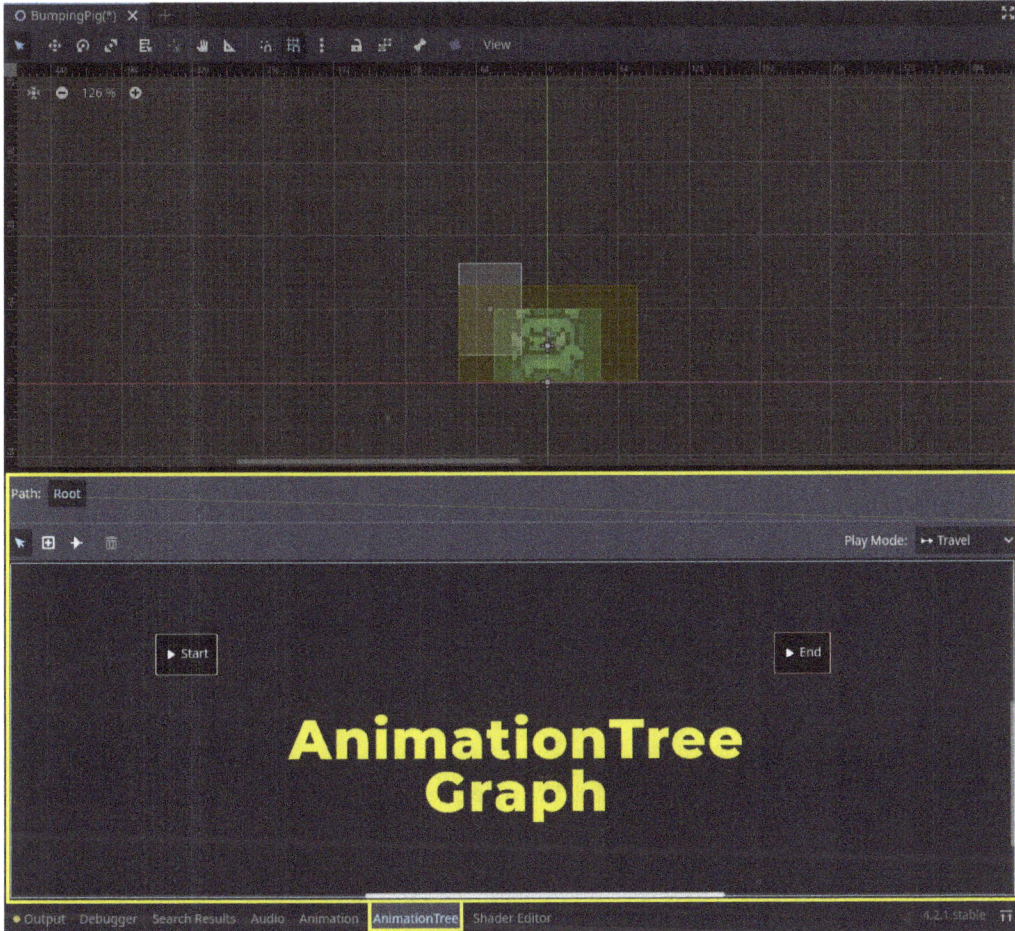

Figure 8.6 – The AnimationNodeStateMachine graph

With that, we have everything we need to access the `AnimationPlayer` node's animations and create transitions between them using the power of this `AnimationTreeStateMachine` node! In the next section, we will finally see this powerful tool in action by making complex transitions between these animations.

Creating animation transitions

Now, it's time to create our states' transitions! In this section, we will arrange all our available animations in a visual graph that makes sense to us and create transitions between them. For that, the first thing we will do is to right-click on the graph and, from the drop-down menu, add all animations except the **RESET** animation:

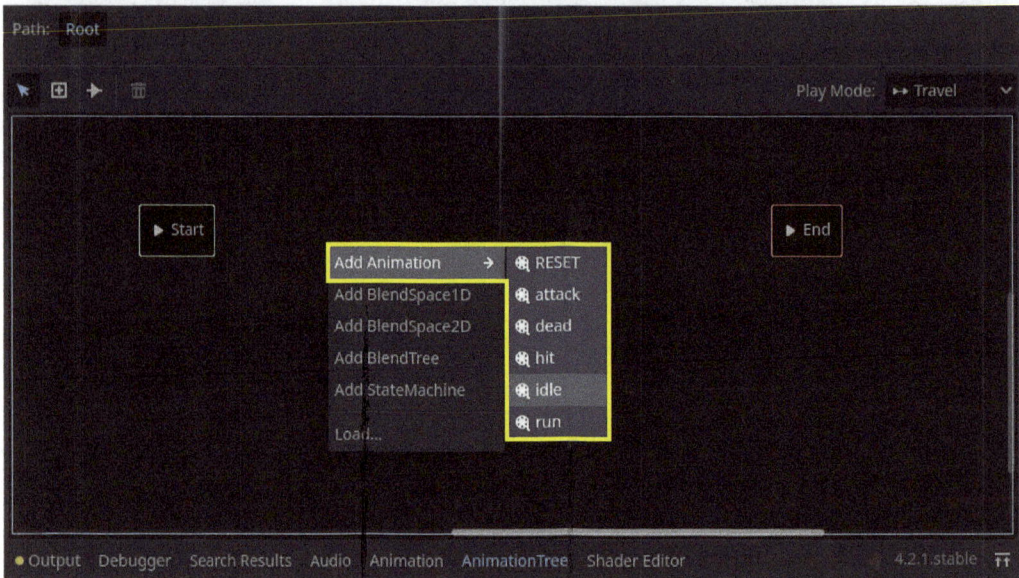

Figure 8.7 – The Add Animation menu displaying the available animations

After adding all the available animations, organize the node so that it makes visual sense to you. Keep in mind the transition order: it starts with the `idle` state, then `run`; from either `run` or `idle`, it can transition to `attack` or `hit`, and from `hit`, it transits to `dead`. Notice that on top of animation nodes, we can also create other node types: `BlendSpace1D`, `BlendSpace2D`, `BlendTree`, and even another `StateMachine` node. This is because they are all `AnimationNode` subtypes, which allows us to create nested graphs. By the way, using an `AnimationNodeStateMachine` node inside another `AnimationNodeStateMachine` node is how we can create sub-state machines and cover sub-states; remember *attack jumping* and *jump dashing* states from the chapter introduction? You could create another `AnimationNodeStateMachine` node to handle `Air` sub-states and `Dash` sub-states. Pretty cool, right? Well, back to our graph; at the end, you should have all the animations organized in such a way that you can visually see their transitions. In my case, I organized it as shown in the following figure:

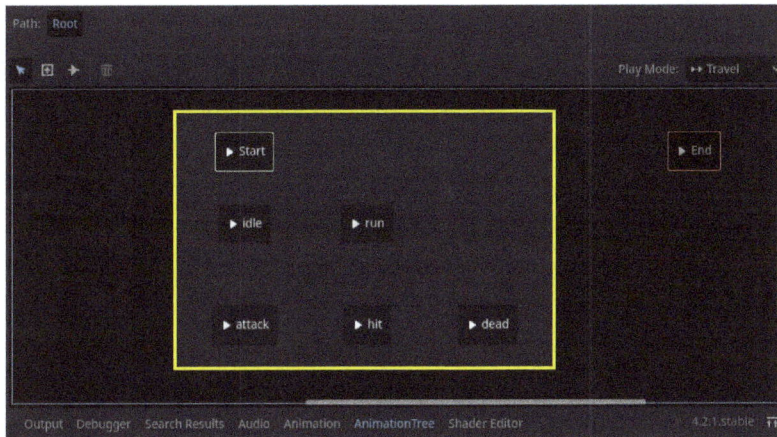

Figure 8.8 – The AnimationNode types arranged in the AnimationTree graph

Now, let's establish the transitions. You can see that there are some icons in this **AnimationTree** interface. Currently, there's an active button in the shape of a selection arrow, like a usual mouse arrow. This is the default mode, and with some hotkeys, we can achieve the other modes as well. But you can see there's also an icon shaped like an arrow with a line in the middle. This is the one that will allow us to connect two `AnimationNode` nodes with a transition by clicking and dragging.

Personally, I like to keep with the selection mode and use the *Shift* key to connect two `AnimationNode` nodes. Choose one of these methods and let's do the following steps:

1.   Make a transition from **Start** to the **idle** node:

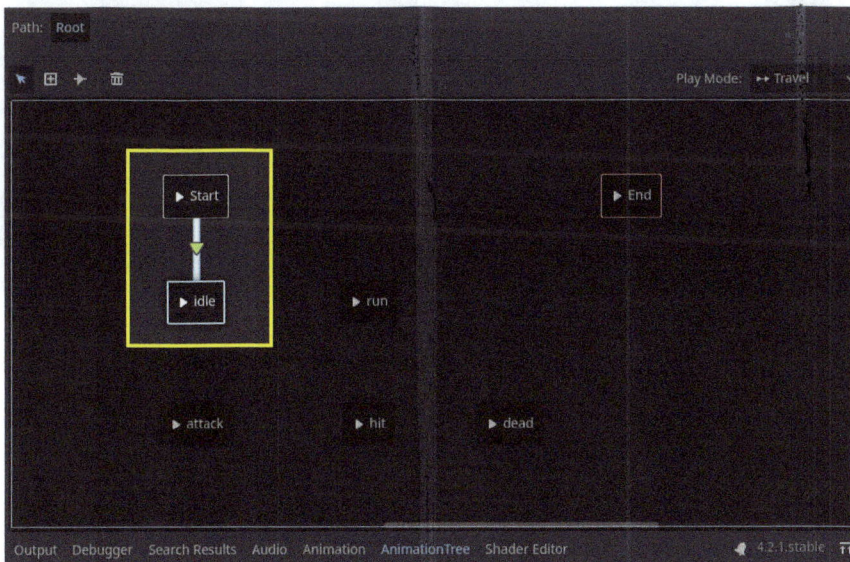

Figure 8.9 – The Start to idle connection

2. Then, make a transition from **idle** to **run**.

3. After that, make a transition from **run** to **idle**. This means that these animation transitions go both ways since the `Bumping Pig` enemy can idle at any moment when it is running and can start running any time when it is idling.

4. Make a transition from **hit** to **dead**. This will be the final state of the `Bumping Pig` enemy, meaning that after reaching death, it doesn't transit back to any other state.

5. Now come transitions that are a bit more complex. Start by making a transition from **idle** to **attack**, then from **attack** back to **idle**.

6. Make a transition from **run** to **attack** and from **attack** to **run**.

7. Now, make another transition from **attack** to **hit** and from **hit** back to **attack**.

8. After that, make transitions from **idle** to **hit**, **hit** to **idle**, **run** to **hit**, and **hit** to **run**. At the end, you should have an **AnimationTree** graph similar to the one shown in the following figure:

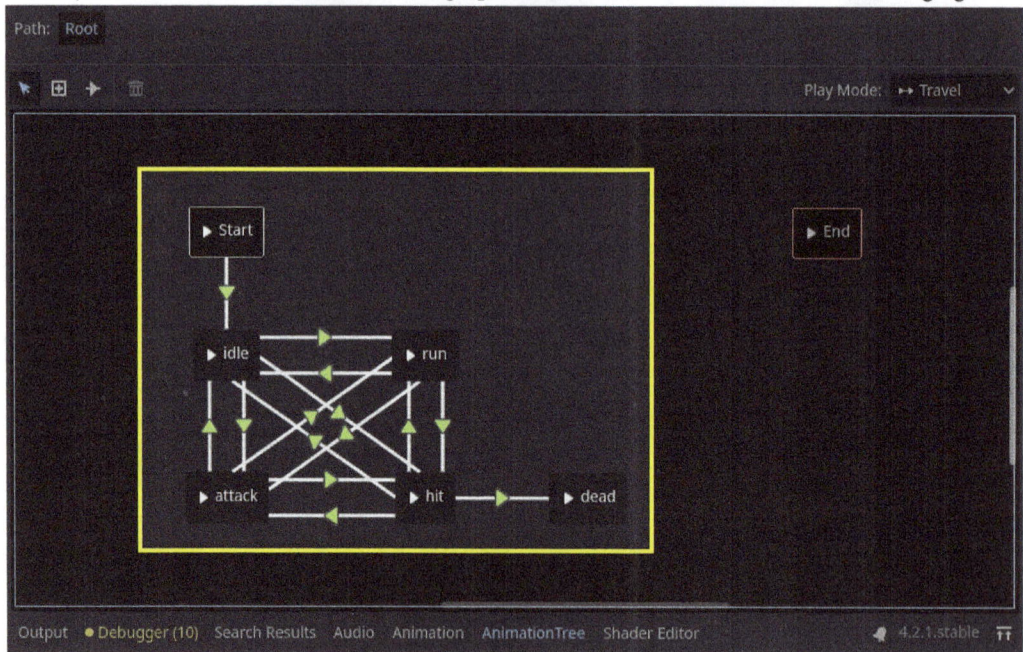

Figure 8.10 – The AnimationTree graph with all available animations as AnimationNode nodes and their respective transitions

With the transitions in place, it's time to use the transitions' properties we saw earlier in this chapter. For context, in Godot Engine, we have two main object classes: **Node** and **Resource**. It turns out that these transitions are Resource objects known as `AnimationNodeStateMachineTransition` and, as such, they bundle some interesting properties that we can access through the Inspector. We will keep our attention to the ones that are relevant to our goal; again, for more information, visit the official tutorial through the link provided earlier in this section.

Moving on with our task, there are some transitions for which we need to change **Switch Mode** from **Immediate** to **At End**. Namely, we need to do that on the **attack** to **idle**, **attack** to **run**, **attack** to **hit**, **hit** to **attack**, **hit** to **run**, and **hit** to **idle** transitions.

We do that because both the **attack** and **hit** animations should finish playing before they transit to other animations. The whole choreography of these animations is important for the gameplay, including their timing. You will notice that transitions that have **Switch Mode** set to **At End** will change their icon in the graph to something that resembles the icon of a **Play Next** button in music players; look at the following figure for reference:

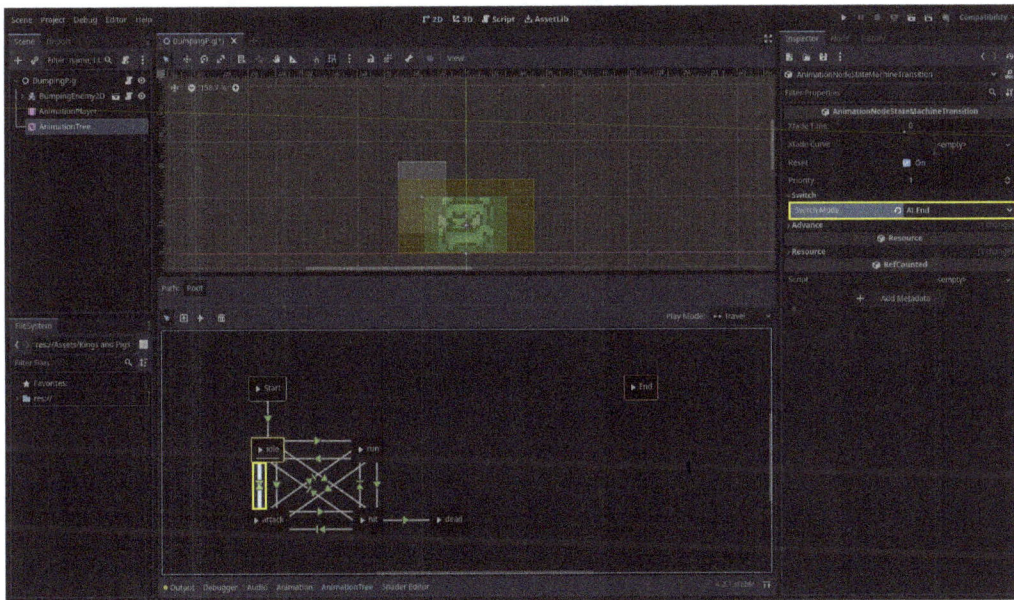

Figure 8.11 – The attack to idle AnimationNodeStateMachineTransition
node with its Switch Mode property set to At End

And with all the transitions in place, it's time to establish their conditions. This is the most important part as it is through the transition conditions that we will control the flow of these animations via code. In the next section, we will understand what conditions are and how to use them, when to use **Advance** expressions instead, and how to access them via code, which will lead us to create an interface for **AnimationTree** node to facilitate accessing and mutating the transition conditions.

Establishing transition conditions and Advance expressions

As we saw earlier in this chapter, the main purpose of `AnimationTree` node is to create advanced animation transitions in an `AnimationPlayer` node. So, we finally reached the main goal of the first part of this chapter. In this section, we will create the conditions that will trigger each transition from one animation (which, through our lens, is a state) to another. For that, we will open the animation graph and, at this moment, it should look like the one showcased in *Figure 8.11*. With the graph opened, we will do the following steps:

1. Select the **idle** to **run** transition and, in the Inspector, under the **Advance** category, set the value of the **Condition** property to **run**. This means that if the **AnimationPlayer** is currently playing the **idle** animation and the **run** condition becomes `true`, it will transit to the **run** animation. Keep that in mind.

2. Select the **run** to **idle** transition and set its **Condition** value to **idle**.

3. In the **idle** to **attack** transition, set the **Condition** value to **attack**.

4. As for the **attack** to **idle** transition, set the **Condition** value to **idle**.

5. For the **run** to **attack** transition, set the **Condition** value to **attack**.

6. For the **attack** to **run** transition, set the **Condition** value to **run**.

7. For the **attack** to **hit** transition, set the **Condition** value to **hit**.

8. For the **hit** to **attack** transition, set the **Condition** value to **attack**.

9. For the **hit** to **run** transition, set the **Condition** value to **run**.

10. For the **hit** to **idle** transition, set the **Condition** value to **idle**.

These are the simple transition conditions that we have for these animations. But I want to present to you the concept of **Advance** expressions. An expression in this context is a logical statement that returns either `true` or `false`. Interestingly enough, it can be written just like any GDScript expression. As mentioned earlier in the chapter, we could use `vision_area.get_overlapping_areas().size() > 0` as an expression in the transitions that transit to the attack animation instead of using the attack condition. But let's keep things simple, there's no need to overcomplicate things if they are still in a manageable complexity. But I feel obligated to show you at least one other expression that can be useful for us in this context.

Since we are using the `BumpingPig` node for **Advance Expression Base Node**, we have direct access to its properties and can use them in these **Advance** expressions. To wrap up our transitions, select the **hit** to **dead** transition, and in the **Advance Expression** property, we will check whether the `BumpingPig.health` property is lower than 1, meaning the enemy should die. The expression should look like the following figure:

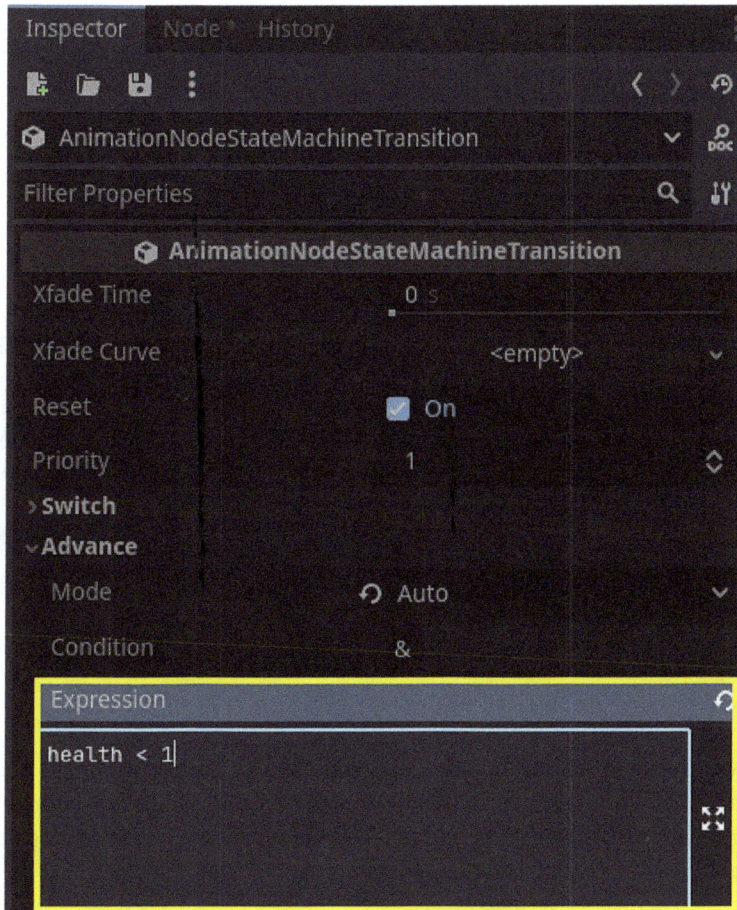

Figure 8.12 – The hit to dead transition's Advance expression

Note that since **Advance Expression Base Node** is the `BumpingPig` node, we can directly refer to its properties and methods. This also allows us to access any of the other nodes referred to in its properties. For instance, we could use an expression such as `body.direction == 0` to transit to the `idle` animation or `not body.velocity.x == 0` to transit to the `run` animation. This would allow us to create complex transitions, as proposed by the `AnimationTree` documentation. But we will keep things simple.

With that, we have everything in place regarding our animations, transitions, and conditions. A nice tip to test these transitions is to select one `AnimationNode` node on the `AnimationTree` graph, then select the `AnimationTree` node, and use the Inspector to toggle the properties displayed under the **Conditions** category. Keep in mind that, ideally, only one condition should be `true` at a time. This is important to remember when we start to code them. In the following figure, you can see the `attack` animation playing after I toggled on the **Attack** condition in the Inspector:

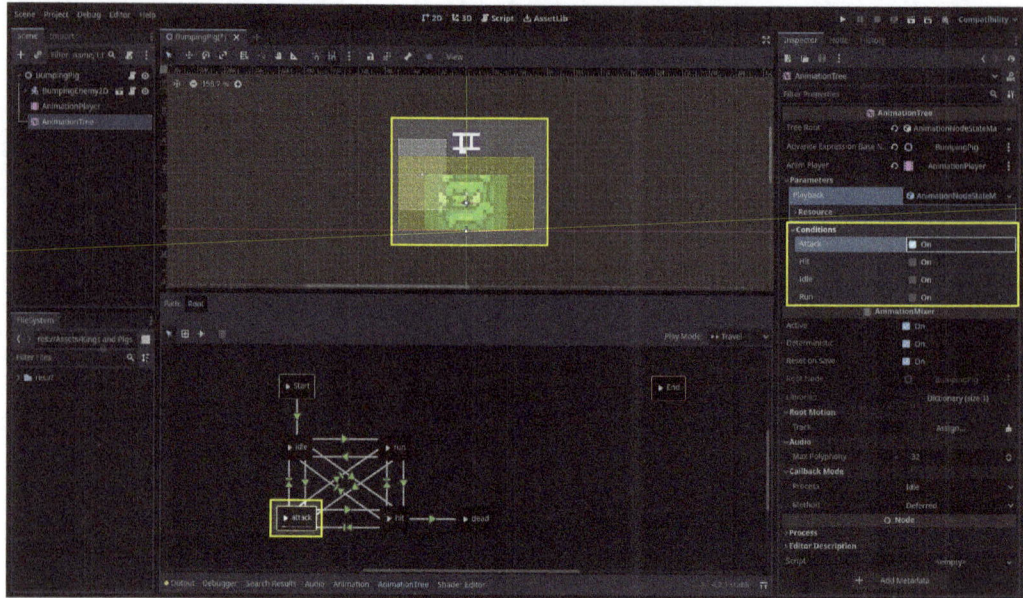

Figure 8.13 – The attack animation playing after the Attack condition value
was set to true; the transition happened from the run animation

This is a nice way to debug your transitions and understand whether there's room for any bugs or if you detect a bug when testing the game. Try to test every condition on every animation and see how `AnimationTree` will respond. You can even try to have multiple conditions toggled on to see whether there's room for this kind of situation in your game.

Before we move on to the next section, where we will create our own custom State pattern implementation using nodes and GDScript, I want to provide you with a nice interface that we will use to toggle these conditions on `AnimationTree` more easily.

By default, Godot Engine documentation suggests that we use the `set()` method to mutate these conditions. For instance, we would use `AnimationTree.set("parameters/conditions/attack", true)` to change the `attack` condition value to `true`. This is not convenient at all. Instead, we will do the following:

1. Attach a new GDScript to the `AnimationTree` node; you can save it as `res://Actors/AnimationTree.gd` since it's a generic script that can be useful for other actors in our game.

2. In the script, create a method that will behave as a shortcut to set conditions; we will name it `set_condition()` and it will ask for two arguments. The first will be `condition`, which will be a `StringName` type referring to the condition's name, for example, `"idle"`. The second argument will be `value`, which is a Boolean representing whether the condition will be set to `true` or `false`:

```
extends AnimationTree



func set_condition(condition: StringName, value: bool) -> void:
```

3. Then, inside this method, we will use the default way to access the `AnimationTree` conditions using the `set()` method with a `%s` placeholder that we will replace using the `condition` argument:

```
extends AnimationTree
func set_condition(condition: StringName,
  value: bool) -> void:

set("parameters/conditions/%s" % condition, value)
```

4. To facilitate the process of changing the `condition` value even more, we will create two other methods: one to directly set a `condition` value to `true` and the other to `false`. We will call them `enable_condition()` and `disable_condition()`, respectively. Both will ask for the `condition` name as a `StringName` argument. The complete `AnimationTree` script should look like this by now:

```
extends AnimationTree

func set_condition(condition: StringName,
  value: bool) -> void:
    set("parameters/conditions/%s" % condition,
      value)

func enable_condition(condition: StringName) ->
  void:
    set_condition(condition, true)

func disable_condition(condition:StringName) ->
  void:
    set_condition(condition, false)
```

With that, we have completed everything we need to integrate the animations and their transitions into the Bumping Pig enemy behaviors. Now, it's time to encapsulate these behaviors into State pattern classes that will handle behavior-specific code and also will be responsible for handling these animation transitions. In the next section, we will see how we can implement the State pattern using GDScript, extracting behavior-specific code and encapsulating it into dedicated State classes that will handle these behaviors properly and prevent undesired overlapping of such behaviors.

Handling state-specific behaviors with the State pattern

Well, if we go back to our game designer's request, one of the main issues presented is that there are multiple overlapping behaviors and there's a lack of predictability and control over how one behavior transits to another. The Bumping Pig looks like having a single messed-up behavior instead of multiple consistent and predictable behaviors. This is because, since the code doesn't explicitly set a boundary between each behavior depending on the BumpingPig enemy state, they bleed and blend on and with each other. This is what we are going to fix in this section by implementing a family of State classes to isolate these behaviors from each other and create a proper transition between them, preventing, for instance, the Bumping Pig enemy from moving while taking a hit or attacking.

Before we get started, I want you to take note that this is not the only way and may not even be the best way to implement the State pattern or a state machine. This is why I'm repeating that you understand the underlying abstract concept behind each pattern, so you can come out with the best solutions that fit your projects or your way of thinking and abstracting problems.

That said, what we are going to do is create multiple nodes as children of a States node, which, in turn, is a child of the BumpingPig node. Each one of them will have its own script, which will inherit from an abstract BumpingPigState class. This abstract class will serve as an interface class; it will have the methods that user classes can expect to access in these BumpingPigState classes but each will have its own implementation of these methods. Without further ado, let's get started. Add a new node as a child of the BumpingPig node and follow these instructions:

1. Rename this node as States to make it visually clear that all its children are supposed to represent states of the BumpingPig enemy, which will be their context object.

2. Right-click on the **FileSystem** dock and, from the drop-down menu, create a new folder inside the BumpingPig folder and name it States. Here is where we will put the BumpingPigState scripts:

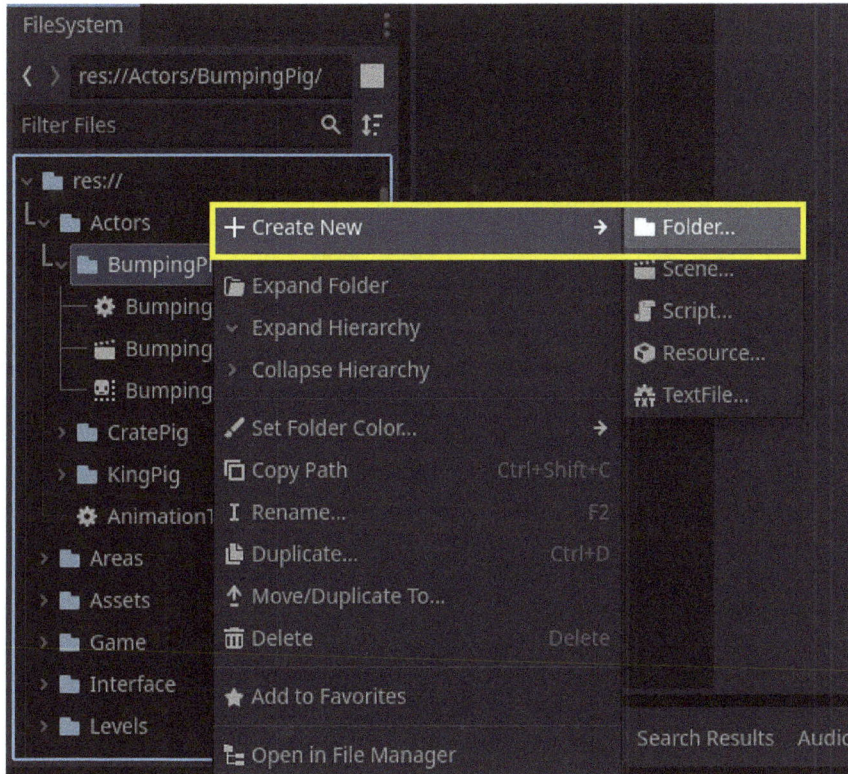

Figure 8.14 – Creating a new folder using the FileSystem drop-down menu

3. Right-click on the States folder and, from the drop-down menu, create a new script. Save it as res://Actors/BumpingPig/States/BumpingPigState.gd.

4. Open the script and the first thing we are going to do is register this as a named class using the class_name keyword followed by BumpingPigState. This will allow us to easily use it as a type on our project. By doing that, we can communicate to our peers the value type that our script expects to receive as an argument or as a variable, among other situations. This prevents errors in the future:

```
extends Node
class_name BumpingPigState
```

5. After that, we will declare our notable context! We will call it context to make it clear that this is the context object the states will use in their code. This variable should be typed as being a BumpingPig variable to make it clear that this class, and subclasses, expect a context with the same interface as the BumpingPig class.

Note that we won't assign any value to this variable here, firstly, because this is not only an abstract class but also because we will use a technique (considered by many as also a design pattern) called dependency injection, where user classes provide the dependencies directly to their service classes:

```
extends Node
class_name BumpingPigState

var context: BumpingPig
```

6. Then, we will also create a variable to hold a reference to the previous state the context was in. This will help us make dynamic transitions back to any state in case we need them. For instance, since the Bumping Pig can transit to the `attack` state from multiple states, it's important to keep them in memory so that when the `attack` state finishes, it can properly transit to the previous state it was in before attacking or getting hit:

```
extends Node
class_name BumpingPigState

var context: BumpingPig
var previous_state: BumpingPigState
```

7. Now comes two fundamental methods that we typically have in State classes: `enter()` and `exit()`. These are super useful methods that we can use to initiate or terminate a state. For instance, in our case, this will be useful to enable and disable the conditions to play the state-equivalent animation:

```
func enter() -> void:
    pass

func exit() -> void:
    pass
```

8. Finally, here goes one of the most important aspects of implementing the State pattern. All state-specific behaviors must be delegated to the states instead of being processed by the context object. It won't be our case, but here we could have `_process()`, `_physics_process()`, or `_unhandled_input()`, among other relevant process-based virtual functions being delegated to states. In these cases, we could use `set_process_*(false)` inside the `enter()` method and the opposite inside the `exit()` method of each State instance. This would prevent overlapping of the logic inside these virtual functions, for instance, the same input event leading to multiple outcomes each from a different state. By delegating that to the `State` instance, we prevent these issues. In our case, we will create a method called `get_hurt()`, which the

context object will call to delegate the behavior to its current `State` instance. We do that because, for instance, the `hit` state and the `dead` state won't need to implement any behavior when the context gets hurt, whereas `idle`, `run`, and `attack` will transit to the `hit` state:

```
func get_hurt() -> void:
    pass
```

Alright, we have our abstract `BumpingPigState` class ready. With that, we can create concrete implementations for each of the states we want the `Bumping Pig` enemy to be in, namely, `idle`, `run`, `attack`, `hit`, and `dead`. In the next section, we will start extracting the behaviors we currently have in the context object into our `BumpingPigStates` class using a factoring technique called extraction.

Extracting the context behaviors into states

Our game designer created some methods in the `BumpingPig` class, but you will notice that things are a bit messy. There is a `match` check in `_physics_process()` just to play some animations in specific states, the `idle()` and `run()` methods just set the `state` variable to their respective state, and while the `hit()` and `dead()` methods have some actual logic, their animation is still being played in the `match` statement for some weird reason. Well, this `match` statement is like a state machine or something, but it's not very well implemented. Let's fix all that; I hope you are ready for some heavy refactoring! Open the `res://Actors/BumpingPig/BumpingPig.gd` script and follow these steps:

1. Since we are not going to use `AnimationPlayer` anymore, we will replace the `anim_player` variable with a reference to `AnimationTree` instead, and rename it `animation_tree`:

    ```
    extends Node2D
    class_name BumpingPig

    @export var initial_direction = -1
    @export var max_health = 3

    @onready var body = $BumpingEnemy2D
    @onready var vision_area =
        $BumpingEnemy2D/Sprites/VisionArea2D
    @onready var animation_tree = $AnimationTree
    ```

2. Then, we can get rid of the `States` enumerator, since we will use the `BumpingPigStates` class instead. After removing the `States` enumerator declaration, change the `state` variable type to `BumpingPigState` and leave it blank with no value set for now:

    ```
    @onready var state: BumpingPigState
    ```

3. After that, we will create a setter method for the `state` variable to encapsulate some procedures that must be performed every time we change its value. So, right after the type declaration, let's create a setter statement to a callable, which we will create in the next step, called `set_state()`:

```
@onready var state: BumpingPigState : set = set_state
```

4. After the `_ready()` callback, let's create the `set_state()` method, which must have an argument with the new value, which we can call `new_state` to help us identify the new, current, and previous state:

```
func set_state(new_state: BumpingPigState) -> void:
```

5. Then, inside the `set_state()` setter method, we will create the state-changing procedure. Start by checking whether there's any state set already; this will prevent errors in case this variable isn't fed yet. If there's a state reference inside the `state` variable, we will call the `exit()` method on it and set `new_state.previous_state` to the current state:

```
func set_state(new_state: BumpingPigState) -> void:
    if state:
        state.exit()
        new_state.previous_state = state
```

6. With the previous state stored and properly exited, we will set the current state to `new_state` and call the `enter()` method on it, effectively finishing our state transition procedures:

```
func set_state(new_state: BumpingPigState) -> void:
    if state:
        state.exit()
        new_state.previous_state = state
    state = new_state
    state.enter()
```

7. The next thing we need to do is inject the missing dependencies that the `BumpingPigState` instances have, which is the context object. For that, in the `_ready()` callback, we will run through every child of the `States` node, which, in our architecture, will be all `BumpingPigState` instances, and set their `context` variable to point to the `BumpingPig` instance using the `self` keyword:

```
func _ready() -> void:
    body.direction = initial_direction
    for state in $States.get_children():
        state.context = self
```

With that, we have a pretty decent state machine ready to perform some state transitions. In the next section, we will create the states themselves.

Creating concrete states

Since we will be extracting some code from the BumpingPig class, this process will have some back-and-forth steps, so take a seat, and let's start by creating the IdleState class logic and work from there. Also, you will notice that the implementation of the State pattern will add a lot of duplication and extra code that might seem unnecessary at first.

The idea is not to decrease the total pool of lines of code in our code base, but instead, to have manageable classes that we can intuitively make sense of. That said, add a new node as a child of the States node and follow these steps :

1. Rename this node as IdleState and, from the **FileSystem** dock, drag and drop BumpingPigState.gd to it, attaching the script to the node.

2. Then, right-click on the **IdleState** node, and from the drop-down menu, select the **Extend Script…** option.

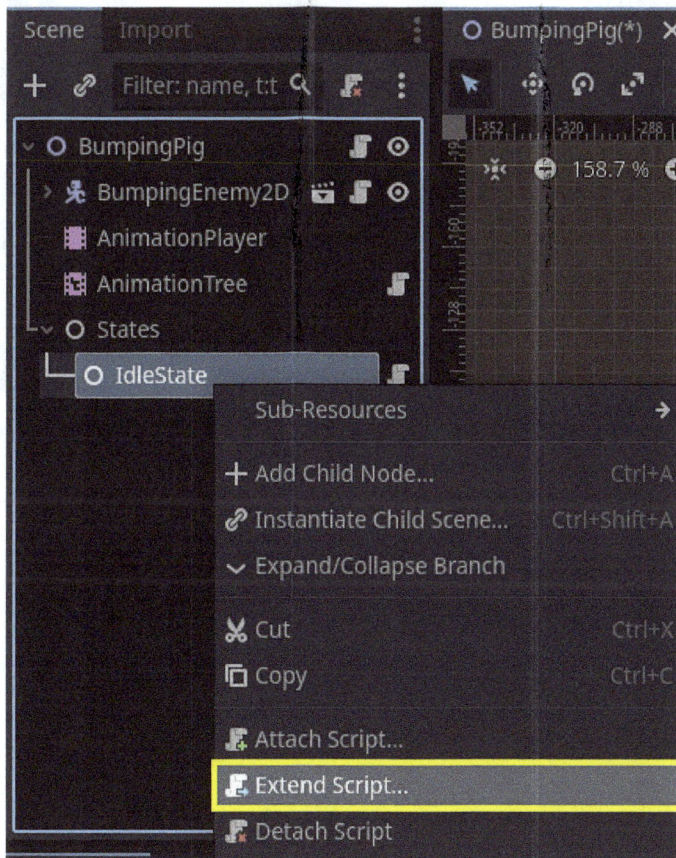

Figure 8.15 – Extending a GDScript using the Scene dock's node menu

3. From the pop-up menu, make sure to save the file under the `States` folder, and for consistency and better communication and searching, name the file `res://Actors/BumpingPig/States/IdleBumpingPigState.gd`. We will follow this pattern in every other state from now on: `res://Actors/BumpingPig/States/*BumpingPigState.gd`, where * is the state name. This will ensure that we know they are all part of the same family of algorithms:

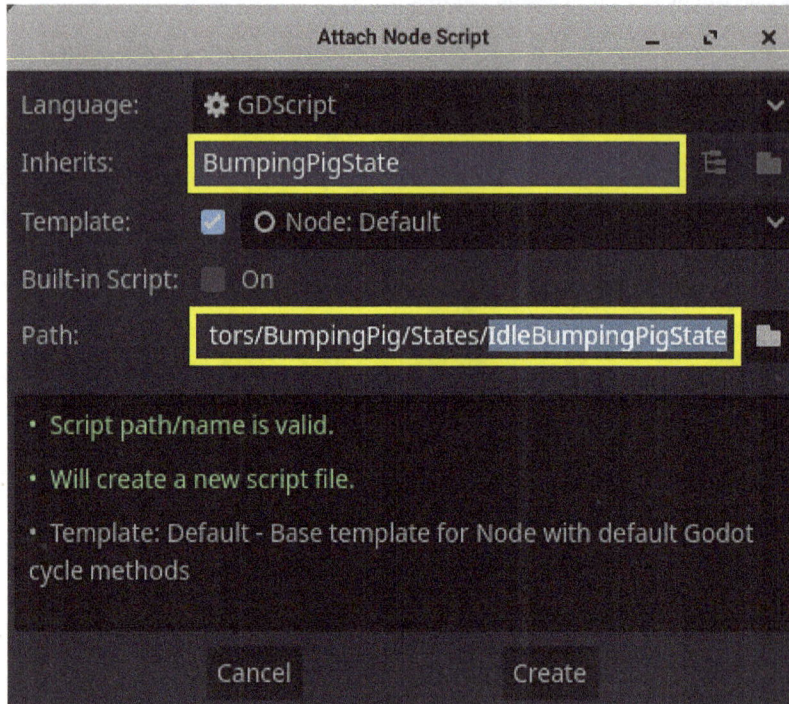

Figure 8.16 – Extending the BumpingPigState script as the IdleBumpingPigState script

4. Inside the script, get rid of the **Node: Default** template methods, and instead, we will implement the methods from the abstract `BumpingPigState` class (`enter()`, `exit()`, and `get_hurt()`):

```
extends BumpingPigState

func enter() -> void:

func exit() -> void:

func get_hurt() -> void:
```

5. Inside the `enter()` method, we will check whether the `direction_changed` signal from the `BumpingPig.body` variable is connected to a method that we will create in the next steps. If it isn't, then we will connect it. The callback method will be named `_on_body_direction_changed`:

```
func enter() -> void:
    if not context.body.direction_changed.is_connected(
      _on_body_direction_changed):
        context.body.direction_changed.connect(
          _on_body_direction_changed)
```

6. After that, we will also connect the `body.vision_area.area_entered` signal to a signal callback that we will name `_vision_area_area_entered()`. We will use this callback to transit to the `attack` state:

```
func enter() -> void:
    if not context.body.direction_changed
      .is_connected(_on_body_direction_changed):
        context.body.direction_changed
        .connect(_on_body_direction_changed)
    if not context.vision_area.area_entered
      .is_connected(_vision_area_area_entered):
        context.vision_area.area_entered
        .connect(_vision_area_area_entered)
```

7. Then, we will enable `AnimationTree`'s `idle` condition using the interface we created:

```
func enter() -> void:
    if not context.body.direction_changed
      .is_connected(_on_body_direction_changed):
        context.body.direction_changed
        .connect(_on_body_direction_changed)
    if not context.vision_area.area_entered
      .is_connected(_vision_area_area_entered):
        context.vision_area.area_entered
        .connect(_vision_area_area_entered)
    context.animation_tree.enable_condition("idle")
```

8. In the `exit()` method, we will essentially undo these. It's important to connect and disconnect the signals because we may want to use them in other states, and if they trigger multiple states' behaviors, we will get into trouble. An alternative for that would be to connect these signals to the `BumpingPig` class and delegate the behavior to each state; we could do that using other methods in the `BumpingPigState` interface, for instance. But I prefer to implement them only in the states that actually need them:

```
func exit() -> void:
    context.body.direction_changed
```

```
        .disconnect(_on_body_direction_changed)
        context.vision_area.area_entered
        .disconnect(_vision_area_area_entered)
        context.animation_tree.disable_condition("idle")
```

9. As for the get_hurt() state, we will use it to trigger a transition to the hit state. Following our architecture, the node that will hold the hit state logic will be named HitState, so we will use the find_child() method to change context.state to HitState:

```
func get_hurt() -> void:
    context.state = context.find_child("HitState")
```

10. Then, let's implement the _on_body_direction_changed() callback, which is another transition. This time, it will transit to RunState if the direction is not equal to 0:

```
func _on_body_direction_changed(new_direction:
  int) -> void:
    if not new_direction == 0:
        context.state = context.find_child("RunState")
```

11. Finally, we will implement the _vision_area_area_entered() signal callback. Here, we will transit to the attack state; following our architecture, it should be named AttackState:

```
func _vision_area_area_entered(area: Area2D) -> void:
    context.state = context.find_child("AttackState")
```

And this wraps up the IdleBumpingPigState class. For reference, the complete script should look like the following:

```
extends BumpingPigState

func enter() -> void:
    if not context.body.direction_changed
      .is_connected(_on_body_direction_changed):
        context.body.direction_changed
        .connect(_on_body_direction_changed)
    if not context.vision_area.area_entered
      .is_connected(_vision_area_area_entered):
        context.vision_area.area_entered
        .connect(_vision_area_area_entered)
    context.animation_tree.enable_condition("run")

func exit() -> void:
```

```
        context.body.direction_changed
        .disconnect(_on_body_direction_changed)
        context.vision_area.area_entered
        .disconnect(_vision_area_area_entered)
        context.animation_tree.disable_condition("run")

    func get_hurt() -> void:
        context.state = context.find_child("HitState")

    func _on_body_direction_changed(new_direction:
      int) -> void:
        if context.body.direction > 0:
            context.sprites.scale.x = -1
        elif context.body.direction < 0:
            context.sprites.scale.x = 1
        if context.body.direction == 0:
            context.state = context
            .find_child("IdleState")

    func _vision_area_area_entered(area: Area2D) -> void:
        context.state = context.find_child("AttackState")
```

In the next section, we will implement the RunBumpingPigState script.

Moving around with the run state

We will repeat *steps 1* to *4* from the previous section. After that, in the RunBumpingPigState script, let's do the following:

1. In the enter() method, we will do what we did in the IdleBumpingPigState.enter() method, but instead of enabling the idle condition, we will enable the run condition:

    ```
    func enter() -> void:
        if not context.body.direction_changed
          .is_connected(_on_body_direction_changed):
            context.body.direction_changed
            .connect(_on_body_direction_changed)
        if not context.vision_area.area_entered
          .is_connected(_vision_area_area_entered):
            context.vision_area.area_entered
            .connect(_vision_area_area_entered)
        context.animation_tree.enable_condition("run")
    ```

2. In the `exit()` method, we will do the opposite of that, disconnecting the signals and disabling the `run` condition. You can see now the importance of connecting and disconnecting these signals every time. Without that, the signals could emit, triggering the callback methods on the `IdleBumpingPigState` and `RunBumpingPigState` classes, which is not desired:

```
func exit() -> void:
    context.body.direction_changed
    .disconnect(_on_body_direction_changed)
    context.vision_area.area_entered
    .disconnect(_vision_area_area_entered)
    context.animation_tree.disable_condition("run")
```

3. Then, inside the `get_hurt()` method, we will transit to `HitState`, just like in the `IdleBumpingPigState` class:

```
func get_hurt() -> void:
    context.state = context.find_child("HitState")
```

4. Then, in the `_on_body_direction_changed()` signal callback, we will extract the code from `BumpingPig._on_body_direction_changed()` that controls the looking direction of the `BumpingPig` scene's sprites:

```
func _on_body_direction_changed(new_direction:
  int) -> void:
    if context.body.direction > 0:
        context.sprites.scale.x = -1
    elif context.body.direction < 0:
        context.sprites.scale.x = 1
```

5. Still inside the `_on_body_direction_changed()` signal callback, if `new_direction` is 0 (meaning the Bumping Pig enemy shouldn't be moving), we will transit to `IdleState`:

```
func _on_body_direction_changed(new_direction:
  int) -> void:
    if context.body.direction > 0:
        context.sprites.scale.x = -1
    elif context.body.direction < 0:
        context.sprites.scale.x = 1

    if context.body.direction == 0:
        context.state = context
            .find_child("IdleState")
```

6. Finally, in the `_vision_area_area_entered()` signal callback, we will transit to `AttackState` as we did in the `IdleBumpingPigState` class:

```
func _vision_area_area_entered(area: Area2D) -> void:
    context.state = context.find_child("AttackState")
```

And our second state is done! I think that, at this point, you are already grasping the gist of how the State pattern works, right? As I mentioned earlier in this section, it's common to have duplication of code, so don't bother about that. Unlike most other architectures, the State pattern classes are aware of their sibling classes. This is necessary for handling transitions between states, so don't be surprised by the cross-references between nodes such as `IdleState`, `RunState`, `AttackState`, and so on. With that said, the `RunBumpingPigState` class should look like the following code after implementing the preceding steps:

```
extends BumpingPigState

func enter() -> void:
    if not context.body.direction_changed
    .is_connected(_on_body_direction_changed):
        context.body.direction_changed
        .connect(_on_body_direction_changed)
    if not context.vision_area.area_entered
      .is_connected(_vision_area_area_entered):
        context.vision_area.area_entered
        .connect(_vision_area_area_entered)
    context.animation_tree.enable_condition("run")

func exit() -> void:
    context.body.direction_changed
    .disconnect(_on_body_direction_changed)
    context.vision_area.area_entered
    .disconnect(_vision_area_area_entered)
    context.animation_tree.disable_condition("run")

func get_hurt() -> void:
    context.state = context.find_child("HitState")

func _on_body_direction_changed(new_direction:
  int) -> void:
    if context.body.direction > 0:
        context.sprites.scale.x = -1
    elif context.body.direction < 0:
        context.sprites.scale.x = 1
```

```
    if context.body.direction == 0:
        context.state = context.find_child("IdleState")

func _vision_area_area_entered(area: Area2D) -> void:
    context.state = context.find_child("AttackState")
```

It's time to make a change and see the real power of encapsulating the context object's behaviors into state classes!

In the next section, we will implement the attack state. It will encompass some really interesting logic that only makes sense because we are working with the State pattern!

Dealing damage in the attack state

Follow *steps 1* to *4* from the `IdleBumpingPigState` class again, naming the node `AttackState`, and let's dive into action by following these steps:

1. In the `AttackBumpingPigState` class, we will start by enabling the `attack` animation in the `enter()` method:

   ```
   extends BumpingPigState

   func enter() -> void:

   context.animation_tree.enable_condition("attack")
   ```

2. Then, we will disable the `Bumping Pig` enemy movement by turning off the physics process:

   ```
   extends BumpingPigState

   func enter() -> void:

   context.animation_tree.enable_condition("attack")

   context.body.set_physics_process(false)
   ```

3. After that, we will wait for the finished signal to be emitted by the `animation_tree` instance. This will mean the Bumping Pig finished its attacking animation so it should leave the `attack` state:

   ```
   extends BumpingPigState

   func enter() -> void:

   context.animation_tree.enable_condition("attack")
   ```

```
context.body.set_physics_process(false)

await context.animation_tree.animation_finished
```

4. Then, we will immediately transition to whatever state preceded the attack state. For that, we will use the previous_state variable:

```
extends BumpingPigState

func enter() -> void:

context.animation_tree.enable_condition("attack")

context.body.set_physics_process(false)

await context.animation_tree.animation_finished

context.state = previous_state
```

5. Moving on to the exit() method, we will disable the attack condition on the animation_ tree instance, and enable the physics processing again:

```
func exit() -> void:

context.animation_tree.disable_condition("attack")

context.body.set_physics_process(true)
```

6. Finally, in the get_hurt() method, we will override it to transition to the HitState node, which is the node carrying the hit state logic. We will implement the hit state behavior in the next section:

```
func get_hurt() -> void:

context.state = context.find_child("HitState")
```

That's it, the complete AttackBumpingPigState class script should look like the following code after following the preceding instructions:

```
extends BumpingPigState


func enter() -> void:

context.animation_tree.enable_condition("attack")
```

```
context.body.set_physics_process(false)

await context.animation_tree.animation_finished

context.state = previous_state


func exit() -> void:

context.animation_tree.disable_condition("attack")

context.body.set_physics_process(true)


func get_hurt() -> void:

context.state = context.find_child("HitState")
```

Moving on to the next state, in the next section, we will finally implement the `hit` state.

Getting hurt in the hit state

This one is interesting because it won't implement the `get_hurt()` method. Since the `hit` animation itself disables the Bumping Pig hurt box, there's no reason to implement the `get_hurt()` method in the `hit` state, as the Bumping Pig can't be hurt while in this state. So, start by following *steps 1 to 4* from the `IdleBumpingPigState` class implementation making the proper adjustments, and then we will perform the following steps:

1. Inside the `enter()` method, we will enable the `hit` condition on `AnimationTree` and disable the `context.body` physics process to prevent it from moving while taking a hit. Remember, this was one of the designer's complaints:

    ```
    func enter() -> void:
        context.animation_tree.enable_condition("hit")
        context.body.set_physics_process(false)
    ```

2. Then, we will adapt the logic from the `BumpingPig.hit()` method. Instead of extracting it directly, we will make some tweaks. First of all, we will increase the player's score:

    ```
    func enter() -> void:
        context.animation_tree.enable_condition("hit")
        context.body.set_physics_process(false)

        context.score.increase_score()
    ```

3. Then, we will use the `await` keyword to wait until the `hit` animation finishes playing:

```
await context.animation_tree.animation_finished
```

4. Now, we can check whether the Bumping Pig is still alive. If it is, we will transition back to the previous state. Otherwise, we will increase the score again and transit to `DeadState`:

```
await context.animation_tree.animation_finished
if context.health > 0:
    context.state = previous_state
else:
    context.score.increase_score()
    context.state = context
        .find_child("DeadState")
```

5. Now, for the `exit()` method implementation, we will enable the `context.body` physics processing again and disable the `hit` condition:

```
func exit() -> void:
    context.body.set_physics_process(true)
    context.animation_tree.disable_condition("hit")
```

At this point, I think you are already noticing some advantages of encapsulating each behavior inside a dedicated State class, right? By doing that, you don't have to be concerned about how each of the behaviors will interact with each other and prevent weird undesired outcomes with brute force. Everything is nice and clean, and this brings some predictability to our code. A good saying states that *"a good code should look like a bad screen script: predictable and boring with no surprises,"* and this is what we get by implementing the proper design patterns. For reference, this is the complete `HitBumpingPigState` class code:

```
extends BumpingPigState

func enter() -> void:
    context.animation_tree.enable_condition("hit")
    context.body.set_physics_process(false)

    context.score.increase_score()
    await context.animation_tree.animation_finished
    if context.health > 0:
        context.state = previous_state
    else:
        context.score.increase_score()
        context.state = context.find_child("DeadState")
```

```
func exit() -> void:
    context.body.set_physics_process(true)
    context.animation_tree.disable_condition("hit")
```

In the next section, we will implement the final state, both practically and philosophically: the dead state.

Killing our character with the dead state

In this one, we won't have transitions to any other state and the Bumping Pig will drop its resources. Quite like in real life. So, without further ado, follow *steps 1 to 4* from the `IdleBumpingPigState` class instructions and follow these steps:

1. In the `enter()` method, we will disable the `context.body` physics processing:

    ```
    func enter() -> void:
        context.body.set_physics_process(false)
    ```

2. Then, we will extract the `loot` logic from the `BumpingPig.die()` method, and this is all we have to do. The complete `DeadBumpingPigState` class script follows:

    ```
    extends BumpingPigState

    func enter() -> void:
        context.body.set_physics_process(false)
        for loot in context.loots.get_children():
            loot.drop()
    ```

With that, we still have two things to do in the `BumpingPig` class. First, we need to initialize the state machine logic by feeding it with an initial state, and we will use `IdleState` in the `_ready()` callback for that. Then, in the `_on_hurt_area_2d_hurt()` signal callback, we will delegate the getting hurt logic to the `state.get_hurt()` method. After that, we can remove everything in `_physics_process()`, which was basically just handling animations. We can also remove the state-specific methods since their behaviors are now self-contained in their respective state classes. The whole `BumpingPig` class script will be way cleaner now; it should look like the following:

```
extends Node2D
class_name BumpingPig

@export var initial_direction = -1
@export var max_health = 3

@onready var body = $BumpingEnemy2D
@onready var vision_area =
    $BumpingEnemy2D/Sprites/VisionArea2D
```

```
@onready var animation_tree = $AnimationTree
@onready var sprites = $BumpingEnemy2D/Sprites
@onready var score = $BumpingEnemy2D/ScorePoint
@onready var loots = $BumpingEnemy2D/Loots

@onready var health = max_health
@onready var state: BumpingPigState : set = set_state

func _ready() -> void:
    for state in $States.get_children():
        state.context = self
    set_state(find_child("IdleState"))
    body.direction = initial_direction

func set_state(new_state: BumpingPigState) -> void:
    if state:
        state.exit()
        new_state.previous_state = state
    state = new_state
    state.enter()

func _on_hurt_area_2d_hurt(damage: int) -> void:
    health -= damage
    state.get_hurt()
```

Note that we call set_state(find_child("IdleState") before setting the initial direction because this will allow the IdleBumpingPigState class to process the direction properly, immediately changing to the RunState instead. This ensures that the whole logic is working!

Well, this was a tough chapter, right? We saw so many things and learned a lot about this popular and controversial design pattern. Let's summarize the chapter so we can revisit some concepts and process them again with a fresher look.

Summary

In this chapter, we learned that changing the behavior of objects using the State pattern allows for more manageable and scalable code. The State pattern is a behavioral design pattern that helps an object alter its behavior when its internal state changes. This pattern provides a cleaner and more organized way to handle state transitions compared to using numerous conditional statements. Each state is represented as a separate class, and the context object delegates state-specific behavior to these classes. By encapsulating state-related behavior, we achieve better code maintainability.

On top of that, the chapter illustrated how state transitions can be implemented in Godot Engine. We explored how to use the `AnimationTree` node to handle animations and transitions based on the object's state. Advance expressions were introduced as a way to create more complex transition conditions. These expressions are logical statements that return `true` or `false`, allowing for dynamic and flexible transitions between animations. The chapter provided practical examples of using these expressions to control transitions between different animations, such as attacking and dying.

To facilitate testing and debugging these transitions, the chapter recommended using the Inspector to toggle conditions and observe the resulting animations. This method helps identify potential bugs and ensure that transitions behave as expected. Additionally, we created a custom GDScript attached to the `AnimationTree` node, providing convenient methods to set conditions and toggle them easily. This script streamlines the process of managing animation states and conditions, making it more efficient to test and debug animations.

The chapter also emphasized the importance of understanding the State pattern and its application in game development. By studying real-world examples and use cases, we gained insights into how the State pattern can solve common problems related to object behavior and state management. The pattern's ability to encapsulate state-specific behavior into separate classes enhances code organization and reduces the risk of introducing bugs when modifying state-related code that would overlap otherwise.

As we move forward to the next chapter, we will explore designing game actors using the Command pattern. This pattern will allow us to enhance our ability to create complex and dynamic behaviors for enemies and NPCs of our games, even for the player character itself. By leveraging the Command pattern, we can encapsulate methods as objects, allowing us to execute, cancel, and even suspend the execution of a method. This approach will provide a powerful tool for managing game actors' behaviors, enabling more sophisticated game mechanics and interactions.

9

Designing Actors with the Command Pattern

The **Command pattern** is a behavioral design pattern that allows us to turn method calls into objects. By doing that, we open up a world of possibilities, such as serializing method calls to pass them through the network, delaying method calls, serializing method calls to save game states, queuing method calls to create turn-based combat systems, and more.

The Command pattern is widely used in applications as the go-to approach to implementing features such as undo/redo systems since they allow the application to create a stack of commands, with each containing the values used to make the method call. Since commands have all the information involved in a method call, they can be used to undo the operation, which can also be useful in games if you want to implement a backtrack or replay system. It's also useful to implement keyboard shortcuts and other input event systems, such as assigning actions to mouse clicks.

In this chapter, we will understand how we turn a request into an object and the advantages of doing that, investigate where game developers typically implement this pattern, and we will implement it on our own in our Godot Engine project to create actors with complex behaviors and map the player character's actions to different input sources, including a GUI controller that will allow the game to be played on mobile devices.

You will cover the following main topics in the chapter:

- Understanding the Command pattern
- Spotting use cases of the Command pattern in games
- Implementing the Command pattern in Godot

You will notice that implementing the Command pattern resembles a lot the idea of the **Callable** type in Godot Engine. However, the Command pattern is different from Callables, especially in the sense that we can store and delay method calls with both. But they are not the same thing, as the Command pattern has all the components involved in invoking the request, including the request's argument values, whereas, with Callables, you will have to provide the method's arguments just in time. Callables use the `Callable.call()` method, which asks for the arguments, so it's not possible to serialize Callables directly.

Technical requirements

To follow this chapter, access the project files located in the `09.designing-actors-with-commands/01.start/` directory. If you run into any confusion, errors, or bugs while working through the *Implementing the Command Pattern in Godot* section, check the files in the `09.designing-actors-with-commands/02.finished/` folder for guidance. Any issues you encounter can be reported using the repository's issue tracker at the following link:

`https://github.com/PacktPublishing/Game-Development-Patterns-with-Godot-4/issues`

If you haven't downloaded the repository files yet, you can get them using the following link: `https://github.com/PacktPublishing/Game-Development-Patterns-with-Godot-4`.

With this in mind, we'll now delve into the fundamental principles of the Command pattern. By understanding the pattern's purpose, characteristics, the problems it addresses, and typical implementation methods, we'll be ready to apply it effectively in Godot, leveraging its built-in features while steering clear of common pitfalls. Let's get started!

Understanding the Command pattern

The whole idea behind the Command pattern is to be able to treat method calls, or requests, as objects.

Imagine that you need to tell something to a colleague in your company. You don't want to forget about the subject, but you will only meet the colleague during lunchtime. So instead of calling them right away, probably messing up with their focus during work, you instead write down the subject and the content on a sticky note. Later on, you meet your peer during lunch and you tell them you have something to ask, but can't remember. You pick up your sticky notes block and there's the note with the subject and the content of the conversation you want to have with them.

This is more or less how the Command pattern works. You can *queue*, *delay*, *store*, and *serialize* the request, which allows you to implement a range of useful features, like the previously mentioned undo and redo feature.

The Command pattern is a behavioral design pattern, which means it solves a problem specifically related to the object's behavior and responsibilities. The Command pattern addresses how objects make method calls on other objects, adding a layer of indirection that prevents a hard coupling and encapsulates possible changes that could affect the health of our code base.

The typical implementation of the Command pattern includes three core aspects:

- An **execution method**, usually called `execute()`, that we use to effectively execute the request
- A **sender object**, which is the object that makes the request
- A **receiver object**, which is the object in which we will actually call the method from inside the `Command` object

Then, we add all the necessary properties to store the parameters, or arguments, that we will need to make the method call on the receiver. Optionally, we can create an `undo()` method to undo the changes made by the `execute()` method.

By doing that, we turn the method call into an object instead of an ephemeral event that we have no control over or reference. One of the major benefits of implementing this pattern is that, by turning the request into an object, we can store it in a variable. We can also pass it as an argument in a function or mutate the variable, allowing us to change which command it stores. This lets us change what happens when the object executes the method later on in the game. Being able to delay the method execution is an additional benefit of turning the request into an object.

On top of all that, since it is an object now, we serialize the request, which solves a very annoying issue of network-based operations. For instance, you can't call a method on an object remotely directly because you don't have access to this object on your machine, since it is a memory reference on your machine. The way we pass data around in the network is through serializing it and deserializing it on the other end of the communication.

Serialization is essentially the process of turning data types into a text string that we can store and reuse later. Godot Engine offers some alternatives to call methods on remote objects, such as **Remote Procedure Calls** (**RPCs**), among other tools and techniques. If you want to know more about that, I highly recommend reading my other book also in partnership with Packt, *The Essential Guide to Creating Multiplayer Games with Godot 4*, available on Amazon and the Packt Learning platform.

Another nice benefit of turning requests into objects is the possibility of storing them in lists, which allows us to create a history of events in the game or application. This is typically how people implement undoable and redoable operations in applications and tools. We are going to talk more about use cases in the next section, *Spotting use cases for the Command pattern*.

You can think about the Command pattern as an object-oriented programming way to implement first-class functions with more specific benefits and the possibility to implement undo and redo operations. But, unlike first-class functions, commands' main benefit is that they completely decouple the sender of the request from its receiver, allowing us to create a much more flexible code base.

This happens especially because by coupling the sender to the `Command` class instead of directly coupling it to the receiver, the sender only needs to know that it should call the `Command.execute()` method, which is very unlikely to change its contract. With that, we adhere to the *Open-Closed Principle* perfectly.

On the other hand, if there are any changes in the receiver object, the `Command` class itself will encapsulate any changes in the code base. Instead of changing all classes that use the receiver class, we only change the `Command` class itself to adapt to the changes in the receiver, preventing unpredictable consequences of changing the receiver class.

The final benefit, and one that will be most useful for us as we move forward with our project, is that the Command pattern allows us to simplify the management of complex behaviors by compositing multiple simpler commands into complex sequences. For instance, if we have a `PickCommand`, `MoveCommand`, `AimCommand`, and `ThrowCommand` command, we can create a sequence of commands that execute one after the other to create an AI that will make an enemy pick up a bomb, move close enough to the player to aim it, and then throw it at the player's character. We can then create a whole library of these behaviors to give our actors complex and meaningful behaviors that will help the player immerse themselves in the game.

To summarize, the Command pattern encapsulates a request as an object, allowing us to treat the request as an object with all the parameters necessary to perform the request. This allows us to delay, queue, serialize, store, and pass the request around to other objects with the main benefit of decoupling the object that invokes that request from the object that performs it.

In the next section, we will see how all this abstract talk turns into concrete implementations that will help us understand how all these benefits turn into features that we can use in our game or as tools that we can use to create our games.

Spotting use cases for the Command pattern

We just saw the potential usefulness of the Command pattern, but outside of the abstract talks, how can it actually help us? In this section, we will see some real-world use cases for the Command pattern, especially related to games and game development.

Using commands such as undo/redo in level editors

Imagine that you have a level designer in your team and they don't like to use the Godot Engine's editor to design and manage levels. They ask you instead to create a custom editor or tool to help them design their levels. You create a very nice tool with the ability to create terrains, position objects, quickly scale them up and down or randomly, a grid-based design tool to create buildings, and more. The level designer goes ahead and tries to make some levels.

But they suddenly notice they can't undo or redo their actions in the level design tool. Since design implies a lot of experimentation, and thus, testing, therefore undoing and redoing things, they ask you to implement an undo and redo system. There you have an excellent opportunity to implement the Command pattern.

Queuing commands in real-time strategy games

Now, let's say you are making a **Real-Time Strategy** (**RTS**) game. In the game, players need to collect some resources such as lumber, gold, and food to create an army and defeat their opponents. *Players*, including AI players, can queue actions in their faction's units. For instance, a unit can be set to collect lumber, deliver it to the main building, then collect gold, deliver it to the main building, hunt some deer, collect food from them, and deliver it to the main building. All of this can be a single queue of actions. Note that an *AI opponent* could queue these actions as well to create a sense of strategy on their part, building their faction to success. We can even adjust how fast, accurate, or effective the AI players would perform these actions based on their difficulty. There we have another opportunity to implement the Command pattern.

Creating strategic encounters in role-player games

Then, we can think the same about battle systems, especially those that are more oriented toward strategy than action. Let's say you are making a **Role-Playing Game** (**RPG**) where you can have a party with three characters. You control the main character and the other two can be set to be controlled by an AI, but you can interfere in their actions by swapping the current character.

In this game, players have visible encounters, in opposition to random encounters. So, before the player engages in a battle, they can queue some actions, such as attacking the monster using the weapon in the character's hand, then casting a fireball spell on an enemy that has fire weakness, casting a protection spell on the ally, and entering in berserk mode with the main character.

Meanwhile, the AI assistants will engage in the battle and will queue some actions based on how the battle unfolds, healing the player character, attacking the weakest enemy, and casting some buffs on the whole party to increase their attributes. To create these complex actions, and especially this AI system, we could definitely use the Command pattern as well.

Making template behaviors in RPGs

Still in the realm of RPGs, we can allow players to create macros based on the available actions. So, let's say the player already has a queue of actions they always want to perform before facing a boss, such as buffering their characters, healing, and crafting items to use during the battle. There we have it, another use case for the Command pattern. Since by implementing the Command pattern we can serialize the action queues, they can be stored as part of the player's save file, allowing them to create and maintain a library of macros that save them time and allow them to fine-tune their strategies.

Backtracking actions in tactical RPG battles

A final example I want to give regarding games is related to tactical turn-based games. Imagine that you want to create a tactical RPG where the player's character has the ability to go back in time. Each of their and the opponents' actions are stored in a stack of events, and during the combat, players can move back to any point in time to try a different approach to defeating their foes. Using the Command pattern, we can play all the combat back and forward so players can see the rewinding of their actions unfolding in real time. How awesome is that?

Well, the Command pattern is useful not only for mechanics but also for basic features that we may want to add in any game, or application for that matter. Imagine that you make a fighting game, a platformer game, or a rhythm game, and you want to give players the opportunity to mess up with your carefully designed controls. By implementing the Command pattern, you don't have to be concerned about what key triggers what action. You add a layer of indirection using the Command pattern; any key can trigger any action in the game and players can finally configure their weird custom inputs that they say are better than the defaults.

With all these potential use cases for the Command pattern, it's time to understand how it can be useful for us in our project. In the next section, we will get yet another request from our game designer. This time around, they say they want to be able to design the game actors with more modularity. For instance, why can the player jump and the Bumping Pig enemy can't? What if they want to make complex actions for the enemies, such as throwing a bomb at the player? We will have to come out with a solution for these requests.

Implementing the Command pattern in Godot

In this section, we will put the Command pattern into practice by paving the way for an AI system that takes the Bumping Pig enemy actions and turns them into commands that we can map to an interface. This all boils down to our game designer's request, as they want to quickly test new behaviors for the Bumping Pig enemy and would like to put them into context instead of creating fake testing scenes.

Let's see what they want so we understand their issues and goals and help them:

"Hey there, it's me again, the game designer.

You did an excellent job with that state thing. Having the Bumping Pig delegate all its actions to the states really helped me have more control over what is possible in each state. Though, there's a lot of duplicate code now. But I think it paid off.

I also managed to understand how to use the AnimationTree's state machine! I managed to make one new animation node. I implemented some bomb-related behaviors and animations using these features. Our code base is really shaping nicely.

With that, I want to start designing its AI. So I need to be able to test these behaviors by putting the Bumping Pig into actual game situations so I can create some nice challenges.

I think that having some interface to play with its actions would be nice. But I don't want to tweak this interface myself if something changes in the BumpingPig code, so try to keep the debug interface completely decoupled from the BumpingPig class.

Thinking about it, it would be nice to have on-screen controls for the player as well, following this same implementation; maybe we want to port the game to mobile. Sounds cool, doesn't it? Well, we never know.

All I need for now is to be able to play with the Bumping Pig behaviors and test them using a visual interface instead of those fake testing scenarios. If you could also create a separate class to put some AI-related code so I understand how I can automate my tests, it would be awesome, since I removed some code from the state classes, especially the ones related to player and object detection, I don't want to mix these things."

Well, our game designer is getting really independent, aren't they? They have made some changes to the code base since our last delivery. This is very common and we typically have to deal with it. Let's take a brief look to ensure everything is still working smoothly.

In the following section, we will review the changes in the `BumpingPig` class, the sub-state machine added to the `AnimationTree` node, and the changes in the `BumpingPigState` class so we know what we are dealing with now.

Evaluating the game designer's changes

Since our game designer is getting more and more familiar with our code, it's common for them to get some autonomy and make changes. As the project engineer, it's our role to evaluate these changes and approve or reprove them, making the necessary adjustments to keep them aligned with our standards and vision.

So, let's start with what they did on the `AnimationTree` node. For that, open the `res://Actors/BumpingPig/BumpingPig.tscn` scene and select the `AnimationTree` node. The `AnimationTree` node graph will now display some new animation nodes; one, in particular, is called **StateMachine**. It represents the state machine that will handle more animation transitions, and it has a *pencil* on it so we can edit it. *Figure 9.1* highlights this, as follows:

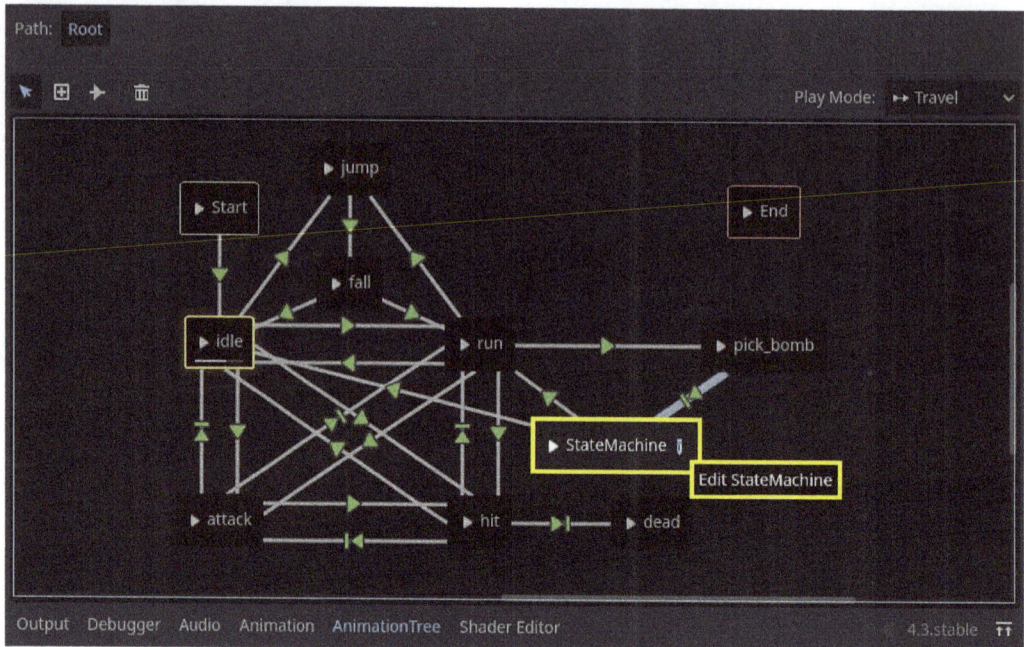

Figure 9.1 – The AnimationTree graph with a StateMachine node about to be edited

If we left-click on this *pencil*, we will enter a new state machine graph with other animations. We typically call these **nested state machines**, when we have a state that transitions to a new State Machine. People also call it **hierarchical state machines** or **sub-state machines**.

Inside this **StateMachine** animation node, there are some animations and two of them lead to the End animation node. This means that once one of these transitions is executed, **StateMachine** will trigger its own transitions. In this case, it will either transition back to the `idle` animation or the `run` animation on the **Root** State Machine. You can navigate back to the **Root** State Machine, or other state machines if this is the case, using the buttons available in the `Path` field of the `AnimationTree` graph, as shown in *Figure 9.2*:

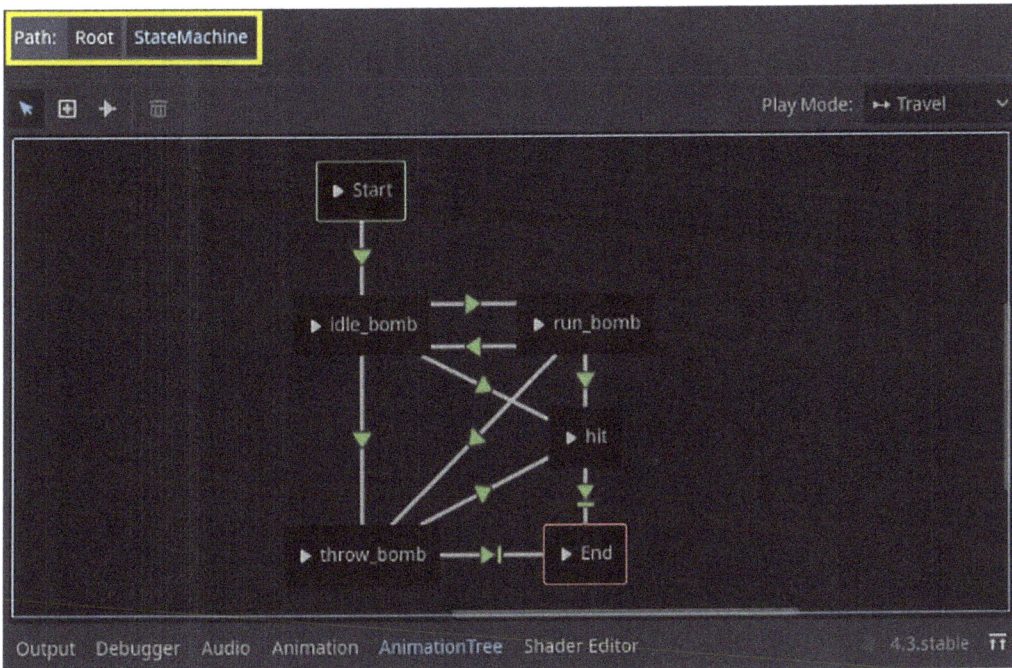

Figure 9.2 – The AnimationTree graph navigation paths

It seems like everything here is done nicely. I wonder how the game designer managed to implement the transition from one State Machine to the other, as this would mean different paths for the conditions we use to trigger the animation transitions.

If you check the **Inspector** panel, there's a new set of conditions. If you hover the mouse over them, you will notice that the paths to these parameters are different from the ones of the **Root** State Machine. *Figure 9.3* highlights the path to the new State Machine's throw condition:

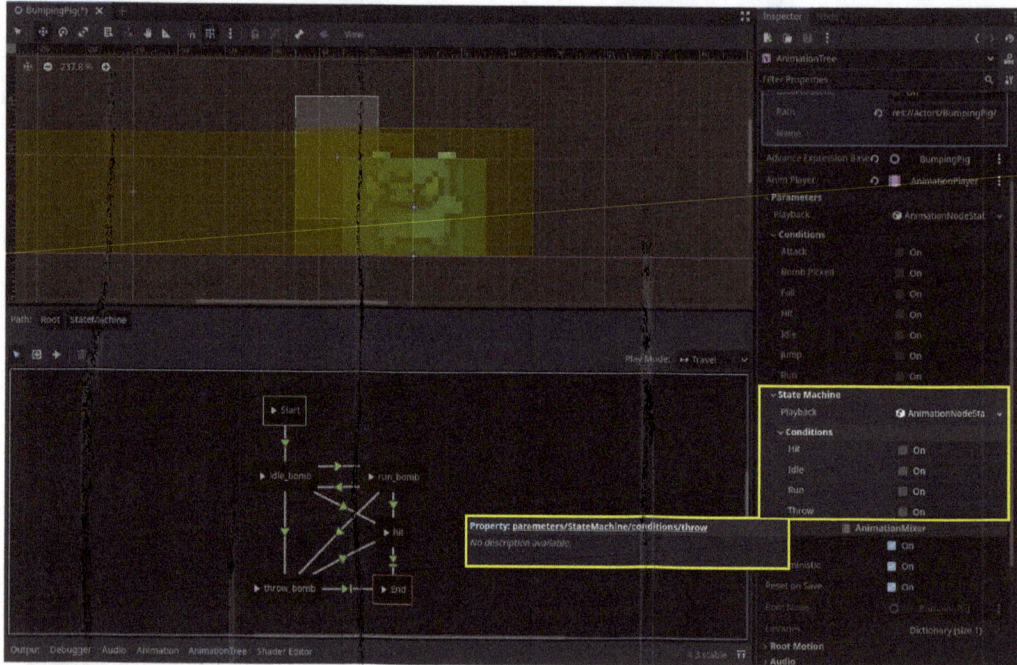

Figure 9.3 – The AnimationTree properties showcasing a new category of custom parameters related to the bomb animations sub-state machine

Let's open `res://Actors/AnimationTree.gd` and see how this is being dealt with. There are surely some changes here – let's have a closer look at these.

If you notice, now we have a property called `condition_path` and instead of directly accessing the path using a hard-coded string, we store a reference and use it to concatenate the final path to the desired condition. Really smart. Now, we can support any number of sub-state machines and hierarchies simply by changing the path.

Notice that the game designer followed the *Open-Closed Principle* by maintaining the `AnimationTree` class interface, so previous user classes wouldn't suffer any damage from this addition. This doesn't necessarily configure a change in the class, as it basically extended its initial interface, maintained its contract with previous classes, and added a new functionality.

This way, the game designer encapsulated the changes in the condition setting implementation, but for all the previous user classes, the `AnimationTree` class stayed the same. This is an excellent approach. We usually refer to that approach as *encapsulate what changes*, and it does exactly that: prevents changes in the implementation itself from causing collateral changes by maintaining the interface and changing just the implementation.

If you want to check how the game designer managed to switch `condition_path`, check the `res://Actors/BumpingPig/States/BombPickingBumpingPigState.gd` script and `res://Actors/BumpingPig/Commands/BombThrowCommand.gd`. They are the states that enter and exit the bomb behavior animations, so it's a good place to have these changes.

Moving on, let's take a look at the new methods created in the BumpingPig class. Open the `res://Actors/BumpingPig/BumpingPig.gd` script and let's take a look at it:

```
extends Node2D
class_name BumpingPig

@export var initial_direction = -1
@export var max_health = 3

@onready var body = $BumpingEnemy2D
@onready var vision_area =
  $BumpingEnemy2D/Sprites/VisionArea2D
@onready var bomb_vision_area =
  $BumpingEnemy2D/Sprites/BombVisionArea2D
@onready var animation_tree = $AnimationTree
@onready var sprites = $BumpingEnemy2D/Sprites
@onready var score = $BumpingEnemy2D/ScorePoint
@onready var loots = $BumpingEnemy2D/Loots
@onready var bomb_factory =
  $BumpingEnemy2D/Sprites/BombFactory

@onready var health = max_health
@onready var state: BumpingPigState : set = set_state


func _ready() -> void:
  for state in $States.get_children():
    state.context = self

for command in $Commands.get_children():
  command.receiver = self
  set_state(find_child("IdleState"))
  move(initial_direction)

func set_state(new_state: BumpingPigState) -> void:
  if state:
    state.exit()
    new_state.previous_state = state
```

```
    state = new_state
    state.enter()

func _on_hurt_area_2d_hurt(damage: int) -> void:
    state.get_hurt(damage)

func move(direction: int) -> void:
    state.move(direction)

func stop() -> void:
    state.stop()

func throw(throw_force: Vector2) -> void:
    state.throw(throw_force)

func jump() -> void:
    state.jump()

func cancel_jump() -> void:
    state.cancel_jump()

func pick_bomb(bomb: Bomb) -> void:
    state.pick_bomb(bomb)

func attack() -> void:
    state.attack()

func turn(direction: int) -> void:
    state.turn(direction)
```

The first thing you will notice is that now there are a bunch of methods and they are all being delegated to the `state` object. This is a good practice, as now we can override specific behaviors and allow each state to handle them differently. For instance, we now have the `JumpState` and `FallState` classes, and their `move()` method does not change the character's state but, rather, just moves it.

The `move()` method from the `IdleState` class, on the other hand, triggers the transition to the `RunState` node. This gives us a lot of flexibility to fine-tune how each method will have different implementations depending on the internal state of the `BumpingPig` class. On the other hand, we now have a lot of duplicate code. This is expected when implementing the State pattern. Talking about it, let's see how the `BumpingPigState` class interface is now, since it now has to support all these new methods that are being delegated from the `BumpingPig` class.

Open the res://Actors/BumpingPig/States/BumpingPigState.gd script and you will notice that the interface has a lot of new methods:

```
extends Node
class_name BumpingPigState

var context: BumpingPig
var previous_state: BumpingPigState

func enter() -> void:
  pass

func exit() -> void:
  pass

func get_hurt(damage: int) -> void:
  pass

func move(direction: int) -> void:
  pass

func stop() -> void:
  pass

func jump() -> void:
  pass

func cancel_jump() -> void:
  pass

func attack() -> void:
  pass

func throw(throw_force: Vector2) -> void:
  pass

func turn(direction: int) -> void:
  pass

func pick_bomb(bomb: Bomb) -> void:
  pass
```

We could say that this would break the *Open-Closed Principle*, but the designer only extended the interface, and there were no changes in the contracts. The only change on the previous contracts was made to the get_hurt() method, which now asks for an argument. This is not ideal, but the only user class, by design, of the BumpingPigState class is the BumpingPig class itself, so we are good.

Understand the State pattern as an extension of its context. Note that the callback method that triggered the get_hurt() call in the BumpingPig class didn't change, so this change on the get_hurt() method only affects, technically, the BumpingPig class itself. All good here. Well, I think our designer did a good job. So, let's move on to the next task.

In the following section, we will create the base class for the BumpingPig class commands and all the commands necessary to test the Bumping Pig enemy behaviors.

Creating the BumpingPig commands

Now, it's time to really understand the power we are about to develop. With the project opened, let's create a new GDScript; you can save it as res://Actors/Command.gd since it will be used as a base for the commands in all actors in our project. With the script opened, let's follow these steps:

1. Create a new variable to store a reference to the receiver object. Remember, the Command pattern has essentially three features: a sender, a receiver, and an execution method. Here, we are creating the reference to the receiver; let's call it receiver:

    ```
    extends Node
    class_name Command

    var receiver
    ```

2. Then, the next step is to create the execution method, which we can call it execute() and it won't return anything. Typically, when we implement the Command pattern, if the target method returns any value, we store it in a variable in the command itself. Remember, the Command pattern parameterizes the request for a method execution. This means that the Command object bundles and stores all the data related to the request such as arguments and returned values:

    ```
    extends Node
    class_name Command

    var receiver

    func execute() -> void:
        pass
    ```

3. Finally, we will also create a method to undo the changes made by the execute() method in case we want to create an undo-redo mechanic or anything of the sort. The final Command class script will look like the following script:

```
extends Node
class_name Command


var receiver

func execute() -> void:
    pass

func unexecute() -> void:
    pass
```

Yes, this is the basic implementation of the Command pattern. Pretty simple right? The real power and responsibility come when we decide what to do with this. Note that we don't have a reference to the sender object. This is because we don't need to; the sender is simply the user class that will take advantage of the Command class. We will implement the user class in the next section, where we will create the graphic interface to debug the actors' behaviors.

Using commands with buttons

Now that we have an interface to work with, we can create a user class and move on to the concrete use cases after that, knowing we have a backbone architecture to build upon. That said, in this section, we will create the CommandButton class, which will execute and unexecute a command based on a button's pressed state. For that, let's do the following steps:

1. Create a new scene using a Button node as the root node and rename it as CommandButton. Save the scene as res://Actors/Debug/CommandButton.tscn.

2. Attach a new GDScript and save it alongside the scene as res://Actors/Debug/CommandButton.gd.

3. Open the script and create an exported variable to get the path to the Command node that this button will interact with. For that, use the @export_node_path annotation and use the Command string to filter all other nodes but the ones that extend from the Command class. Let's name this variable command_path:

```
extends Button

@export_node_path("Command") var command_path
```

4. Then, right below `command_path`, we will actually retrieve this node. Note that this is a method that I particularly don't recommend for production because it implies that the `CommandButton` node will always trigger the `_ready()` callback after its target `Command` node, which may not always be the case and depends on their arrangement in the node hierarchy. Ideally, we inject these dependencies from a topmost node. But for a debug class, we don't need to be as strict, since they are likely to be discarded in the middle of the production anyway:

```
extends Button

@export_node_path("Command") var command_path
@onready var command: Command = get_node(command_path)
```

5. Now, we will use the Editor interface to connect the `button_up` and `button_down` signals to their respective callbacks:

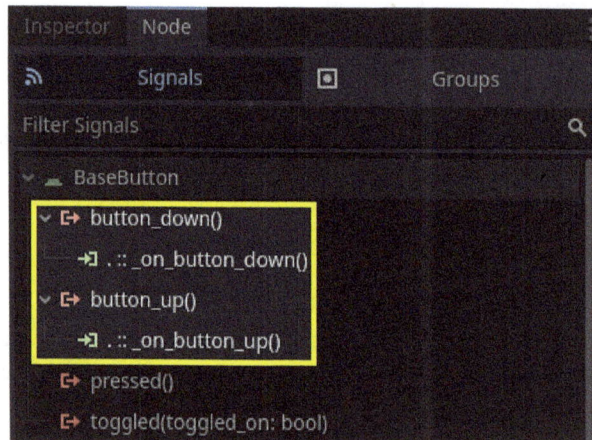

Figure 9.4 – The button_up and button_down signals connected to
their callback methods in the CommandButton class

6. Back to the script; inside the `_on_button_down()` callback, we will call the `execute()` method on the `command` object:

```
func _on_button_down() -> void:
    command.execute()
```

7. And in the `_on_button_up()` callback, we will call the `unexecute()` method on the `command` object. Note that this may vary. We may not want to unexecute a command upon releasing a button. But since we don't have any use case for that and since we can extend the `CommandButton` class to change this behavior when we find it necessary, let's keep it that way:

```
func _on_button_up() -> void:
    command.unexecute()
```

And this wraps up the `CommandButton` class. With that, we can assign a `Command` node to a `CommandButton` node and create a direct trigger to test the actors' behaviors. There's something still missing at this point. We need to actually create concrete `Command` classes for our actors!

In the next section, we will see how to implement concrete commands based on the abstract `Command` class we created previously. With that, we will have that layer of indirection that the Command pattern offers, where we will be able to call methods on an object from any object in our code base without coupling them to the `BumpingPig` class.

Implementing the concrete commands

We now have the bread and butter to experience the advantages of the Command pattern. In this section, we will create a series of commands, extending the `Command` class, inside the `BumpingPig` scene. Using this approach, where we have nodes as commands, is nice because it will give us a visual cue about the possible behaviors of the Bumping Pig enemy without the need to investigate its class.

Now, let's get into action. Open the `res://Actors/BumpingPig/BumpingPig.tscn` scene and follow these steps:

1. Create a new node as a child of the `BumpingPig` node and name it `Commands`. This will be the container node for all the commands we will create. Doing this helps us have a better structure for our scene and also allows us to do some batch procedures, such as injecting the `BumpingPig` node into the commands:

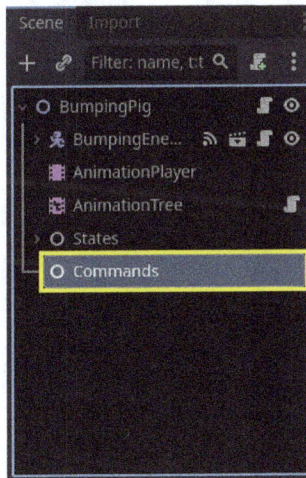

Figure 9.5 – The Commands container node as a child of the BumpingPig node

2. With that, create a new node and attach the `Command` class script to it. Name it `JumpCommand`:

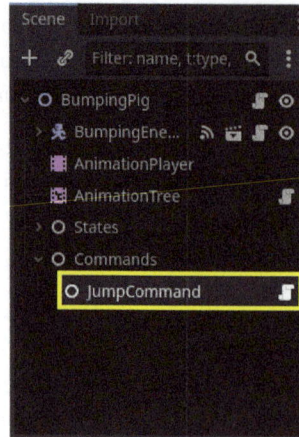

Figure 9.6 – JumpCommand as a child of the Commands container

3. Then, duplicate the `JumpCommand` node to create the `MoveLeft`, `MoveRight`, `TurnLeft`, `TurnRight`, `Stop`, `Attack`, `PickBomb`, and `Throw` commands:

Figure 9.7 – All the commands available in the BumpingPig scene

With that, we have everything in place to make the concrete implementations of our commands. Let's start with the `JumpCommand` class.

4. Right-click the `JumpCommand` node and extend the script, saving it as `res://Actors/BumpingPig/Commands/JumpCommand.gd`.

5. Open the script and let's override the `execute()` method by calling the `jump()` method on `receiver`:

```
extends Command

func execute() -> void:
    receiver.jump()
```

6. Then, in the `unexecute()` method, we will call the `cancel_jump()` method on `receiver`. We do that so we can control the Bumping Pig enemy jump height if we want to:

```
func unexecute() -> void:
    receiver.cancel_jump()
```

That's it! This was quite simple, right? But this is very powerful. We now have three layers of indirection: one from the `JumpCommand` class, then the delegation from the `BumpingPig` class to its states, and from the state to the final context, in this case, the `BumpingPig.body` variable.

It may sound too complex but, in fact, this adds layers of encapsulation that will help us create a reliable framework that we can isolate the changes from one point in the system and prevent them from bleeding into other parts of our code base. Think about our code base as a reservoir and from time to time the water floods. These layers of indirection help us contain the flood into sectors, like floodgates, and bring us other benefits on top of helping us contain the damage.

That said, let's move on to the `MoveLeftCommand` and `MoveRightCommand` classes. There's something really interesting about them. Repeat the first step from the `JumpCommand` class instructions but, this time around, we will only have a single script, the `MoveCommand` class, which we will save as `res://Actors/BumpingPig/Commands/MoveCommand.gd`. After that, follow these steps:

1. Export a variable to store a reference to the direction of the movement; let's name it `direction`:

```
extends Command

@export var direction := -1
```

2. Then, in the `execute()` method, we will call the `move()` method on the `receiver` object, passing the `direction` variable as an argument:

```
func execute():
    receiver.move(direction)
```

And we are done! We won't override the `unexecute()` method this time, but it's not a problem. This is because the `Command` class interface provides an empty method, ensuring that when the `CommandButton` class calls the `unexecute()` method on the `MoveCommand` class, it won't throw any errors. If you prefer, you can override it by calling the `stop()` method on the `receiver` variable. However, since we will have a `CommandButton` node dedicated to that, we will only implement the `execute()` method for now.

Notice that, this time, we have a property to store the movement direction. Since the Command pattern is meant to allow us to serialize the request, we can serialize a request using `direction` set to `-1` for the `MoveLeftCommand` node and using the same script on the `MoveRightCommand` node but setting `direction` to `1`.

As a side note, using the `@export` annotation is a way to serialize the exported property within the `PackedScene` file, which is a serialization of how the scene nodes are structured and their properties' values. In *Figure 9.8*, you can see the `MoveLeftCommand` and `MoveRightCommand` nodes' properties in **Inspector**:

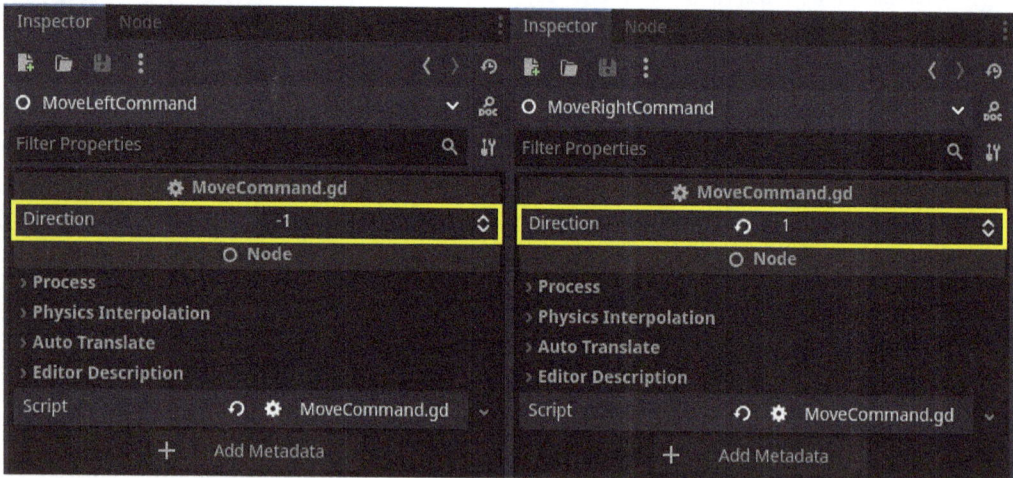

Figure 9.8 – The MoveLeftCommand and MoveRightCommand difference in the Direction property

With that, we will be able to properly map these commands to their respective buttons with the proper changes to reflect what each button should do as if they were calling the `move()` method on the `BumpingPig` class, but note that the `CommandButton` class itself is completely unaware of the existence of the `BumpingPig` class.

Moving on, we will do the same thing with the TurnLeftCommand and TurnRightCommand nodes, but instead of calling the move() method on receiver, the TurnCommand class will call the turn() method. The TurnCommand class should look like the following script:

```
extends Command

@export var direction: int = -1

func execute() -> void:
    receiver.turn(direction)
```

Again, we change the direction property of TurnRightCommand to 1 using the **Inspector** panel. Then, let's make the StopCommand class – it's the simplest of them all. It will essentially call the stop() method on receiver. The StopCommand class should look like the following code:

```
extends Command

func execute() -> void:
    receiver.stop()
```

The AttackCommand class follows the same approach; its code should look like the following code:

```
extends Command

func execute() -> void:
    receiver.attack()
```

Then, we have the PickBombCommand class. In this one, we need to store a reference to the Bomb object because the BumpingPig.pick_bomb() method asks for an object of the Bomb type as an argument. So, we will store it in the PickBombCommand class. This can be useful if we want to create something such as object polling. By keeping the Bomb node stored, we can use it in the throw behavior instead of creating a new Bomb node every time. But since we don't have hundreds of Bomb nodes being thrown, we don't need to poll them.

The PickBombCommand class script should look like the following code:

```
extends Command

var bomb: Bomb

func execute() -> void:
    receiver.pick_bomb(bomb)
```

Note that the bomb variable is empty, so this means the user class will need to inject it.

Now, the `ThrowCommand` class is the most complex one. So, let's follow the extending, naming, and saving processes. Save it as `res://Actors/BumpingPig/Commands/ThrowCommand.gd` and let's follow these instructions:

1. Since the `BumpingPig.throw()` method asks for a `throw_force` argument, we will export a variable to store the impulse force that we will use to throw the bomb. This will allow the game designer to easily change the values using the **Inspector** panel if they want. Let's use `Vector2(600, -600)` as the default impulse force:

    ```
    extends Command

    @export var impulse := Vector2(600, -600)
    ```

2. The actual `throw_force` will be stored separately because this will be the force used by the request itself. In other words, `impulse` is to keep in memory the default force, but the force used in the request is stored separately in case we want a history of all the values used each time the enemy threw a bomb. The `throw_force` variable will be equal to the `impulse` variable by default:

    ```
    extends Command

    @export var impulse := Vector2(600, -600)

    var throw_force := impulse
    ```

3. Then, in the `execute()` method, let's call the `throw()` method on `receiver` passing `throw_force` as an argument:

    ```
    func execute() -> void:
        receiver.throw(throw_force)
    ```

We have everything in place now. Each of these commands does its job as a layer of indirection to access the `BumpingPig` class methods. This brings us a layer of safety to work knowing that if there are any changes in the `BumpingPig` class methods, they will be contained to their respective `Command` class.

Not only that, but the commands also serialize the requests allowing us to directly design the values we want to use on each respective request without touching the code and having extra `if` statements. On top of that, since we now have the requests as objects, we are able to store and queue them. This will be an important feature moving on in our approach.

In the next section, we will finally use the `CommandButton` nodes to create the debug interface, allowing us to map each of these commands to their respective button.

Mapping the commands to buttons

Now that we have all the commands available, we can take advantage of the fact that they are objects (more specifically, nodes) and use them in the `CommandButton.command` property. This will allow us to create a graphical interface for our game designer to test the `Bumping Pig` enemy behaviors.

In this section, we will create this interface mapping each button to a command. By the end of the section, we will have buttons around the Bumping Pig enemy each with an action that the Bumping Pig enemy can perform and, once clicked, will execute the command, allowing the game designer to quickly and visually test the Bumping Pig enemy without having to code tests or create fake scenarios to test specific behaviors.

That said, open the `res://Actors/BumpingPig/BumpingPig.tscn` scene, and let's follow these steps:

1. Create a new `Node2D` as a child of the `BumpingEnemy2D` node and name it `DebugButtons`, as shown in *Figure 9.9*. Again, we will use this node as a container for our `CommandButton` nodes. We use a `Node2D` node because this will allow the `CommandButton` nodes to follow the `BumpingEnemy2D` node transform.

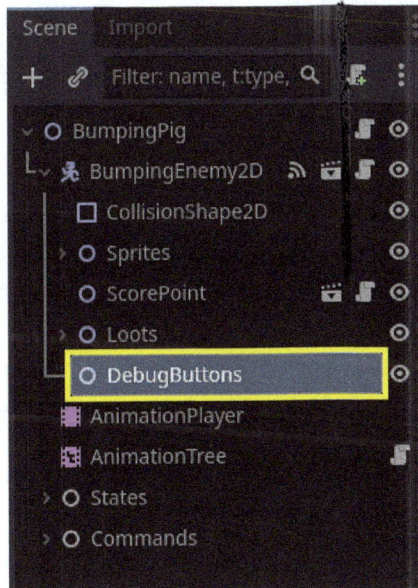

Figure 9.9 – The DebugButtons container node as a child of the BumpingEnemy2D node

2. Then, we will create an instance of the `CommandButton` scene as a child of the `DebugButtons` node and duplicate it for each `Command` node we have inside the `Commands` node except the `PickBombCommand` node, as this will be an automatic command triggered when the Bumping Pig enemy gets close to a `Bomb` object.

3. Name each `CommandButton` node according to the `Command` object it will execute. By the end, the `DebugButtons` node hierarchy should look like the one in *Figure 9.10*:

Figure 9.10 – All the CommandButton nodes as children of the
DebugButtons node, one for each necessary command

4. After that, using the **Inspector** panel, set the **Command Path** property. A pop-up menu will appear, and from there, select the `Command` node you want to link to this `CommandButton` node.

Figure 9.11 showcases the `JumpButton` node assigning the `JumpCommand` node using the mentioned menu. Repeat this step for all the other `CommandButton` nodes assigning their respective `Command` node.

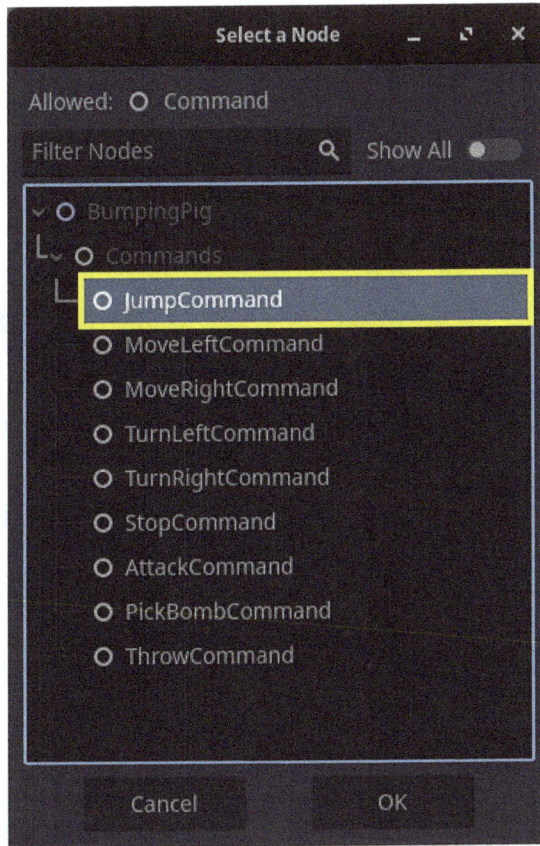

Figure 9.11 – Assigning JumpCommand as the node to get NodePath from the JumpButton node

5. At this point, everything is technically done and each `CommandButton` node will invoke its respective `Command` node. But to make it easy for the game designer to know which button refers to which command, let's use the `CommandButton` node's `Text` property to indicate the `Command` node it's bound to and position the `CommandButton` node around the Bumping Pig enemy so that each button has its position in a place that makes sense and they don't overlap each other.

    Figure 9.12 displays how I organized it in the final project. Note that I turned the visibility of the `ThrowVisionArea` node off; you can see the buttons arranged better:

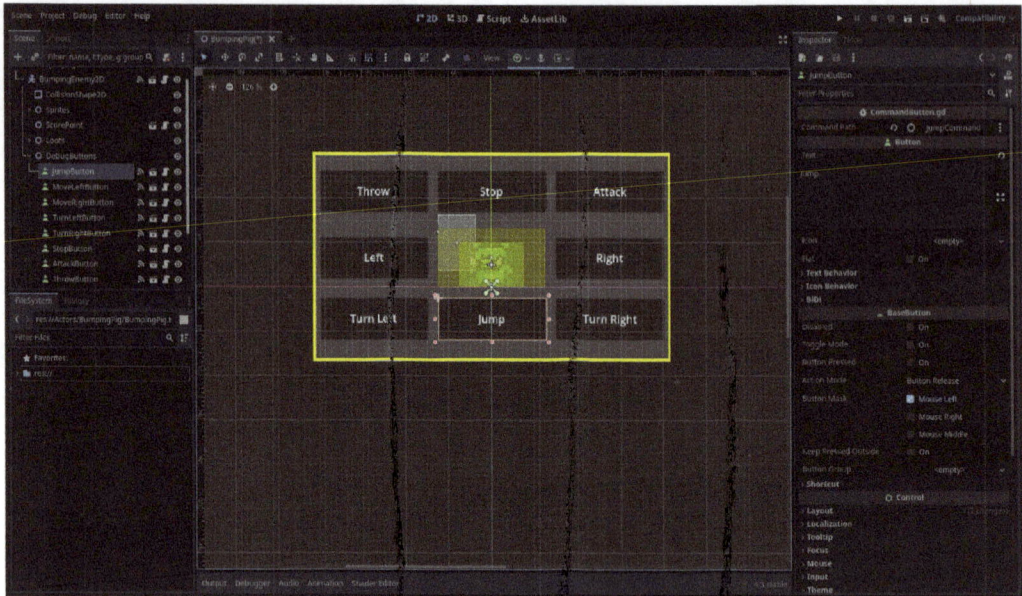

Figure 9.12 – The CommandButton nodes arranged around the Bumping Pig

Now, if you open the `res://Levels/Level1/Level1.tscn` scene and play it, you will be able to see the Bumping Pig enemies mindlessly running until they hit a wall and keep running in its direction. It's your chance to end their misery. Play around with the `Debug` buttons we just created. Make them stop running, jump, grab and throw the bomb, move in the direction of the player, and maybe even attack the player a bunch of times.

In this section, we mapped the `Command` nodes we created in the *Implementing the concrete commands* section to `CommandButton` nodes and arranged them around the Bumping Pig enemy to create a debugging interface that allows us to visually test the behavior of the Bumping Pig enemy within our game without messing around with code.

In the next section, we will create a primitive AI that will automatically trigger these behaviors using the same `Command` objects interface. Again, since we are using the `Command` subclasses, we will take advantage of the fact that they have a simple interface that won't change through the project, effectively safeguarding this AI class from changes in the `BumpingPig` class itself.

We will also see how we can queue multiple `Command` objects to execute more complex behaviors, which is another excellent by-product of the Command pattern: the ability to mix and match multiple commands to create complex behaviors.

Designing the Bumping Pig brain

The main feature that distinguishes an object from an actor is the actor's ability to make intelligent decisions. In this context, *intelligent* just means the ability to solve a problem that will move it toward its goal. For instance, a flamethrower is a hazard that has no purpose in itself. It mindlessly throws flames from time to time, and if the player manages to maneuver it, it will keep throwing flames as it used to.

An actor, on the other hand, may have the purpose of preventing the player from passing from a given section of a level, and one way to accomplish that is by killing the player's character. For that, it can chase the player, attack it, flee when it is with critical health, recover the health, and chase the player again.

Another actor may have the purpose of protecting a treasure chest, and it may throw objects when the player is getting close, and attack the player when the player is in melee range. It may even pick up the treasure chest and run away from the player. The fact is, actors are purposeful and their behavior reflects their purpose, whereas objects are mechanical and don't have any intelligence behind their behavior.

In this section, we will give our `BumpingPig` scene a brain, a class whose sole purpose is to ensure that the `BumpingPig` class is fulfilling its purpose of wandering around bumping into walls and attacking the player when disturbed. For that, we will rely on the robotics sensors and actuators paradigm.

Essentially, we have objects that detect and measure the environment and objects that transform and interact with the environment, respectively, sensors and actuators. These objects have an interesting inter-play where sensors provide data to the system, or a controller, which then sends commands to the actuators to perform specific actions. Actuators take these commands and output them, which, in turn, affect the system's environment.

Very abstract talk, but since you are a smart person, you already catch some core keywords in this description, right? Environment, data, interaction, command, actions, and system. So, for us, we will apply this to our context as the following:

- The environment is our game's levels, with the ground, walls, and other objects that the `BumpingPig` scene can interact with
- The Bumping Pig enemy sensors will be the `VisionArea2D`, `BombVisionArea2D`, and `ThrowVisionArea2D` nodes, and the very `BumpingEnemy2D` node itself, which provides the data we need about the environment
- Our actuators will be the `BumpingEnemy2D` and `BombFactory` nodes, which are the nodes that can effectively interact with the environment
- All the actions we need are available through our `Command` nodes, which are the means through which our actor will interact with the environment
- The system, or controller, will be the `Brain` class itself

Sounds complicated, but once we get our hands dirty, it will all make sense. You will start to think in terms of sensors, controllers, and actuators all the time when you design your AIs. Well, without further ado, let's open the `res://Actors/BumpingPig/BumpingPig.tscn` scene and implement the following instructions:

1. Create a new node as a child of the `BumpingPig` node and name it `Brain`. Make sure the `Brain` node is at the very bottom of the hierarchy so it will be the last node to process before the `BumpingPig` node itself, as shown in *Figure 9.13*. This is because the `Brain` class will need the `Commands` and `BumpingEnemy2D` nodes to be ready and inside the `SceneTree` object to work.

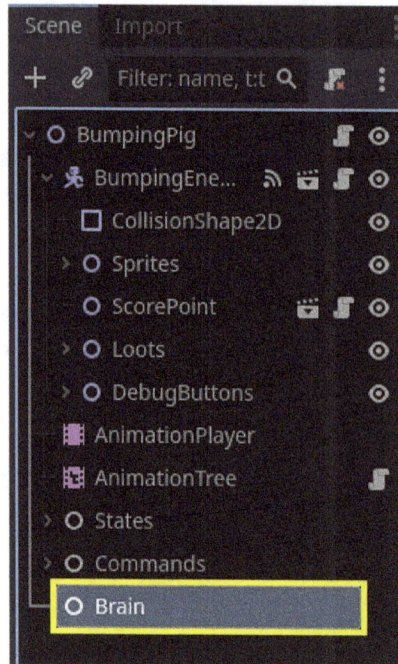

Figure 9.13 – The Brain node position in the BumpingPig node hierarchy

2. Attach a new script to the `Brain` node and save it as `res://Actors/BumpingPig/Brain.gd`.

3. Open the script and let's start by exporting a variable to store the path to the `BumpingEnemy2D` node. We will call it `actor_path` and we will use the `@export_node_path` annotation filtering only nodes of the `BumpingEnemy2D` type:

```
extends Node

@export_node_path("BumpingEnemy2D") var actor_path
```

4. Then, right below it, let's get the node from this path using an `@onready` variable and the `get_node()` method:

```
extends Node

@export_node_path("BumpingEnemy2D") var actor_path
@onready var actor = get_node(actor_path)
```

5. Then, it's time to store references to our commands. For that, we will first export a variable to the `Commands` node as it is the container node for all commands. This will make it easier for us to access the commands moving on. Let's call this variable `commands_path`:

```
extends Node

@export_node_path("BumpingEnemy2D") var actor_path
@onready var actor = get_node(actor_path)

@export_node_path("Node") var commands_path
```

6. Just like before, we will also create an `@onready` variable to store the actual node using `commands_path`:

```
extends Node

@export_node_path("BumpingEnemy2D") var actor_path
@onready var actor = get_node(actor_path)

@export_node_path("Node") var commands_path
@onready var commands := get_node(commands_path)
```

7. With that, we have an easy path to access all the `Command` nodes. Let's create one variable for each `Command` node available; don't forget to use the `@onready` annotation to ensure `Brain` will only try to set these variables once it triggers its `_ready()` callback. Also, use the commands as a base reference to access the `Commands` node using the `get_node()` method. It should look like the following snippet after you finish:

```
extends Node

@export_node_path("BumpingEnemy2D") var actor_path
@onready var actor = get_node(actor_path)

@export_node_path("Node") var commands_path
@onready var commands := get_node(commands_path)

@onready var attack_command: Command = commands
```

```
  .get_node("AttackCommand")
@onready var jump_command: Command = commands
  .get_node("JumpCommand")
@onready var pick_bomb_command: Command = commands
  .get_node("PickBombCommand")
@onready var throw_command: Command = commands
  .get_node("ThrowCommand")
@onready var turn_left_command: Command = commands
  .get_node("TurnLeftCommand")
@onready var turn_right_command: Command = commands
  .get_node("TurnRightCommand")
@onready var move_left_command: Command = commands
  .get_node("MoveLeftCommand")
@onready var move_right_command: Command = commands
  .get_node("MoveRightCommand")
```

8. And here comes the cool and novel part. Once BumpingEnemy2D bumps into a wall, we want to perform two commands: turn and move. For that, we will create two arrays, each of them for each direction, and they will contain their respective commands as elements.

    Note that we could create a node and use it as a container for these behaviors that rely on multiple commands, then we could loop through its children using the get_children() method and execute each child. But using arrays will do the trick for now:

    ```
    @onready var bump_left_queue := [turn_right_command,
      move_right_command]
    @onready var bump_right_queue := [turn_left_command,
      move_left_command]
    ```

9. Now that we have all the commands, and therefore the actions, and the actuators of our AI, it's time to use the sensors to create the right controls for each command. Let's start by connecting the BumpingEnemy2D node's bumped signal using the Editor interface to a signal callback in the Brain class; we can name the callback _on_bumping_enemy_2d_bumped().

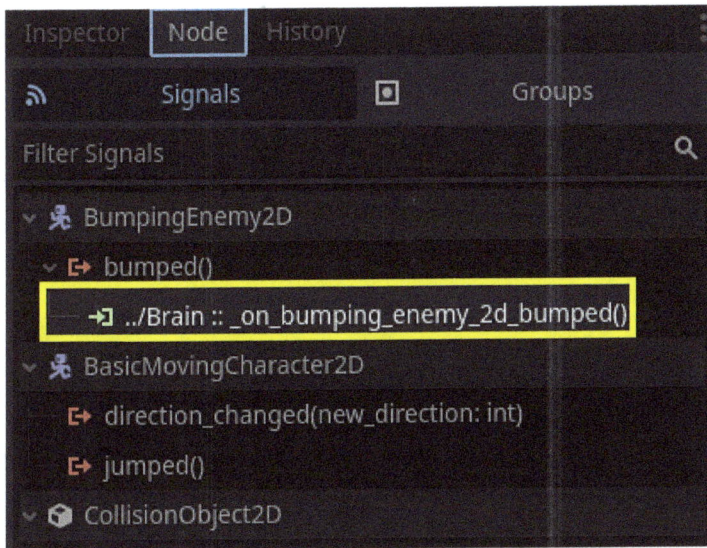

Figure 9.14 – The BumpingEnemy2D bumped signal connected to the
Brain _on_bumping_enemy_2d_bumped() callback

10. Then, back to the script, inside the _on_bumping_enemy_2d_bumped() callback, we will check actor.direction to see whether it bumped while moving to the left or the right.

   If actor.direction is greater than 0, it bumped while moving to the right, so we can loop through the commands in bumped_right_queue and execute them. Otherwise, we execute the commands in bumped_left_queue:

```
func _on_bumping_enemy_2d_bumped() -> void:
    if actor.direction > 0:
        for command in bump_right_queue:
            command.execute()
    else:
        for command in bump_left_queue:
            command.execute()
```

11. The next sensor we will work with is VisionArea2D. Let's use the Editor interface to connect its area_entered signal to a callback in the Brain class, which we will name _on_vision_area_2d_area_entered(). Inside this method, we will execute attack_commmand so that when the player enters the Bumping Pig enemy's melee attack area, the Bumping Pig enemy will try to land an attack:

```
func _on_vision_area_2d_area_entered(area:
  Area2D) -> void:
    attack_command.execute()
```

12. Then, let's connect the `BombVisionArea2D` node's `area_entered` signal to a callback named `_on_bomb_vision_area_2d_area_entered()`.

13. Inside the `func _on_bomb_vision_area_2d_area_entered()` callback, we will assign `area.owner` as the value of the `pick_bomb_command.bomb` property. We do that because the owner of the area detected by `BombVisionArea2D` will be the Bomb node itself, which is the node we need to pass as an argument in the `BumpingPig.pick_bomb()` method that the `PickBombCommand` class invokes:

```
func _on_bomb_vision_area_2d_area_entered(area:
  Area2D) -> void:
    pick_bomb_command.bomb = area.owner
```

14. After that, we can execute `pick_bomb_command` and do something interesting. We will connect the `ThrowVisionArea2D` node's `area_entered` signal here instead of using the Editor. We do that because we will need to dynamically connect and disconnect this signal to prevent it from triggering the throwing behavior if there's no Bomb object to throw:

```
func _on_bomb_vision_area_2d_area_entered(area:
  Area2D) -> void:
    pick_bomb_command.bomb = area.owner
    pick_bomb_command.execute()
    actor.find_child("ThrowVisionArea2D")
    .area_entered.connect(
    _on_throw_vision_area_2d_area_entered)
```

15. Finally, let's implement the `_on_throw_vision_area_2d_area_entered()` callback. We start by disconnecting the `ThrowVisionArea2D` node's `area_entered` signal from it:

```
func _on_throw_vision_area_2d_area_entered(area:
  Area2D) -> void:
    actor.find_child("ThrowVisionArea2D")
    .area_entered.disconnect(
    _on_throw_vision_area_2d_area_entered)
```

16. Then, we calculate the direction in which the Bumping Pig enemy will throw the bomb. For that, we use the `actor.global_position`.

17. `direction_to()` method, passing `area.global_position` and only using the x axis of this vector to store the throw direction:

```
var throw_direction: int = actor.global_position
  .direction_to(area.global_position)).x
```

18. Then, we will change the throwing force we will use to match the throw direction on the x axis:

```
var throw_direction: int = actor.global_position
    .direction_to(area.global_position).x

var throw_force := Vector2(600 * throw_direction,
    -600)
```

19. Assign the `throw_force` variable we just created as `throw_commmand.throw_force` and execute `throw_command`:

```
throw_command.throw_force = throw_force
throw_command.execute()
```

Well, this should give our game designer an idea of how to use the capabilities of the Command class we created to design the Bumping Pig actor. If you want to test it out, open the res://Levels/Level1/Level1.tscn scene and play it. Use the DebugButtons we created in the *Mapping the commands to buttons* section to make the Bumping Pig enemy jump and pick a bomb. Then, move the player close to the Bumping Pig enemy to see whether it will throw the bomb at the player. Play around with other commands as well to see whether everything is working; for instance, make the Bumping Pig enemy bump into a wall to see whether it will turn and move in the opposite direction, and so on and so forth.

In this section, using the Command class, we've created a means to create an AI for our Bumping Pig actor. We used the paradigm of sensors, controllers, and actuators to abstract the approach in which we would design its behaviors and add layers of intelligence and decision-making. We also saw how we can queue Command objects to mix and match them and create more complex behaviors.

At this point, you already understood how the Command pattern can be a powerful ally to create dynamic systems that can be easily re-arranged without being worried about changes in the target object, or rather, the receiver object interface. Using the same principles and the CommandButton node, I mapped the move left, move right, jump, and attack methods on the KingPigPlayer2D scene, effectively adding on-screen controls to the character. Please, do check it in the res://Actors/KingPig/KingPigPlayer2D.tscn scene.

With this, we wrap up this chapter! So, let's take a look at what we've learned in the next section.

Summary

In this chapter, we learned about the implementation of actors in our game using the Command pattern, which is a powerful design pattern that decouples the sender of a request from its receiver. This decoupling allows for more flexible and maintainable code, especially as the complexity of interactions in the game increases.

We began by discussing the fundamentals of the Command pattern, including how commands are created and executed, and the advantages of using this pattern, such as the ability to queue, log, and undo actions. The chapter provided practical examples to help you grasp these concepts and illustrated how to apply them within the context of a game developed using the Godot Engine.

The Command pattern was then applied to control the actions of different actors in the game, such as player characters and enemies. We explored how this pattern can be used to manage actions such as moving, attacking, and interacting with objects, which are crucial to gameplay. By implementing commands as objects, we can dynamically assign and execute actions, leading to a more versatile and scalable game architecture. This approach also allows for greater flexibility in designing the game's user interface and controls, as commands can be easily mapped to different inputs.

On top of that, the chapter discussed the role of commands in creating a more interactive and dynamic game environment. We examined how commands can be used to trigger events, interact with game objects, and influence the behavior of other actors. This allows for a richer gameplay experience where the actions of the player and **Non-Playable Characters** (NPCs) are more intertwined and responsive to the game world. The Command pattern was shown to be a key tool in creating these interactions, enabling us to design more engaging and complex scenarios.

This chapter laid the groundwork for implementing more sophisticated game mechanics and AI behaviors in subsequent chapters. In the next chapter, we will extend the AI system we began developing in the *Designing the Bumping Pig brain* section by implementing AI with the Strategy pattern, enhancing the intelligence and adaptability of our game's actors. See you there!

Part 3:
Advanced Design Patterns

At this point, we are already familiar with what design patterns are and how we use them to solve issues that we find in our project. Previously, we relied a lot more on Godot Engine's built-in features, but now we are going to implement design patterns directly into our code, learning how to create class instances without depending on nodes, wrapping objects, and working with class mediation and data structures to achieve the project goals.

This part includes the following chapters:

- *Chapter 10, Implementing AI with the Strategy Pattern*
- *Chapter 11, Creating a Power-Up System with the Decorator Pattern*
- *Chapter 12, Cross-Fading Transitions with the Service Locator Pattern*
- *Chapter 13, Improving Game Feel with the Event Queue Pattern*

10

Implementing AI with the Strategy Pattern

The Strategy pattern is the simplest yet most useful pattern we can learn. I consider the Strategy pattern to be the mother of all patterns and the concretion of the **composition over inheritance** principle.

By applying the Strategy pattern, we can decouple the algorithms from the user class, allowing other classes to mutate the algorithm they want to be executed in at runtime. In this chapter, we'll note some similarities between the Strategy pattern and other patterns we've seen so far, especially the other behavioral design patterns.

With the Strategy pattern implemented, our code base will have a safe framework to extend. Similar to the Command and State patterns, it turns elements of our class into interchangeable objects that we can inject and mutate at runtime. With that, we can dynamically compose object behaviors depending on the events that happen in our game.

Using the Strategy pattern adds yet another layer of flexibility and protection to our code base. Since we encapsulate the object's algorithms into individual classes, these classes ensure that changes in the algorithm don't affect the code base, thus promoting resilience and maintenance while allowing us to extend our code base.

In this chapter, we'll take advantage of the Strategy pattern to create an AI for the Bumping Pig enemy so that it can pick up and throw multiple objects, depending on the current strategy it's using. This will pave the way for us to implement new pickable objects in the game.

In this chapter, we'll cover the following topics:

- Understanding the Strategy pattern
- Spotting use cases for the Strategy pattern
- Implementing the Strategy pattern in Godot

Get yourself ready, and let's get started!

Technical requirements

To work through this chapter, open the project files available in the `10.implementing-ai-with-strategies/01.start/` directory. If you face any confusion, errors, or bugs while following the steps in the *Implementing the Strategy pattern in Godot* section, please refer to the files in the `10.implementing-ai-with-strategies/02.finished/` directory. Any issues can be reported via the repository's issue tracker: `https://github.com/PacktPublishing/Game-Development-Patterns-with-Godot-4/issues`.

If you haven't downloaded this repository's files yet, you can obtain them here: `https://github.com/PacktPublishing/Game-Development-Patterns-with-Godot-4`.

Now, let's dive into understanding the core concepts of the Strategy pattern. Comprehending its purpose, characteristics, the problem it addresses, and typical implementation methods will enable us to find suitable use cases and integrate them efficiently into Godot while leveraging its built-in features and avoiding technical pitfalls.

Understanding the Strategy pattern

To understand the Strategy pattern, we need to understand the main advantage of using the **Object-oriented programming** (**OOP**) paradigm. In *Chapter 1*, we learned that this paradigm presents a data structure called **objects** that bundles data and behavior together to allow its algorithm to have direct access to the data and mutate it according to its responsibilities. We also learned that one of OOP's main features is inheritance, but instead of abusing it, we should use it purposefully and always favor composition over inheritance. By doing that, we decouple the object's functionalities from its class, whereas by using inheritance, we always bind – or rather, couple – a subclass with its superclass, instead of turning them into individual classes that can be composed by having them become users of different other classes.

In *Chapter 8*, we learned how to turn the object's states into interchangeable classes that we can dynamically change at runtime, instantaneously mutating an object's state to predefined states that encapsulate the object's behavior depending on its current state. In *Chapter 9*, we learned how to turn requests to an object's method into objects themselves, allowing us to serialize them, pass them around, reference them, mutate the reference, and even combine multiple requests to create more complex behaviors. In *Chapter 7*, we learned how to turn the instantiation of an object into an object itself, allowing us to dynamically create an object in our game without having to add new lines of code to our code base. Instead, we simply pass the reference object serialized as a `PackedScene` interface. With that, I want you to notice that, fundamentally, design patterns turn elements of our code into objects, allowing us to quickly instantiate, mutate, serialize, reference, store, and combine them. The Strategy pattern is the root of this approach.

Essentially, the Strategy pattern is a behavioral design pattern that takes an object's algorithm and turns it into a family of interchangeable classes that execute different versions of the same main algorithm. It may sound complex, but it's the simplest and my favorite pattern.

To understand the Strategy pattern better, imagine that you're at a festival, and you have a date set with another person. You plan to arrive early at the festival to secure a spot before all the seating areas fill up. Since there are several reference points, you decide to create a code with the bartender because you won't know where you'll settle until your date arrives. You instruct the bartender to tell your date you're near the angel statue if they ask for a Negroni. If they ask for a Margarita, the bartender will direct them to the food trucks. For an Old-Fashioned, they'll be told you're near the stage. Wanting to keep things a bit mysterious, you wander around, looking for the perfect spot away from the crowd. As the festival becomes busier, you decide that the area near the angel statue is best and tell your date to grab a Negroni when they arrive. 10 minutes later, they find you at the table and bring you a Negroni.

In this analogy, each location paired with a specific drink represents a different strategy that the bartender will use based on your date's request. This helps us understand how each element of the Strategy pattern functions.

The Strategy pattern is composed of a context object, an execution method, and a user class. Does it remind you of other patterns we've already seen?

Using our analogy, the context object is the bartender, the execution method is the drink request, and the user class is the person dating you. Based on the request, the bartender changes their strategy, adapting their behavior.

That's exactly how the Strategy pattern works – we take the possible branching statements from an object's algorithm and turn them into interchangeable classes that a user class can inject, depending on events in our application. In our analogy, the event is the change in the place where you'll be waiting for the person you're dating.

One good indicator that the Strategy pattern may be a good fit to implement in our code base is places where we have `switch` statements. Similarly, `match` statements and `if` statements followed by `elif` statements are also good candidates. Note that binary branching – in other words, `if` statements followed by a single `else` statement or `elif` statements – aren't good candidates. The idea of the Strategy pattern is to support further logic branches, allowing us to extend our class by simply creating new strategy classes instead of breaking the open-closed principle by directly changing the implementation details of a class.

Note that a positive side effect of the Strategy pattern is that it ensures that we'll subscribe to the open-closed principle since instead of directly changing the class' code to implement new conditional statements with their respective logic branching, we create a completely decoupled class that will ensure that the context object's interface is left intact when we extend its functionalities.

With all that said, we can start to think about situations where the Strategy pattern would fit perfectly in a game's code base. In the next section, we'll see some common use cases for this pattern and also elaborate on other possible use cases that can benefit from this pattern.

Spotting use cases for the Strategy pattern

The Strategy pattern is by far one of the most versatile patterns. Since it essentially conveys a framework to implement the principle of favoring composition over inheritance, we can extrapolate it to create whole systems and even code bases for our game project or even to create a custom engine. One close example that we have in this direction is Godot Engine's `Area2D` and `CollisionShape2D` relationship. The `Area2D` region is composed of multiple `CollisionShape2D` classes but each `CollisionShape2D` can be composed of different `Shape2D` interfaces: `CircleShape2D`, `RectangleShape2D`, `CapsuleShape2D`, and so on.

In that example, the `Shape` property of `CollisionShape2D` supports multiple strategies; every single strategy inherits the `Shape2D` interface and implements its methods, such as `collide()`, `draw()`, and `get_rect()`, in different ways. So, `CircleShape2D` may implement it by calculating the circle's radius, whereas `RectangleShape2D` may calculate it using the rectangle's size instead. This could be a field in the `CollisionShape2D` class with multiple options and a `switch` statement to calculate the collision or drawing, depending on the option selected. However, by implementing the Strategy pattern, we delegate each of these scenarios to the strategy in the `shape` field, leaving the `CollisionShape2D` class cleaner and adaptable.

Note that `CollisionShape2D` doesn't decide which strategy it's going to use; it's provided from outside. This is important to understand because the Strategy pattern would lose its purpose if we still had to check for specific parameters within the class to decide on the strategy. This would mean modifying the class's code every time a new strategy is introduced. However, that's not the case. The Strategy pattern allows us to extend the context class without altering its original code while adhering to the open-closed principle. This is one of the main advantages of the Strategy pattern.

Now, let's consider use cases directly related to games. Picture the following scenario: you're making a **role-playing game** (**RPG**) and you have various skills and spells a character can use and cast. Depending on the environment, these skills can cause different damage and effects. For instance, if you cast a wind spell in a humid level with fog, the fog object could inject a new strategy into the object that instantiates the wind spell, telling it to cast a lightning spell instead. The same goes when you're within a volcano dungeon and cast a water or ice spell that turns into some steam. Remaining within the realm of RPGs, imagine PVP combat where we have some cool visual effects of blood spilling when a sword slashes through a character's flesh. But if the character's wearing iron armor, this visual effect wouldn't reflect the damage accurately. So, what if the armor object injects the damage visual effect strategy upon hit instead? The iron or steel armor could emit some sparks when hit by a sword. The possibilities are endless!

Moving away from RPG games, let's see how the Strategy pattern can be useful for **first-person shooter** (**FPS**) games. Let's say your game has a weapon system where weapons have multiple firing modes, such as single shot and rapid-fire. The weapon logic itself is simple – it shoots when you press the left mouse button. But everything changes depending on which firing mode the player selects, such as the animation played, the amount of bullets shot, and the amount of ammo that gets used. We can create two firing strategies, `SingletShotStrategy` and `BurstShotStrategy`, and within these classes, we can state exactly what happens in each mode. Then, using the `Controller` class, we can pass the new strategy to the weapon based on the mode selected by the player. The weapon algorithm stays intact. This allows us to extend this behavior if we want to, such as by adding more shooting modes as our design expands.

Now, let's consider some good use cases for our project. The Strategy pattern is amazing for implementing AI. Let's say we're making a real-time strategy game where neutral units wander around the map or a specific spawn point. But we don't want to be concerned with how they wander or their movement pattern just yet, so we don't waste time implementing each movement pattern for enemies that we don't even know about yet. We can create a class called `MovementStrategy` and work with its interface and maybe create a `LinearMovementStrategy` class to test some things. Once we have the main logic all set, we can start to design new units that use different movement strategies, such as `ZigZagMovementStrategy` or `CircularMovementStrategy`. All we have to do is change which strategy it uses in its movement logic, leaving the AI code intact.

Now, imagine that we're making a rogue-like game where the player fights small amounts of really smart enemies and the player has to defeat all of them to move on to the next room of a dungeon. The enemies may have different strategies to interact with the player, depending on their core goal. Initially, the goal is to prevent the player from progressing by defeating them. However, if they sense that the player is stronger than them (since the player's goal is to defeat them so that they can move to the next room), they can still perform their antagonist role by fleeing from the player, preventing the player from killing them. Effectively, this prevents the player from progressing. In that sense, we can create a family of `EngageStrategy` algorithms. When the enemy detects the player within its engage area and they're strong enough to fight against the player, they use a `FightStrategy` algorithm. However, as soon as their health drops below 30%, the strategy changes to a `FleeStrategy` algorithm so that whenever the player gets close to them, they run away from the player until their health heals above 30%, changing their strategy back to the `FightStrategy` algorithm.

At this point, you may have noticed that the Strategy pattern is similar to the Command pattern. It all boils down to intent. The Strategy pattern intends to encapsulate behaviors based on logic branching within a class, whereas the Command pattern intends to encapsulate a method call request. Besides their structure being similar, their benefits are unique. We use the Strategy pattern when we have multiple ways to perform the same task and we want to switch them at runtime based on user classes, whereas we use the Command pattern when we want to decouple the sender and the receiver of a given method request. In the next section, we'll learn how to apply the Strategy pattern in practice by implementing an interaction system in our Bumping Pig enemy so that we can rely on a single detection area and allow objects it detects to dictate how the Bumping Pig will interact with them.

Implementing the Strategy pattern in Godot

Once our project progresses and reaches a stage where the game designer can fully express their ideas, the code base has matured into a healthy state. We're now at a point where implementation details are merely that – details. The game designer made many improvements alone and they managed the code very well. This is one of the most important byproducts of making good code bases. When the code base is well structured, the team can follow up with its architecture by themselves, promoting less work on our end.

At this point, the game designer is thinking about making the Bumping Pig enemy smarter and the game world more alive by allowing the Bumping Pig to interact more with the environment. Well, let's take a look at their current request so that we understand what they want and how we can help them solve this.

"Hello! It's your friendly neighborhood game designer.

Our project is finally taking shape as a game and I'm very proud of our teamwork. The work you've done adding that Command pattern is amazing! I made some improvements to the debug interface so that I can click on the enemy I want to debug and the interface will appear. It's pretty nice; take a look when you have some time.

I also managed to create more commands and states! I'm really liking the process. I don't have to be concerned about how things will take shape. I can just follow the framework you created: make new animations, set their transitions, create new states, and use the commands to keep them more generic instead of coupling the Brain class to the BumpingPig methods.

In the meantime, I decided that the AI I was creating was too primitive. The Bumping Pig just... bumps around and hits the player when they interact. I saw that our artist provided some objects that we can expand upon. Since I implemented the bomb-picking and throwing behavior, I thought that it would be a good idea to also use the art of the pig carrying a crate and lighting a match to fire a cannon. I'm really looking forward to implementing this cannon thing.

The problem is that the Brain class became a mess! I had to keep on creating new exclusive VisibleArea2Ds for each type of interaction I wanted, including attacking the player. If we keep on doing that, every time I want to add a new type of interaction, I'll have to create a new method to support a new VisibleArea2D and use a new exclusive Collision Layer. I don't think this will scale nicely. Not to mention the filtering I have to do using conditional statements for each type of interaction.

I think that if I keep doing that, I'll break the Brain code at some point. Please help!"

There's some really good information we can take out from this request. The first thing to note is that the game designer is trying to support multiple types of interactions for the Bumping Pig, each of which triggers a slightly different behavior: attacking the player, picking up a bomb, picking up a crate, and lighting and firing a cannon. Fundamentally, these are all interactions. They just have different implementations.

The second important point to notice is that the game designer is struggling to keep up with all the mess caused by trying to filter which interaction the Bumping Pig should perform. This may be because it's hard to keep up with how each conditional will interact with each other and with the whole context of what's happening in the `Brain` class.

The third problem is that our game designer, very wisely, is afraid that by modifying the `Brain` class every time they want to add a new object that the `BumpingPig` class can interact with, the `Brain` class will break at some point. This is exactly why we try to keep up with the open-closed principle as much as we can. If the class is working, we shouldn't modify it.

Taking all these signals into account, it's safe to say that we can use the Strategy pattern to help our game designer have a safe tool to work with and expand their design, adding yet another piece to our platformer development framework. The Strategy pattern will help them add all the behaviors listed without having to modify the `Brain` class code. We'll create a family of `InteractionStrategy` classes that are interchangeable so that the `Brain` class can simply tell the current instance to execute its algorithm, leaving the `Brain` class unaware of the implementation details. This will also reduce the scope of the class, moving it closer to the single-responsibility principle – that is, the `Brain` class should only be concerned about executing a behavior based on an interaction, not about what the behavior is or how this behavior is implemented.

Since we're going to use the Strategy pattern, the `Brain` class in itself doesn't need to select an algorithm to execute. Instead, whatever object `VisionArea2D` interacts with will provide what it's interacting with and the proper `InteractionStrategy` class to interact with it, unbloating the `Brain` class from conditional or `switch` statements. This is excellent and some programmers would defend that this is ideal.

There's a branch in programming that advocates that the fewer conditional statements we use, the better. They say that service classes should inject algorithms into the user class, which, in turn, would use polymorphism to implement multiple possible algorithms that would be provided by the service class. Doing that would get rid of unnecessary – if not all – conditional statements. Their motto is to use polymorphism over logic branching. I would be as extremist as they are, but less logic branching is always better because doing so facilitates thinking about the application structure and communicating it to other team members. Think about it – isn't it simpler to say *"The proper interaction behavior is provided by the crate"* than to say *"In the brain, there's a method that checks if the enemy is interacting with a crate. If it is, we call the interacting with crate method"*?

Another reason to use the Strategy pattern is that it will unbloat the `Brain` class from conditional statements, allowing us to clearly understand what it's doing at a high level, without being concerned with implementation details and how each one of them can or can't lead to a specific behavior. By using the Strategy pattern, all we need to do is know that the context class will execute a strategy. If we want to understand the implementation details, we can check the available strategies.

Since the Strategy pattern essentially forces us to subscribe to the composition over inheritance principle, our code base becomes more flexible and open to extension. The game designer will be able to extend the `Brain` class without being afraid of messing up the code that already works. All in all, the Strategy pattern is excellent. I decided to add it alongside advanced patterns – not because it's complex, but because it's a pattern that advanced programmers mastered to the point it's natural for them to use it. You're about to add it to your toolbelt as well. In the next section, we'll create our very own family of algorithms that follow the Strategy pattern so that we have the necessary framework to adapt our project's code to support this new architecture and explore the new possibilities that it allows.

Creating the InteractionStrategy family

The Strategy pattern is maybe the simplest pattern to exist. Some programmers may even say that OOP was supposed to be made by implementing the Strategy pattern. This statement alone illustrates the importance of mastering this pattern. In this section, we'll understand why its simplicity is so beautiful to the point it's considered must-have knowledge for any serious programmer. We'll start by opening the `10.implementing-ai-with-strategies/01.start/` project and creating the first Strategy family of algorithms in our project. Follow these steps:

1. Create a new GDScript and save it as `res://Actors/BumpingPig/ InteractionStrategies/InteractionStrategy.gd`.

2. Open the script. The first thing we'll do is remove the `Node` inheritance line. By doing so, it will be a plain script that won't be coupled to any superclass other than GDScript itself. This is important because, being a strategy, it works as a code snippet that complements the context class. Then, use the `class_name` keyword followed by `InteractionStrategy` to make sure that other classes know that this class exists and to make it clear that this is an `InteractionStrategy` class:

    ```
    class_name InteractionStrategy
    ```

3. Then, we'll create a variable to store the context object. Remember, the Strategy pattern is made up of three major elements. The first item is a context object – that is, the object that will execute the strategy instead of implementing the algorithm replaced by the strategy. The second item is an execution method that the context will call. The third item is a service class that will tell the context object which strategy it should use. In that sense, let's call this variable `context` and make it of the `BumpingPigBrain` type:

    ```
    class_name InteractionStrategy
    var context: BumpingPigBrain
    ```

4. Next, we'll create a variable to store the `VisibleArea2D` node, which will provide this strategy to the `Brain` class. Note that this step isn't necessary to implement the Strategy pattern, but it will be useful for us to have a reference to the `VisibleArea2D` node that the Bumping Pig interacted with, especially to access its parent:

```
class_name InteractionStrategy

var context: BumpingPigBrain
var interacted_area: Area2D
```

5. Finally, we'll create a method called `execute()` to serve as an interface to execute this strategy. With that, we have our `InteractionStrategy` interface:

```
class_name InteractionStrategy

var context: BumpingPigBrain
var interacted_area: Area2D

func execute() -> void:
    pass
```

Congratulations – you've just acquired one of the most essential pieces of knowledge you need. Remember, with great power comes great responsibility. Use the Strategy pattern wisely, but abundantly. This is one of the patterns that I would advocate that you can use without much moderation as it will help you more than not. To be honest, specifically regarding the Strategy pattern, you should think about reasons to not use it instead of to use it.

With our `InteractionStrategy` class in place, the next step is to understand how we're going to make it known to the `VisibleArea2D` node so that it can provide the proper strategy to the `Brain` class moving forward. The next section will explain that. We'll also understand the caveats of using the Strategy pattern in Godot Engine.

Using the target object to provide a strategy

The main advantage of the Strategy pattern is that the algorithm that the context class will use isn't provided by the context class itself but by a service class.

To understand how this works, imagine that you've been selected to cook some meals in a local Japanese restaurant, but you don't know anything about that particular cuisine, as Italian food is your specialty. The person who hired you said that you don't need to be concerned about what and how to cook as this is part of the experience, just be at the restaurant by 7 P.M. So, at 7 P.M., you go to the restaurant, enter the kitchen, and wait to be taught how to cook the restaurant's main dish. But instead, the restaurant opens and customers start to arrive. You look around and you see all the ingredients in place, pans of all kinds, and utensils. You have everything available to cook – you just don't know what and how to cook.

As the customers arrive, you start to get some orders, but instead of getting the order with the name of the dish the customer wants you to cook, every order itself is a recipe, with all the ingredients and the preparation instructions provided. All you have to do is follow the recipe to deliver the meal the customer wants to eat.

This is an excellent analogy for why the context object doesn't need to know how to implement each strategy. Since the service classes will provide them to the context object, all the context object needs to do is execute them. That said, in this section, we'll understand how we can provide such a recipe – or rather, strategy – to the `Brain` class. For that, let's open the `res://Recipes/VisionArea2D/VisibleArea2D.tscn` scene. With the scene open, follow these steps:

1. Attach a new script to the `VisibleArea2D` node and save it as `res://Recipes/VisionArea2D/VisibleArea2D.gd`.

2. Open the script and start by exporting a variable that will store the path to the GDScript file alongside the `InteractionStrategy` class that the `Brain` class will use to interact with whatever object will use this `VisibleArea2D` node. Here, we'll use an export annotation specific to get file paths – the `@export_file` annotation. It allows us to add a filter using a String value in parenthesis to only allow files that match the filter. In our case, we'll filter files with `"*InteractionStrategy.gd"` in their name. Note that `*` means it will accept anything, so long as it ends up with whatever comes after `*`. Let's call this variable `interaction_strategy_file`:

    ```
    extends Area2D

    @export_file("*InteractionStrategy.gd") var
      interaction_strategy_file
    ```

3. After that, we'll create a variable that will hold a new instance of the `InteracctionStrategy` class we pointed out in the `interaction_strategy_file` variable. But before we instantiate, we need to load the instance. Since the `VisionArea2D` class doesn't know the exact path to the file until the game starts, we'll use the `load()` keyword to load the file at runtime and the `@onready` annotation to ensure that it will only create the instance when it's ready inside the **SceneTree** area. This will prevent loading and instancing errors:

    ```
    extends Area2D

    @export_file("*InteractionStrategy.gd")
      var interaction_strategy_file

    @onready var interaction_strategy:
      InteractionStrategy = load
        (interaction_strategy_file)
    ```

4. Then, to create the actual instance, we just need to append the `.new()` method at the end of the following line:

```
@onready var interaction_strategy:
    InteractionStrategy = load
    (interaction_strategy_file).new()
```

5. To ensure we don't have any null instance errors when we load the game, let's set a default `InteractionStrategy` class using the **Inspector** area. Left-click on the file icon that appears on the **Interaction Strategy** file property slot under **VisibleArea2D.gd**:

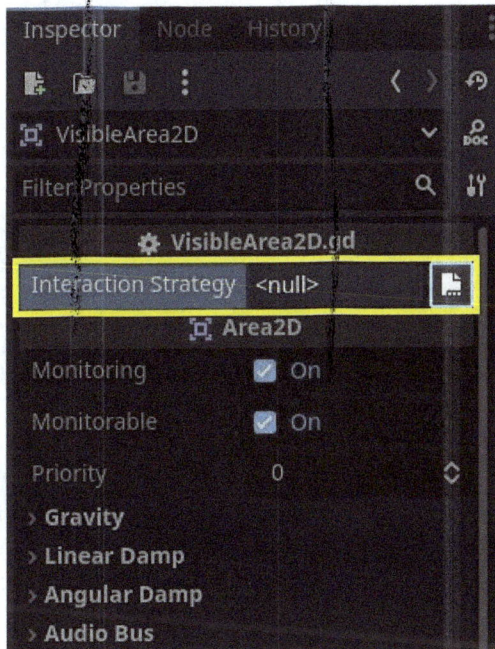

Figure 10.1 – The VisibleArea2D.gd Interaction Strategy File property slot in the Inspector area

6. From the pop-up menu, look for the `res://Actors/BumpingPig/InteractionStrategies/InteractionStrategy.gd` file. You'll notice that as you search for it in the project's folders, no other files appear. This is our filter working!

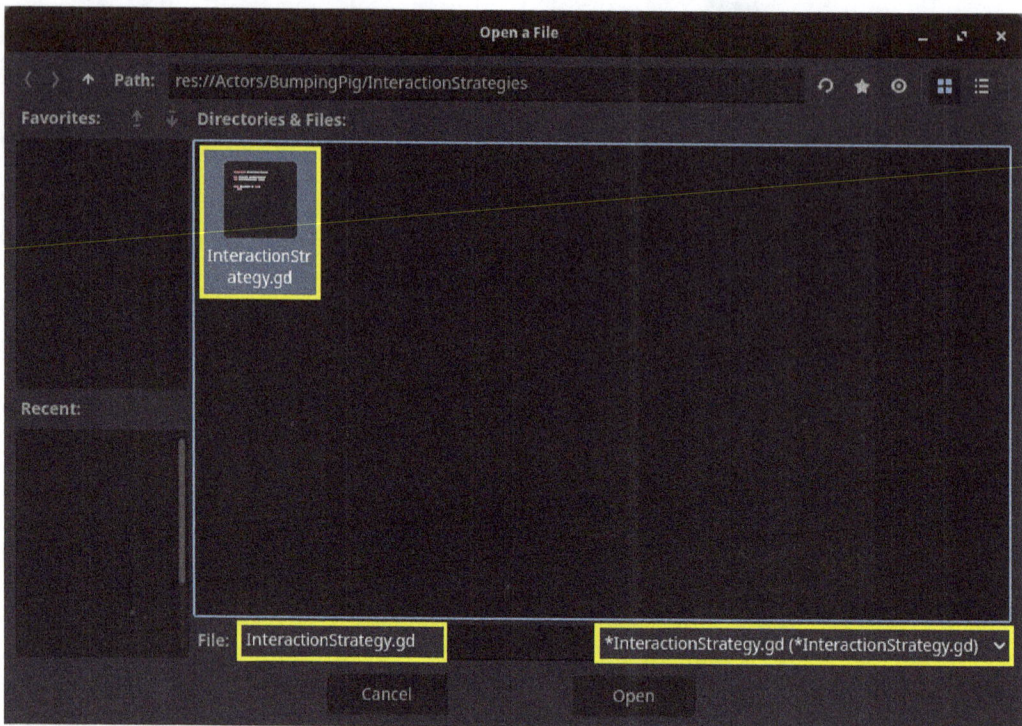

Figure 10.2 – Selecting the InteractionStrategy.gd file from the Open a File menu

This is all we have to do to inject the proper `InteractionStrategy` class into each type of object we want the `Brain` class to interact with. Talking about the `Brain` class, we can now clean up the mess that's been made by the designer to support multiple interactions and replace it with a simpler, cleaner strategy-based approach. We'll do that in the next section!

Cleaning up the Brain class with strategy executions

Now, it's time to clean up the `Brain` class and remove the conditional statements that will only get bigger as the game designer adds new objects that the Bumping Pig enemy can interact with. In this section, we'll use the extract class method to take the multiple interaction approaches that the `Brain` class currently has when the Bumping Pig enemy's `VisionArea2D` node overlaps with a `VisibleArea2D` node and put them into distinct strategies. For that, open the `res://Actors/BumpingPig/Brain.gd` script and perform the following steps:

1. Right before the declaration block, which contains variables to store the references to the commands, create a variable where you'll store the current `InteractionStrategy` class:

    ```
    extends Node
    class_name BumpingPigBrain
    ```

```
@export_node_path("BumpingPig") var actor_path
@onready var actor = get_node(actor_path)

@export_node_path("Node") var commands_path
@onready var commands := get_node(commands_path)

var interaction_strategy: InteractionStrategy
```

2. Then, we will move on to the _on_vision_area_2d_area_entered() signal callback method. The game designer ensured that only one VisionArea2D node was used instead of creating separate instances for each type of interaction. This is a significant improvement over our previous approach, where we had one VisionArea2D node for detecting the player and another for detecting bombs. However, this still results in a multi-conditional statement, with the interaction behaviors divided among each conditional branch. From here, we'll do the following:

I.   Create a new script that inherits from InteractionStrategy and save it as res://Actors/BumpingPig/InteractionStrategies/PlayerInteractionStrategy.gd.

II. Copy the lines inside the if area.owner is KingPigPlayer2D statement.

III. Open the PlayerInteractionStrategy script and override the execute() method, paste the lines of code we copied, and prepend the context variable when necessary:

```
extends InteractionStrategy

func execute() -> void:
    context.attack_command.execute()
```

IV. Let's do the same for each conditional branch. The CannonInteractionStrategy node should look like this:

```
extends InteractionStrategy

func execute() -> void:
    context.light_cannon_command.cannon =
      interacted_area.get_parent()
    context.light_cannon_command.execute()
```

V. As for `BombInteractionStrategy` and `CrateInteractionStrategy`, we'll
    have to access `interacted_area` instead of directly accessing the `area` variable
    since the `area` variable was passed to the signal callback and we don't have access to it in
    the `InterationStrategy` classes. At this point, `BombInteractionStrategy`
    should look like this:

```
extends InteractionStrategy

func execute() -> void:
    context.pick_command.object =
      interacted_area.owner
    context.actor.picking_object_type = "bomb"
    context.actor.throwable_factory
      .product_packed_scene = preload
        ("res://Objects/Bomb/Bomb.tscn")
    context.actor.throwable_factory
      .target_container_name = "Bombs"
    context.pick_command.execute()
```

VI. The `CrateInteractionStrategy` node should look like this:

```
extends InteractionStrategy

func execute() -> void:
    context.pick_command.object =
      interacted_area.owner
    context.actor.picking_object_type = "crate"
    context.actor.throwable_factory
      .product_packed_scene = preload
        ("res://Objects/Crate/Crate.tscn")
    context.actor.throwable_factory
      .target_container_name = "Crates"
    context.pick_command.execute()
```

3. Back to the `Brain` class, we can delete all the conditional statements inside the `_on_vision_area_2d_area_entered()` callback method. Here, we'll set up the `interaction_strategy` variable by setting its value to `area.interaction_strategy`:

```
func _on_vision_area_2d_area_entered(area: Area2D) ->
    void:
      interaction_strategy = area.interaction_strategy
```

4. Then, we'll inject the `Brain` instance into the `interaction_strategy.context` variable by using the `self` keyword:

```
func _on_vision_area_2d_area_entered(area: Area2D) ->
  void:
    interaction_strategy = area.interaction_strategy
    interaction_strategy.context = self
```

5. At this point, we'll inject the `VisibleArea2D` node that passed the current `InteractionStrategy` class to the `Brain` class in the `interaction_strategy.interacted_area` variable:

```
func _on_vision_area_2d_area_entered(area: Area2D) ->
  void:
    interaction_strategy = area.interaction_strategy
    interaction_strategy.context = self
    interaction_strategy.interacted_area = area
```

6. Finally, we'll call the `execute()` method on the `interaction_strategy` instance, effectively executing the proper `InteractionStrategy` class provided by the `VisibleArea2D` node:

```
func _on_vision_area_2d_area_entered(area: Area2D) ->
  void:
    interaction_strategy = area.interaction_strategy
    interaction_strategy.context = self
    interaction_strategy.interacted_area = area
    interaction_strategy.execute()
```

From now on, all we have to do to create new interaction behaviors for the Bumping Pig enemy is to create a new `InteractionStrategy` subclass, override its `execute()` method, and pass its file to the `VisibleArea2D` node of the object that we want the Bumping Pig to interact with. To understand how this works, in the next section, we'll set up all the necessary `VisibleArea2D` nodes inside the current objects that the Bumping Pig can interact with.

Implementing interaction strategies

We currently have the bread and butter to fulfill our task. If you test the `res://Levels/Level1/Level1.tscn` scene, you'll note that everything is working, with no errors or crashes, but the Bumping Pig enemy simply doesn't interact with anything – it passes right through the `Bomb`, `Crate`, `Cannon`, and even the `KingPigPlayer` scene objects. This is because the current `InteractionStrategy` class they're using has nothing implemented inside its `execute()` method.

As a quick tip, if you want to avoid this kind of situation and risk losing hours trying to understand why your implementations aren't working, I recommend that you add a breakpoint to the main methods in the abstract classes that we use as base classes for our patterns. For instance, in the `InteractionStrategy` class, you should add a breakpoint to the line where the `pass` statement is inside the `execute()` method.

You can do the same thing for the `Command` class. As for `BumpingPigState`, you can add a breakpoint in the `enter()` and `exit()` methods' `pass` statement. By doing that, you ensure that you'll use the concrete classes and not the abstract class. If you use the abstract class, Godot Engine will trigger the breaking point to remind you of that.

Was that an anecdote for an experience that I had while writing this very chapter? We'll never know. The fact is, in this section, we'll add the final touches to the scenes, setting up the proper `InteractionStrategy` classes they'll provide to the `Brain` class. Let's start with the player. Open the `res://Actors/KingPig/KingPigPlayer2D.tscn` file and follow these steps:

1. Use the **Scene's** dock **Filter** area field to find the `VisibleArea2D` node:

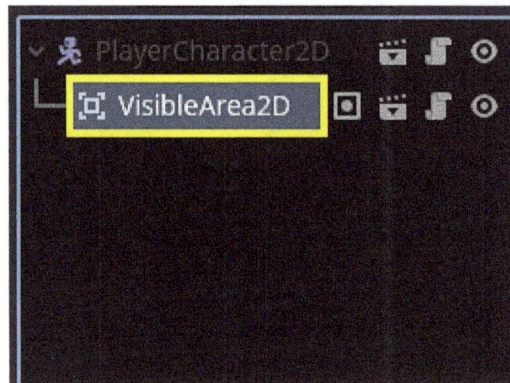

Figure 10.3 – The KingPigPlayer2D VisibleArea2D node

2. Then, using the **Inspector** area, select the `PlayerInteractionStrategy.gd` file from the **Interaction Strategy File** property pop-up menu:

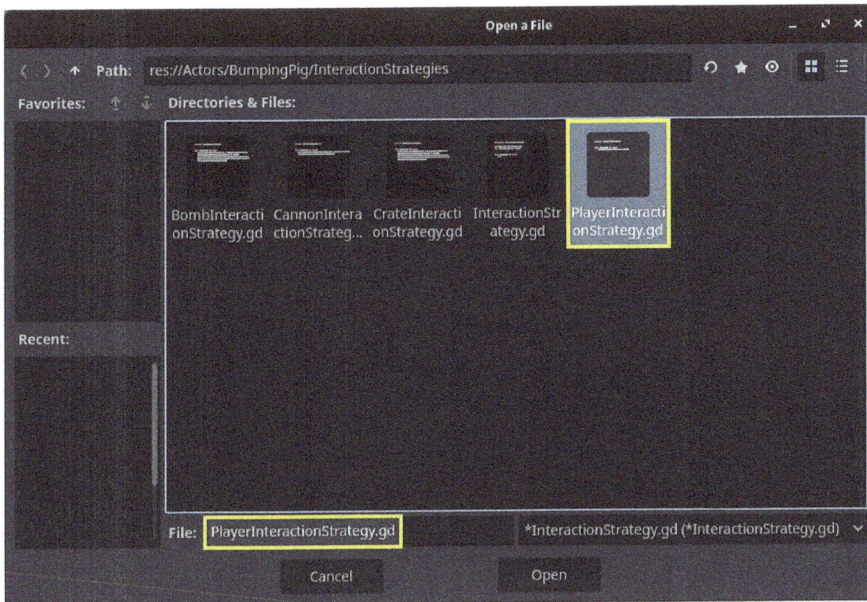

Figure 10.4 – Selecting PlayerInteractionStrategy from the Open a File menu

3. Save the scene!

That's it. You can test the `res://Levels/Level1/Level1.tscn` scene and move close to a Bumping Pig enemy to see if it will attack you. If everything goes well, you should see it attacking the King Pig Player scene, as shown in the following figure:

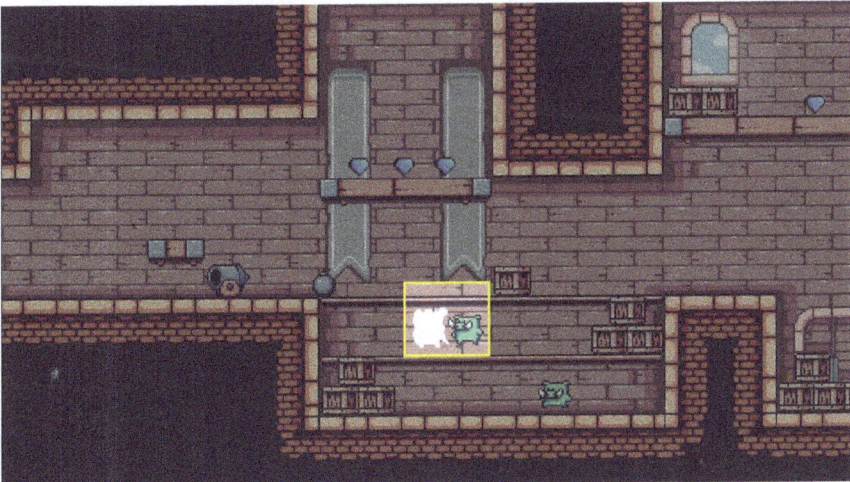

Figure 10.5 – The Bumping Pig enemy attacking the King Pig Player
scene, confirming that PlayerInteractionStrategy is working

This means our framework is working! Naturally, we already had the appropriate commands, states, and animations established for the successful implementation of the Strategy pattern. As new interactions appear further on in the development process, we'll have a good architecture ready to support them. All we'll have to do is create a new `InteractionStrategy` class to implement the `Brain` class' new behavior and, if necessary, new commands and states. By implementing these patterns for the `BumpingPig` scene, we now have a reliable workflow with a pipeline that can be a bit tedious to work with but ensures that we don't waste time figuring out new ways to solve each problem. We now have a tested and reliable architecture to scale our Bumping Pig actor. At this point, it's time to move on to other aspects of our game.

Feel free to set up the `Cannon`, `Bomb`, and `ThrowableCrate` scenes as well. All you have to do is replicate the steps outlined in this section by choosing the proper `InteractionStrategy` file. If you want to, take a look at the project inside the `10.implementing-ai-with-strategies/02.finished/` repository folder, where we already have everything in place. You can use this as a reference. Now, let's wrap up this chapter by recapping what we learned!

Summary

In this chapter, we learned how to implement AI behaviors using the Strategy pattern, which is one of the simplest yet most versatile design patterns. The Strategy pattern allows us to encapsulate algorithms within individual classes, making them interchangeable and enabling dynamic behavior changes at runtime. By decoupling the algorithms from the classes that use them, this pattern offers flexibility and scalability, allowing us to extend and modify behavior without altering the underlying code base. This approach aligns with the principle of composition over inheritance, making it a fundamental tool for building scalable and maintainable game architecture.

We applied the Strategy pattern to enhance the AI of the Bumping Pig enemy in our game, enabling it to attack, fire, pick up, and throw objects based on the current strategy. By doing so, we created a modular and flexible system that allows the AI to adapt its behavior depending on the game's context. The Strategy pattern was particularly useful in managing different interaction types, such as attacking the player or using objects such as bombs and crates. Each interaction type was encapsulated in its own strategy class that the AI could execute without the need for complex conditional logic in the `Brain` class.

This chapter also highlighted the importance of reducing logic branching in our code. By using the Strategy pattern, we were able to simplify the `Brain` class, making it easier to understand and maintain. Instead of relying on multiple conditional statements to handle different interactions, the `Brain` class simply executed the appropriate strategy provided by the object it interacted with. This not only made the code cleaner but also ensured we adhered to the open-closed principle, guaranteeing that the `Brain` class could be extended without modification.

We also explored multiple use cases for the Strategy pattern, both within our game and in other game genres. From handling different movement patterns to creating diverse combat strategies, the Strategy pattern proved to be a powerful tool for building sophisticated AI systems. This chapter provided practical examples of how to implement these strategies in Godot, reinforcing the pattern's utility in real-world game development scenarios.

As we move forward to the next chapter, we'll explore how to create a power-up system using the Decorator pattern. This system will allow us to stack score points in the `Diamond` object, creating a combo system where collecting multiple `Diamond` objects within a short time frame yields increasing points. After picking up five `Diamond` objects, the player will become invulnerable for a brief period, adding an exciting new layer of gameplay to our project.

Get This Book's PDF Version and Exclusive Extras

UNLOCK NOW

Scan the QR code (or go to `packtpub.com/unlock`). Search for this book by name, confirm the edition, and then follow the steps on the page.

Note: Keep your invoice handy. Purchases made directly from Packt don't require an invoice.

Creating a Power-Up System with the Decorator Pattern

Sometimes, we may want to add new behaviors for our objects but we don't want this behavior on all instances of a class. They may even be just temporary behaviors that are added and removed dynamically. It may be a punctual feature triggered by a specific event. Or we may want our object to carry out its usual responsibilities with extra features during the game run. Well, usually when we face this kind of situation where we want to add new behaviors to an object in runtime, instead of having them statically set, we use the Decorator pattern.

The Decorator pattern is a structural pattern that allows us to wrap an object inside a decorator, and people often refer to it as a wrapper. The wrapper, or decorator, looks exactly the same from the client class perspective but it carries a reference for the decorated object and delegates requests to it, altering the behavior of the decorated object, or wrappee, either before or after delegating the request.

This may sound a little bit too abstract, right? Well, in this chapter, we will get our hands dirty with a concrete case to use the Decorator pattern. We will take our project's `Diamond` class and give it the ability to behave as power-ups by altering the player character's attributes such as movement speed, jump height, attack strength, and more.

The Decorator pattern is a powerful solution that follows the composition over inheritance principle in depth, as most design patterns tend to do. However, with the Decorator pattern, we will note that inheritance is not the solution most of the time, especially when we want to simply add new behaviors for a class that is already in production and should have its code closed, adhering to the open-closed principle. So, without further ado, let's understand what exactly this pattern is, the problem it typically solves, and when to use it.

We will cover the following topics in this chapter:

- Understanding the Decorator pattern
- Spotting use cases for the Decorator pattern
- Implementing the Decorator pattern

Technical requirements

To follow this chapter, access the project files in the `11.creating-power-ups-with-decorator/01.start/` folder. If you run into any confusion, bugs, or errors while working through the *Implementing the Decorator pattern in Godot* section, refer to the files in the `11.creating-power-ups-with-decorator/02.finished/` folder. Any issues can be reported via the issue tracker at `https://github.com/PacktPublishing/Game-Development-Patterns-with-Godot-4/issues`.

If you haven't downloaded the project files yet, you can get them here: `https://github.com/PacktPublishing/Game-Development-Patterns-with-Godot-4`.

Let's start by diving into the Decorator pattern's core concepts, functionality, advantages, and common use cases in Godot, ensuring we leverage Godot's built-in capabilities efficiently and avoid unnecessary technicalities.

Understanding the Decorator pattern

The Decorator pattern is a structural design pattern used to dynamically add behaviors to an object without altering its original class' code. It provides an alternative to subclassing by allowing you to "wrap" objects with additional responsibilities. This can be useful when you need to extend the behavior of a class in a flexible and reusable manner without affecting the code base or introducing inheritance complexities. The main idea is that the object itself doesn't change; instead, additional functionalities are stacked over it through decorator objects.

This pattern typically solves the problem of adding features to objects in a way that adheres to the open-closed principle, which states that software entities should be open for extension but closed for modification. Picture a situation where you have a base class representing a game character, and you want to add multiple features such as new skills, attributes, or magical effects. Without the Decorator pattern, you might be tempted to create subclasses for each combination of these features, leading to a bloated and hard-to-maintain class hierarchy. The Decorator pattern solves this by letting you add features dynamically, without the need for numerous subclasses.

You would typically use the Decorator pattern when you want to add functionality to individual objects at runtime, rather than to a whole class or through inheritance. This is particularly useful in scenarios where different combinations of behaviors are needed. For instance, in a game, a player could gain a speed boost or shield power-up, and these enhancements can be applied in different orders and combinations. The decorator allows these features to be mixed and matched, applied, and removed flexibly.

The way the Decorator pattern works is by defining a decorator class that implements the same interface or inherits from the same base class as the object it decorates. Inside this decorator class, you store a reference to the original object and implement additional functionality that can be executed before or after calling the original object's methods. This allows you to modify or extend the object's behavior seamlessly while keeping the core logic intact.

The structure of the Decorator pattern consists of a few key components. At its core, there is a base interface or abstract class that defines the behavior common to both the original object and the decorators. The concrete component, which is the object being decorated, implements this interface, providing the default behavior. Decorators also implement this same interface and wrap the original object, allowing additional behavior to be introduced. Each decorator stores a reference to the object it wraps, which could either be the base object or another decorator. This composition allows decorators to add or modify functionality without affecting the underlying object's code.

In a typical implementation, the client class is responsible for applying the decorators to the base object. First, the client creates an instance of the original object, and then it dynamically decorates the object by wrapping it in one or more decorator instances. The decorator, in turn, holds a reference to the object it wraps, or decorates, allowing it to call the original object's methods while extending or altering the behavior as necessary. Since each decorator also implements the same interface as the base object, they can be stacked, with each decorator adding its own functionality while still allowing the decorated object's methods to be invoked. This approach provides a lot of flexibility, as the client can control how many decorators to apply and in what order.

The Decorator pattern is ideal when you need to add or enhance the functionality of an object in a modular and dynamic way. It avoids the pitfalls of deep inheritance trees, making your code base more maintainable and flexible. It's particularly beneficial in game development, where object behaviors often need to be modified or extended at runtime based on power-ups, effects, or other gameplay mechanics. By using decorators, you can combine these behaviors efficiently, ensuring that your system remains scalable and adaptable to change.

It sounds too abstract at this point, right? Well, in the next section, we will explore some concrete use cases so we can see, with real-world examples, how this pattern can be used to implement game systems.

Spotting use cases for the Decorator pattern

The Decorator pattern is a powerful tool for solving a wide range of design challenges in game development. It shines particularly in situations where objects need to be extended or modified dynamically, allowing us to avoid rigid inheritance hierarchies and instead compose behaviors in a more flexible, modular way. However, knowing when and where to apply the pattern can be tricky, especially in such a complex field as game development. The key to spotting good use cases is understanding how often behavior changes and extensions are needed without altering the core functionality of objects.

In many games, such as platformers, dungeon crawlers, or RPGs, objects such as characters, weapons, or enemies need to adapt their behavior based on the player's actions, environmental effects, or temporary power-ups. These objects often share common behaviors but require varying enhancements over time. This is where the Decorator pattern becomes an essential tool. By wrapping objects in decorators that apply new functionalities, we can ensure that these behaviors evolve without the need for clunky inheritances or hardcoded solutions.

In this section, we will explore some concrete use cases for the Decorator pattern, focusing on common scenarios in game design where dynamic behavior extensions are essential. From adding power-ups to characters to handling score multipliers and weapon enhancements, these examples will show how the pattern can be applied in practice to make games more dynamic, scalable, and maintainable. Each use case will demonstrate how decorators provide a clean solution to complex behavior management, ensuring that objects can be extended without rewriting or complicating existing code.

For instance, imagine a player character in a platformer game that can pick up various power-ups such as speed boosts, shields, or double jumps. Instead of creating multiple subclasses for each possible combination, you could use the Decorator pattern to apply these power-ups dynamically. For instance, when the player collects a speed boost, a `SpeedBoostDecorator` object can be applied to the `player` object, increasing movement speed for a limited time. If they collect a shield, a `ShieldDecorator` object could be stacked on top of that. Once the effects expire, the decorator is removed, restoring the original behavior.

One important thing to keep in mind is that a limitation of the Decorator pattern is the difficulty in removing specific decorators from a stack once they've been applied. Since they are all linked together, it is hard to maintain the decoration stack working without the interdependency of the decorators. For instance, in this example, the player character could hit a trap that removes its speed boost power-up. How will you remove it without messing up the whole decoration stack? Another downside of the Decorator pattern is that designing decorators usually leads to behaviors that depend on a specific order of the decoration stack. This is not mandatory, and we can find new ways to avoid it. However, it's not a problem if done well and mindfully. Now let's see more examples.

In a dungeon crawler game, such as *Torchlight 2*, players can enhance their weapons and armor by adding enchantments or embedding gems. Instead of subclassing every weapon or armor type to account for different combinations of effects (for instance, fire damage, life steal, or defense boosts), this can be another use case for the Decorator pattern. For example, a `FireEnchantmentDecorator` object could be applied to a sword to add fire damage, and a `LifeStealGemDecorator` object could be applied to steal health with each hit. Players can mix and match enchantments and gems, stacking multiple decorators onto the same weapon or piece of armor, giving it new abilities and effects. These decorators modify the behavior of the base item dynamically, adding and removing enchantments and gems, allowing for diverse and customizable equipment to allow players to explore multiple builds!

Another good use case is strategy and RPG games. In these games, certain enemies might receive buffs or debuffs, such as increased damage or reduced movement speed, as a result of spells or environmental effects. Instead of hardcoding these changes into the enemy classes, we can use decorators to modify their behavior dynamically. For example, a `FrozenDecorator` object could reduce an enemy's movement speed, while a `RageDecorator` object could increase its attack power. These effects can stack and be removed as conditions change, providing more flexibility for balancing game mechanics and allowing players to play with multiple strategies.

In games with combo-based scoring systems, such as in fighting games or platformers such as *Super Mario World*, the Decorator pattern can be used to handle combo streaks and multipliers. When a player defeats multiple enemies in succession without taking damage or landing, a `ScoreMultiplierDecorator` object can be added to the player's score system. With each successful hit, the multiplier increases. If the player continues the combo, additional decorators stack, and after reaching a certain threshold, for instance, eight enemies, they earn an extra life. If the player fails to continue the combo, the decorators are removed, and the score returns to normal.

Finally, and this one is particularly interesting for us, in games where the player's state frequently changes, such as gaining invincibility after collecting a star in a platformer, gaining boosted movement speed, or temporary stealth effect in a stealth-based game, the Decorator pattern can manage these transitions. When the player becomes invincible, for instance, an `InvincibilityDecorator` object could be applied, modifying how damage is handled and allowing the player to pass through enemies. Once the invincibility period ends, the decorator is removed, reverting the player to their normal state. In the next section, we'll be implementing a power-up system using the Decorator pattern, applying it to the `Diamond` objects in our game!

Implementing the Decorator pattern in Godot Engine

In many games, power-ups play a crucial role in enhancing the player's abilities and providing a sense of progression and excitement. Whether by increasing the player's speed, boosting their attack strength, or granting extra lives, power-ups can add layers of strategy and fun to the gameplay experience. In this section, we'll delve into a flexible system for managing power-ups in your game using the Decorator pattern, which allows for dynamic changes to player stats in a clean and modular fashion.

The Decorator pattern is particularly well-suited for handling temporary or stackable power-ups because it allows us to extend the functionality of the player's core stats without modifying the underlying code. By creating Decorators that "wrap" the player's stats, we can easily introduce new power-ups that modify attributes such as speed, jump height, and attack power. These power-ups can be applied when the player collects specific items, such as our project's Diamonds, and will automatically expire after a given duration, one after the other until they return the player's stats to their original values.

Godot Engine's architecture presents specific challenges for implementing the Decorator pattern, especially due to the way our project was also designed. Nodes have their own virtual methods and callbacks running in the background, and the very way they are processed through the `SceneTree` object also makes it difficult to wrap them, especially their life cycle and how their position in the node hierarchy is important. The same happens to resources, which, as we will see, have their own challenges as well, especially due to initialization and deserialization procedures. These are not problems exclusive to Godot Engine, and there are certainly better situations to implement the Decorator pattern, which is a powerful and useful pattern. I decided to put the Decorator pattern in *Part 3* of this book, where we talk about advanced patterns. I made this choice because of the way it is implemented in our project, which demands an extra layer of abstraction and understanding of both the engine and the pattern itself, and also about how object-oriented design and programming work.

In this section, we'll implement a power-up system step-by-step. We'll cover how to abstract the player's stats as an object that we can pass around and wrap, how to create Decorator classes that modify these stats, and how to manage the life cycle of power-ups using a singleton to apply and remove them over time. We will have power-ups that are easy to implement, extend, and maintain, making it a perfect fit for games with a variety of player abilities and pickups.

With all that said, let's take a look at how we came out with this system because you can bet that it didn't come from a deliberate desire! It came as a request from our beloved game designer. I believe they want the best for our game, but the guy is surely demanding, as you can see in the following request:

Hi, there! I have an idea and I need your help!

I love how we were able to make our Bumping Pig intelligent and alive in the game, allowing it to interact with everything in the environment. I'm really excited to test it out, that strategy thing works wonders!

I think we can change our focus now to the player's character, poor King Pig got abandoned as we were focusing on polishing the enemies.

As I played the game I noticed that there are no real incentives for the player to rush through levels, and the action aspect of our game is lagging behind. Players can score points, sure, but they can carefully craft strategies that lead them to the most optimal outcome in terms of score, without any attrition. And our game is supposed to be mainly an action game.

Since action-based games are closely related to player's reaction time and hand-eye coordination, I want to use time in our favor to promote a sense of urgency in players. But I don't want to punish them, instead reward them as they use their time well. So instead of having something like a timer that would make the player fail the level if they don't finish the level within a given amount of time, I want a power-up system that gives players some status buffs, like increasing their movement speed, jump height, and attack strength. Particularly I thought about adding these power-ups as bonus effects when collecting diamonds, but not every diamond, and each diamond can give different buffs.

These buffs have a time span, though. So players must use them as much as they can before they go away! To compensate for this, I want these power-ups to stack. So if players pick two movement speed buffs, they will have double the effect, until the first buff disappears.

Thinking about it…this can be a really cool statuses system! Depending on how you do it, try to make it so that I can make negative effects as well, like debuffs. For instance, making the player move slowly and dizzy when they get hit by an enemy, hehe. This sounds fun!

Thanks in advance,

Yours truly, Game designer of the fictional studio

Good, the game designer is having some fun playing with the strategies we implemented previously, I'm glad about that as it is my favorite design pattern and it's good that it was useful. This is the most important aspect of any implementation: its usefulness. Optimization and performance are nice when they are necessary, but knowing that you helped someone and they enjoyed your work is the most rewarding aspect of being a programmer. Now to the analysis of the request.

Our game designer wants us to create a power-up or status effect system, as they also want us to support negative effects. Note that one of the fundamental aspects here is that these effects can stack. All of these effects mess with the player's attributes: movement speed, jump height, and attack strength. So, we are talking about altering some properties of the `KingPigPlayer2D` class, more accurately, in the `BasicMovingCharacter2D` class, which the `KingPigPlayer2D` class inherits from.

Another important aspect is that these effects will be provided by another object, the `Diamond` nodes in this case. However, it's not their responsibility to manage status augmentations on the player, especially due to their life cycle. Note that the buffs are supposed to disappear after some time, whereas `Diamond` nodes disappear as soon as the player picks them. Thus, we would have to keep them stored in memory to manage their buff's duration, which is nonsense as this would explode the memory very quickly, or we delegate that to a single object that would manage all these statuses. This object should be globally accessible to all Diamonds and probably for the player, as it will need a reference to the player.

Well, we can see two problems with distinct solutions here. The most obvious one is, you guessed it, a globally accessible class that manages power-ups. We can create a singleton to solve that. The second problem is a way to stack objects, which should be treated as being of the same class, but with different behaviors. Not only that, they must be interchangeable and alter each other behavior in run time, since instead of providing just the plain attribute, for instance, speed, they will alter this speed before the final user class uses it. There may be many different types of alterations involved. For instance, we can add more speed, or multiply the speed. Maybe for a debuff, we would need to set the final speed to a specific value, such as being dizzy. In the dizzy effect, the player character could always move at a fixed slower speed instead of a fraction of its final speed.

All of this points to a wrapper class, but not only a wrapper but a wrapper of the same type of what it wraps. This class must use the same interface as its wrappee so that the wrappee user classes don't recognize if they are dealing with a wrapper or with a wrappee. From this description, it sounds like we need a Decorator, but what is it supposed to decorate? The player? How? The Diamond? The Singleton? You are about to see **Object-Oriented Programming (OOP)** at its finest. In the next section, we will create a new class to represent all the player character's attributes, allowing us to treat them as objects!

Turning properties into the Stats class

One of the advantages of working with programming languages that support OOP is the ability to turn anything into objects. You may be asking yourself what the advantages of doing that are, right? Well, as we saw throughout this book, by using objects, we can reference them, pass them around to other objects, encapsulate, and abstract our thoughts. Think about objects as we did in *Chapter 1*: concrete instances of abstractions for problems we are solving.

Currently, we are dealing with a problem related to the player character's attributes such as speed, attack strength, and jump height. So, using an OOP paradigm, in other words, a way to think in terms of objects, let's turn these attributes into an object so that we can treat it as such. Remember, the Decorator pattern is essentially a wrapper object that wraps an object of the same base type. So if we need to add layers of power-ups that mutate these attributes, the best approach is to wrap these attributes directly, and to do that, we can turn them into an object itself. For that, open the project available at the repository's `creating-power-ups-with-decorators/01.start/` folder. From there, let's follow these steps:

1. In the **FileSystem** dock, right-click on the `res://Recipes/BasicMovingCharacter2D/` folder. From the drop-down menu, select **+Create New | Script…** to create a new GDScript.

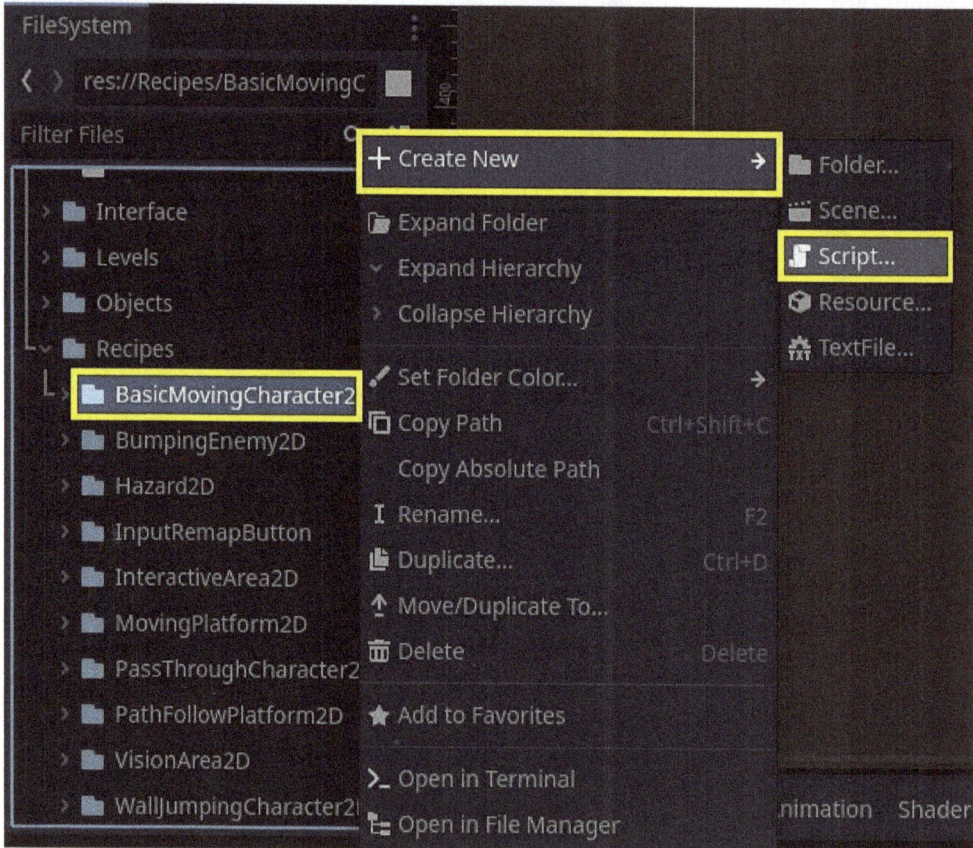

Figure 11.1 – Creating a new script from the FileSystem drop-down menu

2. This script will inherit from the `Resource` class and we will call it `Stats` as it will represent the actors' stats.

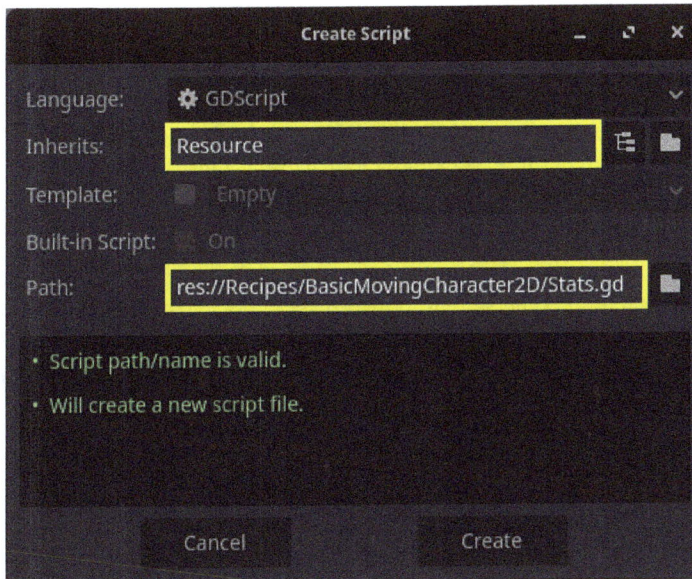

Figure 11.2 – The Stats script settings

3. In this script, we will transfer all the properties related to the `BasicMovingCharacter2D` behavior and its subclasses, as instead of carrying the data themselves, they will access the `Stats` instance. We will export all the properties in the `Stats` class so that we can create new instances with serialized values that we can configure through the **Inspector** tab on each instance of the `BasicMovingCharacter2D` class. The properties include the following: `gravity`, `speed`, `jump_strength`, `max_lives`, `lives`, `attack_strength`, `wall_jumpstrength`, `slide_gravity_factor`, `horizontal_gravity`, and `max_slide_speed`:

```
extends Resource
class_name Stats

@export var gravity := 2000.0
@export var speed := 500.0
@export var jump_strength := 800.0
@export var max_lives := 3
@export var lives := 0
@export var attack_strength := 1
@export var wall_jump_strength := Vector2(800, -800)
@export var slide_gravity_factor := 0.2
@export var horizontal_gravity := 8000
@export var max_slide_speed := 200
```

4. The first thing we will do after that is to override the `_init()` callback method and initially set the `lives` variable to the `max_lives` variable value. We do that because since the values will be serialized, the `max_lives` variable value may have a different value. Also, as the `lives` variable should initially have the same value as `max_lives`, we will ensure that in the `_init()` callback, which is called by Godot Engine as soon as an instance of the class is created:

```gdscript
func _init() -> void:
    lives = max_lives
```

5. Now we will use setters and getters to encapsulate these values into methods and create an interface that we can use in the Decorator class to add new behaviors to the `Stats` class. This approach ensures that any class using the `Stats` class will invoke the setter and getter methods whenever accessing these properties. We will take advantage of that to manipulate the accessed values:

```gdscript
extends Resource
class_name Stats

@export var gravity := 2000.0 : set = set_gravity,
    get = get_gravity
@export var speed := 500.0 : set = set_speed,
    get = get_speed
@export var jump_strength := 800.0 :
    set = set_jump_strength, get = get_jump_strength
@export var max_lives := 3 : set = set_max_lives,
    get = get_max_lives
@export var lives := 0 : set = set_lives,
    get = get_lives
@export var attack_strength := 1 :
    set = set_attack_strength, get = get_attack_strength
@export var wall_jump_strength := Vector2(800,
    -800) : set = set_wall_jump_strength,
    get = get_wall_jump_strength
@export var slide_gravity_factor := 0.2 :
    set = set_slide_gravity_factor,
    get = get_slide_gravity_factor
@export var horizontal_gravity := 8000 :
    set = set_horizontal_gravity,
    get = get_horizontal_gravity
@export var max_slide_speed := 200 :
    set = set_max_slide_speed, get = get_max_slide_speed
```

6. After that, we will implement the setters and getters methods. In this implementation, they will essentially do nothing really impressive. The setter method will set the variable value to the new value, and the getter will return its current value. In the following code, I'll use the `gravity` variable's setter and getter methods as a reference so we don't get confused and save some space. However, you should replicate the same approach on every other setter and getter method we declared in the previous step. You can refer to the same script in the `11.creating-power-ups-with-decorators/02.finished` project for reference:

```
func set_gravity(new_gravity: float) -> void:
    gravity = new_gravity

func get_gravity() -> float:
    return gravity
```

This wraps up our `Stats` class, but this is not everything yet. We now need to refactor our classes so that they use the `Stats` class instead of handling their attributes themselves. For that, we will have to revisit several classes in our code base, starting with the `BasicMovingCharacter2D` class. Open the `res://Recipes/BasicMovingCharacter2D/BasicMovingCharacter2D.gd` file and let's do the following:

1. Let's start by removing the variables that we extracted from the `Stats` class, namely the `gravity`, `jump_strength`, and `speed` variables. Then, export a variable that will carry the reference to an instance of the `Stats` class instead:

```
class_name BasicMovingCharacter2D
extends CharacterBody2D

signal direction_changed(new_direction: int)
signal jumped

@export var stats: Stats

@export var direction = 0:
    set(new_direction):
        direction = new_direction
        direction_changed.emit(new_direction)
```

2. Then, we should fix all the errors pointing out the missing variables. To fix them, we will prepend the stats variable. The _physics_process() callback and the jump() methods should look like the following code:

```
func _physics_process(delta):
    velocity.y += stats.gravity * delta
    velocity.x = direction * stats.speed
    move_and_slide()


func jump() -> void:
    if is_on_floor():
        velocity.y = -stats.jump_strength
        jumped.emit()
```

3. Now, we need to look at other classes. Moving on to the res://Recipes/WallJumpingCharacter2D/WallJumpingCharacter2D.gd file, we will do the same, removing the slide_gravity_factor, horizontal_gravity, max_slide_speed, and wall_jump_strength variables. Just as in the previous step, we will fix the errors that will appear by prepending the stats variable where there were only references to these variables we deleted.

My padawans, I will allow you to do the tedious job of refactoring the following classes by implementing the same approach I highlighted in the previous instructions, removing the variable declarations of the properties we extracted to the Stats class when necessary, and prepending the stats reference where there were direct references to the variables carried by the Stats class. For that, I recommend you use the built-in text editor **Find in Files** feature. Look for references to the variables declared in the Stats class and fix the ones that don't use the stats property reference yet. In the following figure, you can see that we have references to the lives property in the KingPigPlayer2D class, for instance. Note that references to this variable appear in other classes as well, but they are not related to the BasicMovingCharacter2D class, so we don't need to refactor them.

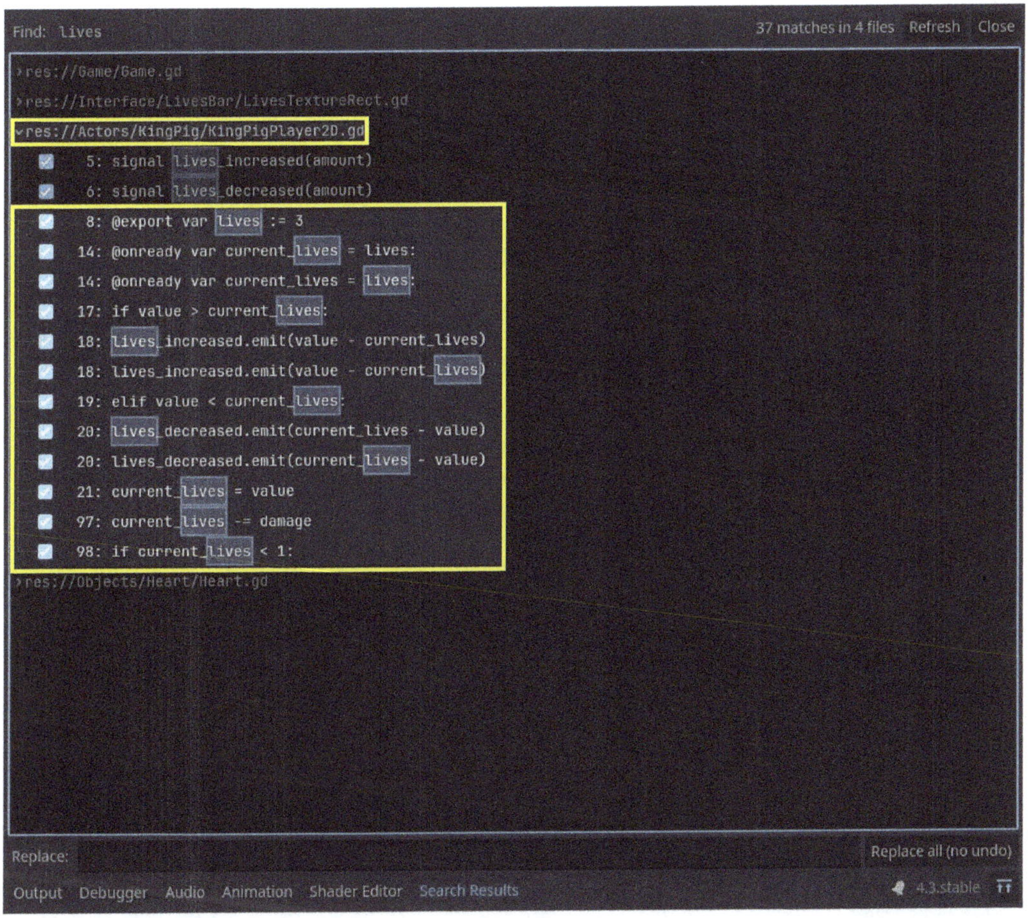

```
Find: lives                                               37 matches in 4 files   Refresh   Close

> res://Game/Game.gd
> res://Interface/LivesBar/LivesTextureRect.gd
⌄ res://Actors/KingPig/KingPigPlayer2D.gd
    ☑    5: signal lives_increased(amount)
    ☑    6: signal lives_decreased(amount)
    ☑    8: @export var lives := 3
    ☑   14: @onready var current_lives = lives:
    ☑   14: @onready var current_lives = lives:
    ☑   17: if value > current_lives:
    ☑   18: lives_increased.emit(value - current_lives)
    ☑   18: lives_increased.emit(value - current_lives)
    ☑   19: elif value < current_lives:
    ☑   20: lives_decreased.emit(current_lives - value)
    ☑   20: lives_decreased.emit(current_lives - value)
    ☑   21: current_lives = value
    ☑   97: current_lives -= damage
    ☑   98: if current_lives < 1:
> res://Objects/Heart/Heart.gd




Replace:                                                          Replace all (no undo)
Output   Debugger   Audio   Animation   Shader Editor   Search Results              4.3.stable
```

Figure 11.3 – The search results in every GDScript file in the project for the "lives" keyword

By doing that, we now have a refactored system that uses the Stats class to access attributes used to perform their behavior. Now, instead of carrying the reference to the movement speed, jump height, attack strength, gravity, and other variables, the BasicMovingCharacter2D classes will be able to access these values from an encapsulated Stats object. This is fundamental for the implementation of our Decorator class, as we will now be able to change the reference to this Stats object, allowing us to point it to a decorated version of the Stats object. For that, in the next section, we will create the StatsDecorator class, which is our project's implementation of the Decorator pattern to create a power-up system.

Creating our StatsDecorator class

We use our abstraction capabilities to understand that we can treat the various attributes of our BasicMovingCharacter2D class and its subclasses as objects instead of primitive types such as integers, strings, Booleans, and floats. Of course, at some point, we will have to use these types as they are the building blocks of programming. However, as we add layers of abstractions, we can encapsulate them into object types that we can have more control over. By doing that, we were able to create setter and getter methods for the properties and encapsulate them, leaving the user classes of our Stats class unaware of what happens when they set or get a value. This is important because, with that, we maintained the previous contract. In this section, we will take advantage of this new interface and implement the Decorator pattern, adding new behaviors in runtime to our Stats objects.

The whole idea now is that we will create a subclass of the Stats class that will use polymorphism to override the setter and getter methods doing extra procedures before setting or returning the Stats properties. Since we will implement the Decorator pattern, we will wrap an actual Stats object and delegate the call to this object either before or after the extra procedures.

There's a small caveat due to how game engines work and to the approach we used of overriding setter and getter methods. In Godot Engine, these methods are called when the object is deserialized and instanced. The problem is that nodes are only ready and available once they are inside the SceneTree object being processed, or in other words, after Godot Engine runs its _ready() callback method. This is not in sync with the step where the setter and getter methods are called. Every time we use a node inside a setter or getter method, it will throw a null instance error, because the node object won't be available. As a result, we will need to not only delegate calls to the decorated Stats object but also check whether one is available. If a decorated object is not present, we will access and return the properties of the StatsDecorator instance instead. This will ultimately allow it to function as a simple Stats object, which goes slightly beyond the intended scope of the Decorator pattern. However, with that said, you will understand that the pattern itself is simple. We just had to adapt it to our context, which is pretty much what we always have to do with all patterns. We just need to understand their concept and then abstract and implement them for the specific problem we are solving, if the problem gives signs that it can be solved by implementing a given pattern.

With this disclaimer, let's get started! Open the project inside the 11.creating-power-ups-with-decorators/01.start/ folder and let's implement the following steps:

1. Using the **FileSystem** dock, create a new folder inside the res://Actors/ folder called Decorators. We will do that inside this folder because both the BumpingPig and KingPigPlayer2D classes will be able to use Decorators.

2. Then, inside the res://Actors/Decorators/ folder, we will create a new script that will inherit from the Stats class and we will call it StatsDecorator.

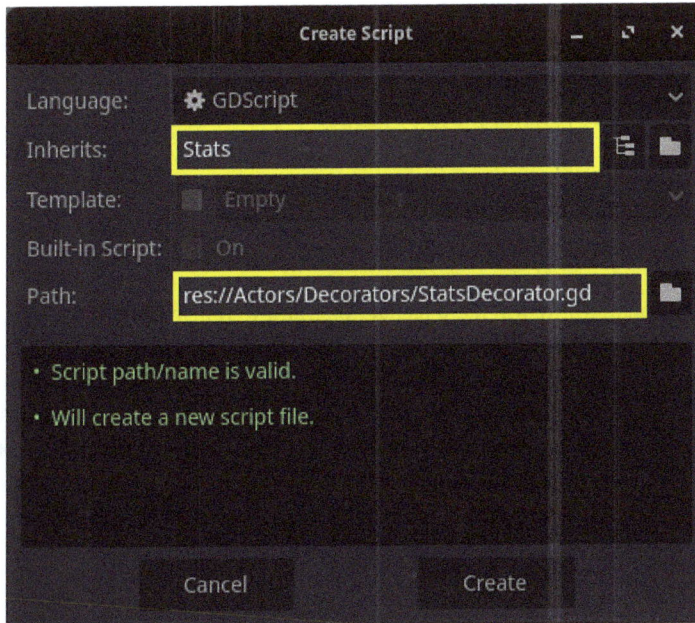

Figure 11.4 – Creating the StatsDecorator script

3. Within the `StatsDecorator` script, we will first declare its trademark property, which is a property that holds a reference to another instance of its superclass. In this case, that's a `Stats` instance. Yep, a Decorator is an object that carries a reference to an object of the same type. This can be confusing to some people, but at this point you already understand why we do that, right? We need to wrap an object but keep all its user classes thinking they are still interacting with it, so our wrapper needs to maintain all the contracts of the wrapped object. For that, we make it inherit the wrappee's class. Let's call this variable `decorated_stats`:

```
extends Stats
class_name StatsDecorator

var decorated_stats: Stats
```

4. Now comes yet another bit of tedious work. We now need to override all the setter and getter methods we created in the `Stats` class and make them delegate their call to the `decorated_stats` object. Remember that we have a caveat here: if the `decorated_stats` variable is currently set as `null`, we will perform the procedure on the `StatsDecorator` instance. Otherwise, we delegate to the object wrapped in the `decorated_stats` variable. Again, I'll use the setter and the getter method that encapsulates the `gravity` property as an example, but you can replicate the same idea on every other setter and getter method. For the setter methods, we will check whether `decorated_stats` is populated with an object. If it isn't, we will use the `super()` method, passing the same arguments to use the `Stats` class setter

procedures instead. This will maintain the `StatsDecorator` behavior consistent with its superclass. Otherwise, we delegate the call to the `decorated_stats` object:

```
func set_gravity(new_gravity: float) -> void:
    if not decorated_stats:
        super(new_gravity)
    else:
        decorated_stats.gravity = new_gravity
```

5. As for the getter method, we will use a ternary operator to return the `decoratated_stats` variable's value if there's a `decorated_stats` object; otherwise, we call the `super()` method. We use a ternary operator here to avoid having a conditional statement with two returning variables explicitly declared, which is ugly and usually a bad practice. An alternative would be to create a new local variable that would store the value of the `decorated_stats` object's variable or the value returned by calling the `super()` method and then returning this variable at the end. However, I personally prefer to use ternary operators for simplicity in this specific case:

```
func get_gravity() -> float:
    return decorated_stats.gravity if
        decorated_stats else super()
```

Well, again to save space, I'll ask you to implement *steps 4* and *5* on all the remaining setter and getter methods to ensure the proper behavior for our `StatsDecorator` class. Again, I want to emphasize that this is not a necessary step to implement the Decorator pattern. Usually, we would just create an abstract or an interface class to override the necessary methods on its wrapped object.

The main reason we are doing all that is because the main use of `Stats` objects is accessing their properties, as they don't have any concrete method. Since we will wrap the `Stats` objects, we need their user class to access the `Stats` object properties' values, and not the decorator object's values. This is a way to bypass the `StatsDecorator` object default values unless we access a variable that has its value altered by the `StatsDecorator` behavior.

For instance, if a character currently has one life and we wrap its `Stats` object with a `StatsDecorator` instance, failing to delegate the getter method call to the original `Stats` object would result in the character suddenly having three lives, even if we are only decorating its movement speed. Got it? I hope so because after overriding all the setter and getter methods from the `Stats` class, we now have our very own first decorator. Congratulations! With that, we can start to play around and test whether our system will work. In the next section, we will create a class that will use the `StatsDecorator` object to decorate `Stats`. By doing that, we will maintain the user classes of the `Stats` class unaware of the existence of the `StatsDecorator` class since a brand new class will be responsible for decorating `Stats` objects.

Wrapping Stats with the power-ups Singleton

Remember our friendly neighborhood Singleton pattern? We are going to revise it. In the game designer's request, they mention we need to manage the duration of the power-ups, and this is not a responsibility of the KingPigPlayer2D, Diamond, or StatsDecorator class. So we will create a new class for that, which the Diamond class can use to add power-ups to the player's character. To make that, every Diamond node must refer to the same instance of the power-ups manager class because the power-ups are supposed to stack. The Singleton pattern is the perfect solution for that. This is what we will do in this section! So let's open the project inside the 11.creating-power-ups-with-decorators/01.start/ folder and perform the following steps:

1. Create a new scene and use a Node instance as the root node. Rename it to PowerUps.

2. Add a Timer node as a child of the PowerUps node. We will use this timer as the buff duration. We are using a default duration for every power-up so it's safe to use a global timer with a default duration. However, if the game designer requires that each buff has its own duration, we will have to add a duration property to the StatsDecorator class. Set the **Timer Wait Time** property to 3.

3. Save the scene as res://Game/PowerUps/PowerUps.tscn and attach a new script to the PowerUps node, saving it as res://Game/PowerUps/PowerUps.gd.

4. Then, in the script, let's start by creating a variable to store a reference to the Timer node using the @onready annotation:

```
extends Node
class_name PowerUps


@onready var timer := $Timer
```

5. It should also store a reference to the KingPigPlayer2D instance. It will wrap the Stats object:

```
extends Node
class_name PowerUps


@onready var timer := $Timer
var player: KingPigPlayer2D
```

6. Since we will need to manage the StatsDecorator life cycle, we need to store them in an array so we are able to order and remove them accordingly:

```
extends Node
class_name PowerUps


@onready var timer := $Timer
var player: KingPigPlayer2D

var decorators_list: Array[StatsDecorator] = []
```

7. With that, we can create a method that user classes can use to add a new power-up to the player. Let's call this method add_power_up(). It will ask for a decorator as an argument:

```
func add_power_up(decorator: StatsDecorator) -> void:
```

8. Inside the add_power_up() method, we will first inject the player's current Stats instance as the decorator object's decorated_stats property value. This effectively wraps the Stats object inside the decorator instance:

```
func add_power_up(decorator: StatsDecorator) -> void:
    decorator.decorated_stats = player.stats
```

9. However, part of what constitutes the Decorator pattern is also substituting the wrapped object with the wrapper decorator object, making it so that the object using the previous wrappee instance will now use the Decorator instead, without even realizing it. For that, we set the player.stats variable to become the decorator instance instead:

```
func add_power_up(decorator: StatsDecorator) -> void:
    decorator.decorated_stats = player.stats
    player.stats = decorator
```

10. After that, we append the current decorator to the decorators_list variable and call the start() method on the timer instance, so when it times out, we remove the power-up:

```
func add_power_up(decorator: StatsDecorator) -> void:
    decorator.decorated_stats = player.stats
    player.stats = decorator
    decorators_list.append(decorator)
    timer.start()
```

11. Speaking of removing the power-up, we need to create a method for that as well. Let's call it remove_power_up():

```
func remove_power_up() -> void:
```

12. Inside the remove_power_up() method, we will check whether there is any power-up in our decorators_list array by checking whether its size is greater than 0:

```
func remove_power_up() -> void:
    if decorators_list.size() > 0:
```

13. If there are any decorators in the list, we will pop the first one using the pop_back() method. In other words, we will remove the power-ups in a first-in first-out fashion. We will store the popped decorator in a variable called decorator as well:

```
func remove_power_up() -> void:
    if decorators_list.size() > 0:
        var decorator := decorators_list
        .pop_back() as StatsDecorator
```

14. Then, we must unwrap the decorated Stats object. For that, we will set the player.stats variable to decorator.decorated_stats, effectively resetting the wrapping. At this point, you must have realized that we can wrap the StatsDecorator object with another StatsDecorator object since they also inherit from the Stats class, right? This is exactly what the Decorator pattern allows us to do. By wrapping wrappers, we can add virtually infinite extra behaviors to the wrappee in runtime. Ultimately, our remove_power_up() method will set the player.stats variable back to the original Stats object:

```
func remove_power_up() -> void:
    if decorators_list.size() > 0:
        var decorator := decorators_list
        .pop_back() as StatsDecorator
        player.stats = decorator.decorated_stats
```

15. If there's nothing inside the decorators_list array, we will call the stop() method on the timer node so we don't try to remove decorators when there are none:

```
func remove_power_up() -> void:
    if decorators_list.size() > 0:
        var decorator := decorators_list
        .pop_back() as StatsDecorator
        player.stats = decorator.decorated_stats
    else:
        timer.stop()
```

16. Speaking of the timer node, we will use its timeout signal to call the remote_power_up() method. For that, let's use the **Inspector** and connect the timeout signal to a callback method called _on_timer_timeout().

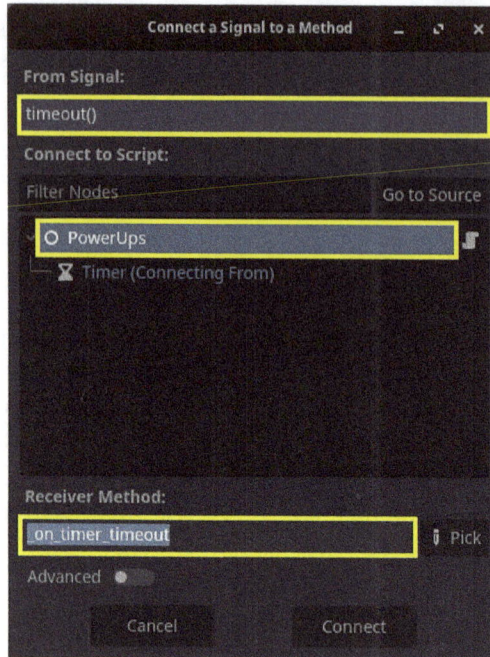

Figure 11.5 – Connecting the timer's timeout signal to the PowerUps' _on_timer_timeout() method

17. Then, in the `_on_timer_timeout()` method, let's call the `remove_power_ups()` method. With that, our `PowerUps` class is done:

```
func _on_timer_timeout() -> void:
    remove_power_up()
```

18. With the `PowerUps` class in place, we now have to turn it into a singleton that both the `KingPigPlayer2D` and the `Diamond` class can access. For that, let's open the **Project Settings** menu. In the **Globals** tab, let's create a new **Autoload** in the **Autoload** tab by loading the `res://Game/PowerUps/PowerUps.tscn` scene. Instead of calling it `PowerUps`, which would generate some errors because the class name is already `PowerUps`, we will call it `PowerUpsSingleton`.

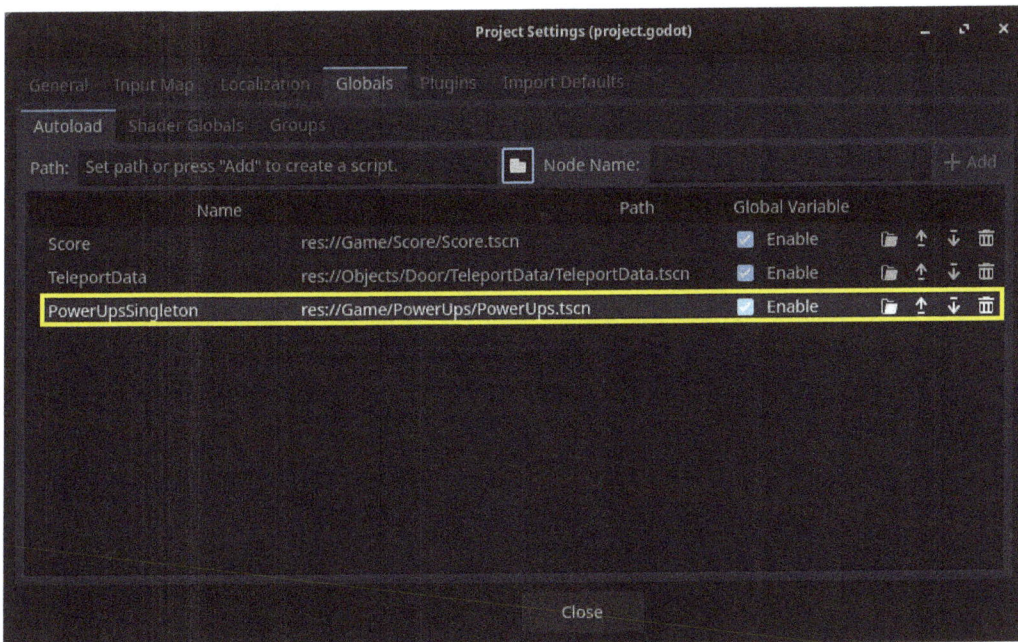

Figure 11.6 – Creating PowerUpsSingleton using the Project Settings | Autoload menu

Well, with that, we have our power-up system in place so that other classes can use it. We have a class that is capable of wrapping the player's attributes and changing them as we wish. For that, we first need to inject the player into it. So, let's open the `res://Actors/KingPig/KingPigPlayer2D.gd` script and add inside its `_ready()` callback method a line setting the `PowerUpsSingleton.player` variable to be the `KingPigPlayer2D` instance using the `self` keyword:

```
func _ready() -> void:
    for command in $Commands.get_children():
        command.receiver = self
    PowerUpsSingleton.player = self
```

With the `PowerUps` and `KingPigPlayer2D` classes ready, we can wrap the `KingPigPlayer2D` class' `Stats` instance with decorators, stacking them up their effects. We can also remove them as their buff duration ends. Now we need to add this functionality to the `Diamond` class, allowing it to pass any type of power-up, or rather `StatsDecorator` objects, to the `PowerUps` class, and that's what we are going to do in the next section!

Using Diamond objects to add power-ups

The missing piece in our puzzle is how we are going to use the power-up system we just built. It's all set and any class can use it. The game designer asked us to add this functionality to the `Diamond` objects first, so let's start there. In this section, we will give `Diamond` objects the ability to wrap the player's `Stats` object with a `StatsDecorator` by using `PowerUpsSingleton`. Then, we will create some power-ups to test the system! To do that, let's start by opening the `res://Objects/Diamond/Diamond.tscn` scene and following these instructions:

1. Open the `Diamond` node script. Let's start by creating a variable that we will use as a reference to the `StatsDecorator` instance that this `Diamond` node will request the `PowerUpsSingleton` object to apply on the player's `Stats` instance. For that, we will use the `@export` annotation and make sure this variable will only accept `StatsDecorator` objects by typing it as such:

```
extends Node2D
class_name Diamond


@export var decorator: StatsDecorator
```

2. Then, inside its `func _on_interactive_area_2d_interaction_available()` callback method, we will add a line calling the `PowerUpsSingleton.add_power_up()` method, passing the `Diamond` object's `decorator` object before performing the other procedures in this method:

```
func _on_interactive_area_2d_interaction_available():
    PowerUpsSingleton.add_power_up(decorator)
    score_points.increase_score()
    queue_free()
```

3. Then, we will create a default `StatsDecorator` resource to prevent getting null reference errors. For that, we will use the **Inspector**. Right-click the **Diamond Decorator** property and from the drop-down menu, select the **New StatsDecorator** option.

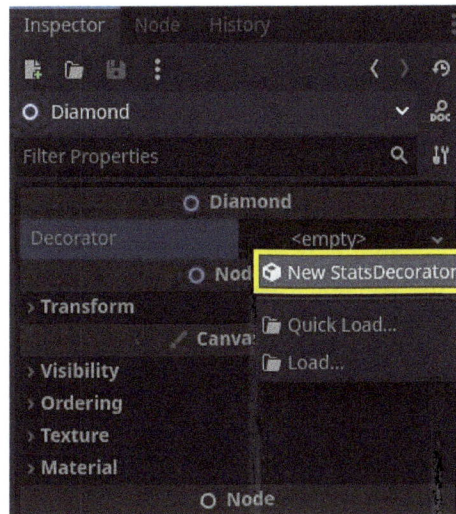

Figure 11.7 – Creating a new StatsDecorator instance using the Decorator property drop-down menu

4. There's something we need to do to prevent getting a stack overflow error. Remember, the Decorator pattern wraps an object that is of the same type as its own. In Godot Engine, objects of the Resource type have shared references unless we make them unique. This means that if we leave things as they currently are, we will run into the situation where a StatsDecorator object will wrap itself as soon as the player collects two Diamond objects. Since we delegate calls to the decorated_stats object inside the StatsDecorator object, it will be delegating calls to itself in an infinite loop. To prevent that, we will make the Decorator variable's StatsDecorator object unique to every instance of the Diamond scene. For that, left-click the newly created StatsDecorator resource and in the **Resource** category, toggle on the **Local to Scene** property.

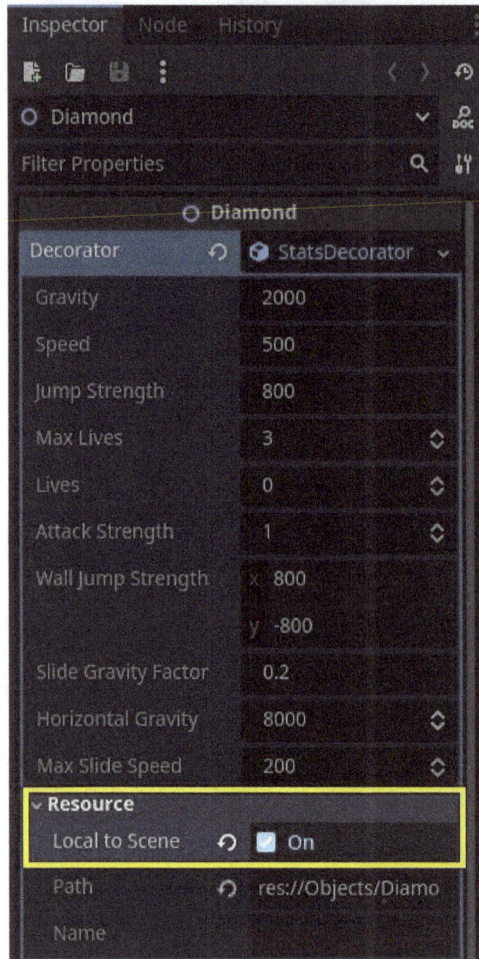

Figure 11.8 – Checking the Diamond object's StatsDecorator Local to Scene property

With that, our system is working, but we won't see any concrete changes in the gameplay as we pick up `Diamond` objects. So let's create some concrete power-ups! In `res://Actors/Decorators/`, create a new script that inherits the `StatsDecorator` class. Let's call it `SpeedStatsDecorator`, as in the following figure:

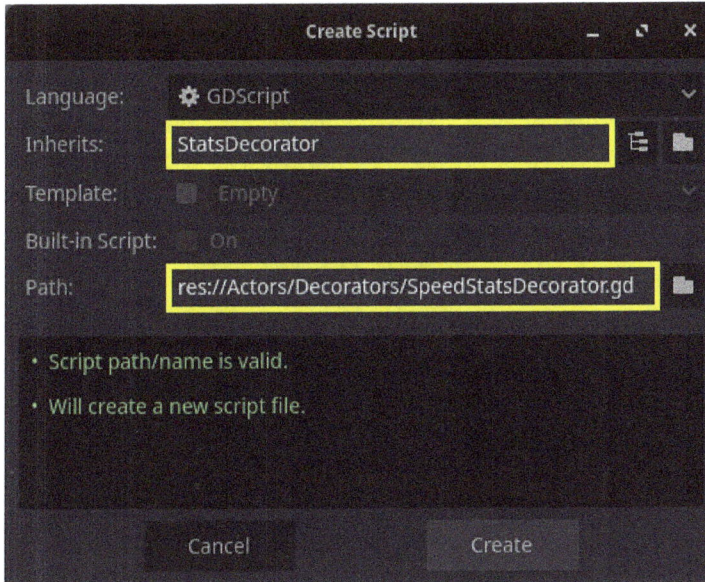

Figure 11.9 – Creating the SpeedStatsDecorator script

Inside this script, we will make sure that we declare its `class_name` field so that we have it available as an option on the **Diamond Decorator** property's drop-down menu. Then, we will serialize a property that will represent how much the player's movement speed will be multiplied when they pick this power-up. Let's call this variable `speed_multiplier`:

```
extends StatsDecorator
class_name SpeedStatsDecorator

@export var speed_multiplier := 1.1
```

Then, since the speed is a variable the player will retrieve from its `Stats` instance, we can intercept this request using the `get_speed()` getter method, returning the `decorated_stats` speed multiplied by the `speed_multiplier` variable. Here, we need to use the same approach we did before where we return the value with the effect applied if we have an object referenced in the `decorated_stats` variable. Otherwise, we call the superclass' implementation using the `super()` method:

```
extends StatsDecorator
class_name SpeedStatsDecorator

@export var speed_multiplier := 1.1

func get_speed() -> float:
    return decorated_stats.speed * speed_multiplier
if decorated_stats else super()
```

That's it! Our first power-up is done. Now, how can we implement it in our game? Well, there are several ways. For instance, you can create a new inherited scene using the `Diamond` scene as the base scene and instead of using an abstract `StatsDecorator` object on its `Decorator` property, it uses a `SpeedStatsDecorator` object. However, we will use a simpler method here. Open the `res://Levels/Level1/Level1.tscn` scene and pick a `Diamond` node. From there, create a new `SpeedStatsDecorator` object on its `Decorator` property, as in the following figure:

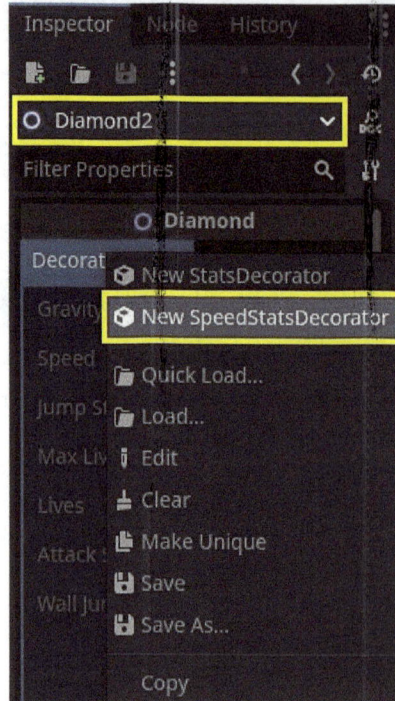

Figure 11.10 – Creating a new SpeedStatsDecorator object using
the Diamond2 Decorator property drop-down menu

I will suggest that you pick at least three `Diamond` instances and do the same so we can see the effects of stacking. Now, if you test the scene, you will see that the `KingPigPlayer2D` instance's `Stats` node gets wrapped when it touches `Diamond` instances. You can feel its movement speed increasing when it picks up the `Diamond` object with the `SpeedStatsDecorator` instance. Pretty nice, right?

Well, this is a very versatile system. For instance, in the project available in the `11.creating-power-ups-with-decorators/02.finished` repository folder, we can see other examples such as the `AttackStatsDecorator` object that adds a bonus to the player's `attack_strength` variable. In particular, the `InvulnerabilityStatsDecorator` object is interesting because it uses the `set_life()` setter method, overriding it only to change the `life` property if the new value is greater than the current value, ultimately preventing the player from losing health as long as the power-up is running.

That said, experiment a bit with this system, and try to create some debuffs as well. Maybe prevent the player from hitting the enemies to simulate a ghost form? Remember, you can add multiple effects! Maybe you can create some basic effects and then combine them to create more complex effects depending on what you want to achieve. Try to attach `StatsDecorator` objects to other game objects, such as a burning effect when the `Bomb` objects explode and hurt the player. The burning effect could make the player move slower and jump lower while also making it deal more damage. Be creative! However, it's time to wrap up this chapter. In the next section, let's see what we learned and highlight some core concepts we saw throughout this chapter.

Summary

In this chapter, we learned about the Decorator pattern and its application in creating dynamic power-up systems for games. The Decorator pattern is a structural design pattern that allows us to wrap objects with additional functionalities at runtime without altering their underlying code, as we learned in this chapter. This approach adheres to the open-closed principle, which promotes extending functionality while keeping the original class intact. By applying this pattern, we learned that we can flexibly add or remove features to an object during the game, such as modifying player attributes, including movement speed, jump height, and attack strength when power-ups are collected.

We explored how the Decorator pattern works by wrapping a base object, in this case, the `Stats` class, with new behaviors through decorator objects. The decorators act as wrappers, allowing us to stack multiple power-ups and apply their effects in different combinations. For instance, when a player picks up a `Diamond` object that grants a speed boost, we can apply a `SpeedStatsDecorator` object to modify the player's speed. If the player collects multiple power-ups, these decorators stack, allowing us to increase the effects dynamically. We covered this in detail in this chapter.

A key challenge we addressed was managing the life cycle of these power-ups, particularly their duration and stacking effects. To handle this, we implemented a singleton based on the `PowerUps` class that tracks and manages active power-ups. The `PowerUpsSingleton` object ensures that buffs such as increased speed or invulnerability are applied and removed in an orderly fashion, preventing overlap and conflicts between multiple decorators. This system makes it easy to scale the power-up system and manage the player's attributes without burdening the game's core logic.

We also tackled some common pitfalls of the Decorator pattern, such as maintaining the integrity of the decorator stack and preventing recursive calls that could lead to stack overflow errors. By making each decorator unique to its respective instance, we ensured that the system behaves consistently without errors. The flexibility of the Decorator pattern also allowed us to experiment with various power-ups and debuffs, making it a highly versatile system for our game project.

As we finish this chapter, we have a solid foundation for implementing power-up systems in games using the Decorator pattern with the available features in Godot Engine. In the next chapter, we will create a cross-fade background music singleton that seamlessly cross-fades between the current and next background music track.

Get This Book's PDF Version and Exclusive Extras

Scan the QR code (or go to `packtpub.com/unlock`). Search for this book by name, confirm the edition, and then follow the steps on the page.

Note: Keep your invoice handy. Purchases made directly from Packt don't require an invoice.

12

Cross-Fading Transitions with the Service Locator Pattern

In games, many classes use a single class to perform common procedures. This is known as a service class. For instance, in Godot Engine, we have the `Input` class, a singleton that offers services related to input that any class can access. Another example is the `Engine` class, which provides data about the very engine itself to any class interested in knowing it; the `Engine` class is also a singleton. When we have singletons that provide services, especially if these services are provided through layers of indirection to other classes, we call them service locators. Well, this is not precisely what a service locator is, but it's a way of understanding its purpose.

In this chapter, we will implement a common case for implementing the Service Locator pattern: audio, specifically, music. There is no reason to implement multiple instances of a class that plays music. This is undesirable, as multiple songs overlapping each other is, usually, unpleasant. At the same time, music is an aspect of the game that changes all the time based on multiple events, so a variety of classes need to access this service. This is a good use case for the Service Locator pattern.

We will discuss the difference between the Service Locator pattern and its cousin, the Singleton pattern, by first understanding what the Service Locator pattern is and how it can be implemented. While the Singleton pattern is often used to implement the Service Locator pattern, the two are not exactly the same, and we'll explore why that's the case.

To make things less abstract and help us visualize the value proposition of the Service Locator pattern, we will see some common use cases that we can spot in games so we can have some scenarios to compare it and gain insights about its usefulness.

After that, we will implement it in our project by understanding our fictional game designer's request, pinpointing the core issues, and abstracting them to find potential solutions.

In this chapter, we will cover the following topics:

- Understanding the Service Locator pattern
- Spotting use cases for the Service Locator pattern
- Implementing the Service Locator pattern in Godot

Technical requirements

To follow along with this chapter, open the project files in the `12.cross-fading-with-service-locator/01.start/` folder. If you face any difficulties or come across errors or bugs while working through the *Implementing the Service Locator pattern in Godot* section, consult the files in the `12.cross-fading-with-service-locator/02.finished/` folder. Any issues can be reported on the repository's issue tracker via this link: `https://github.com/PacktPublishing/Game-Development-Patterns-with-Godot-4/issues`.

If you haven't downloaded the repository files yet, you can find them here: `https://github.com/PacktPublishing/Game-Development-Patterns-with-Godot-4`.

Let's start with exploring the essential concepts of the Service Locator pattern, including its purpose, features, and common use cases in Godot, ensuring we make full use of its built-in functions while adding our own custom touch to achieve the chapter's purpose.

Understanding the Service Locator pattern

The Service Locator pattern is a creational design pattern, similar to the Singleton pattern. It provides a centralized point of access where user classes can obtain services without being tightly coupled to the specific classes that implement those services. This allows for more flexibility and decoupling in the system's architecture.

For instance, instead of instancing `AudioStreamPlayer2D` nodes to play sound effects, a node could rely on a `SoundEffectService` class that would instantiate, play, and handle the life cycle of the `AudioStreamPlayer2D` node that would play the requested sound effect. This adds a layer of indirection between the user class and the concrete service class, effectively decoupling them.

By providing a centralized registry where any class can retrieve a given service, the Service Locator pattern allows for loose coupling between different components in the system. It's especially useful if you think about protecting your code base from external changes in an API. For instance, if Godot Engine changes the interface of the `AudioStreamPlayer2D` node instead of updating many classes, we would only have to change the implementation details of our sound effect's service locator class, maintaining its interface and its contract with other classes.

This approach is also interesting to remove common responsibilities from classes and centralize them into a single one. For instance, instead of each object in our game's code base knowing about the `AudioStreamPlayer2D.play()` method and the `AudioStreamPlayer.finished` signal to handle playing a sound effect and freeing the instance once the sound effect finishes playing, we can move this responsibility entirely to a service locator that would handle everything and would offer a simpler interface for user classes, encapsulating the implementation details about how the sound effect life cycle works, for instance.

One common discussion about the Service Locator pattern is in regard to how it differs from the Singleton pattern, as both centralize access to shared resources. However, they differ a lot when you understand their foundations, principles, and intent. While the Singleton pattern aims to provide a unique instance of a class to user classes, so that they all mutate the same object's state and are all aware of such state, the Service Locator pattern aims to provide a single point of access to a given service. Typically, the easiest way to do that is by using a singleton as such a point of access, but it can be a static class, or we can even achieve that through dependency injection, by injecting instances of a service locator on user classes. Note that, differently from the Singleton pattern, having a single instance of a service locator is not mandatory, as long as the class itself can be used as a centralized provider of a service.

For instance, the `Input` and `Engine` classes in Godot Engine are good examples of the Service Locator pattern implemented using the Singleton pattern. They offer specific services globally to any class interested in their services without having to pass references around. At the same time, different from a singleton, their state, especially the `Engine` instance, with very rare exceptions, is not meant to be mutated. In that sense, they just provide a service to user classes, and don't necessarily alter their state and don't necessarily need to know about their current state. To make it clearer, there is no reason why we need to mutate the `Input` class state if we use it as a hub to access the state of input methods.

On top of helping us with decoupling classes and centralizing services, the Service Locator pattern also helps us by simplifying tests and modularity. By centralizing services within a single class, we can test different implementation approaches and new behaviors to the system knowing that this won't affect other classes and that the `ServiceLocator` class itself will be the only class we will need to fix or update. This also allows us to make logging easier; for instance, if we want to create a custom monitor in Godot Engine to monitor how many sound effects we create throughout a play run, we can make it in a single place and remove it in a single place as well.

Now that you understand the differences between the Service Locator and the Singleton patterns, how we typically use the Service Locator pattern, and its value proposition, let's try to find some good use cases for it so that it becomes clear in our heads when it is applicable. In the next section, we will spot some common features in games that can benefit from implementing the Service Locator pattern.

Spotting use cases for the Service Locator pattern

As a versatile pattern, the Service Locator pattern can be implemented in many systems in our game. Since it is meant to be a centralized point of access to a given service, we can apply it to a variety of situations. Something we should keep in mind is that making many classes rely on a single instance of a class, like in the Singleton pattern, can be dangerous. For instance, if, for some reason, this instance is removed at some point, all the other instances of classes that depended on it will be broken. This is less likely to happen when we have multiple instances with short life cycles. Also, the fact that many user classes rely on a single class is a double-edged sword since if we decide to make a change to said class, we will break all its user classes. That said, in this section, we will explore common use cases for the Service Locator pattern in games.

Localization is an interesting system in games. We need to ensure that every element that needs to be localized will fetch its appropriate version upon loading the game and also update dynamically if the player decides to change the language settings while playing. This is a good use case for the Service Locator pattern; when a class initializes, it fetches its data, and in Godot Engine's case, this can be a `Resource` object, containing all the localized versions of its content, including image, text, and audio. In this example, `LocalizationService` could be the class providing the localized files to all other classes that could simply use a `LocalizationService.get_localized_resource()` method, passing a string or integer as an ID to get the specific resource for the requesting class.

As we saw previously, handling inputs is another good use case for the Service Locator pattern, as Godot Engine itself does that. But we could go a little bit further and make a class, maybe a singleton, that would be customized for our game. For instance, I do that to check for specific mouse events to check for gestures that are relevant to entities in my game. This allows me to create and emit signals and subscribe some entities to events such as `Gestures.swiped_left`, `Gestures.cricle_drawn`, and `Gestures.pinched_inwards`. In this case, the service of recognizing gestures is located by the `Gestures` locator, which uses the built-in `Input` singleton to detect when the player managed to draw a relevant gesture.

In many game engines, such as Godot and Unity, we have multiple game states that we typically call scenes. To transit between these scenes, we can make use of a Service Locator pattern to handle all the necessary steps that such transition needs, such as a loading screen or specific transition effects such as fade in and out. In Godot Engine, I used to implement that for my games as well: an `Autoload` node that uses a `CanvasLayer` node to play transitions and load the next scenes using `get_tree().change_scene_to_file()`.

Saving and loading game data is a fundamental feature to implement if we want to maintain the player's progression through game sessions. Usually, save files are populated with thousands of pieces of data about the game state that must be replicated once the player loads the game again. This is done by allowing objects to feed the saved files with relevant data, and for that, they need a central point of access that will perform the service of handling and managing the saved file, ultimately storing it in the player's disk. As you can imagine, this is yet another excellent use case for the Service Locator pattern.

Finally, and this is our hook, handling audio is stereotypically a good use case for the Service Locator pattern, especially when it is used to handle music. Playing multiple songs at the same time is usually not desired in games. But making transitions between songs is! For instance, if the player engages in battle, we can change the current background music to match the fast-paced battle. Or if the player enters an area where it's necessary to perform stealthy actions, we can change the music in runtime to adapt to that. Changing music to play the current level's theme is also common. And for all that, we use different parts and components of the game, but all of them need to use the same service to handle music transitions and management, thus a good opportunity for a service locator!

Now that you have had a glance at some concrete use cases for the Service Locator pattern, it's safe to assume that the concept is starting to take shape in your head, right? Well, fear not; if this isn't the case, with the next section, it will be! We will get yet another feature request from our game designer and we will understand how to implement the Service Locator pattern in our project to allow the game designer to make background music transitions that will allow the game to adapt its atmosphere to the feeling that the designer wants to convey using the proper music!

Implementing the Service Locator pattern in Godot Engine

The Service Locator pattern is a simple pattern conceptually, as we saw in this chapter. It essentially provides a wrapper class for common services in our game's code base, allowing user classes to decouple from repetitive procedures, delegating them to the Service Locator. To make it clear again, this pattern can be implemented in many ways: as a static class, as a dependency injected on the user class upon initialization, and as a globally accessible instance. In this section, we will take our fictional game designer's request and see the proper approach to solve their demand, and, based on that, we will use Godot Engine's built-in features to implement this useful pattern in our project. That said, let's take a look at the game designer's request.

"Hey hey!

It's your friend, the game designer!

You know, that power-up thing was amazing! It took me some time to understand that it's like one of those matryoshka dolls, or an onion, where we keep on adding layers of the same thing to stack properties. Pretty clever!

As I was playing with those diamonds, I figured that we are about to get into some world design, adding some multi-layered atmosphere to the game. I thought about that because I was playing with the Doors system and I made a secret room, to which I thought it would be cool to have a stealthy song playing as we enter it.

This led me to the realization that we don't have any background music yet! It's fundamental to create a living world for our game that we have themed music playing. Not only that, I think we will need to have multiple pieces of music playing based on different situations in our game: when players engage in combat with a boss enemy, when players enter a secret room, when players reach specific areas of a level such as the end of the level, even different kinds of music depending on the very level itself; each level needs its own theme, and each screen needs its own screen as well!

But we can't just make music play out of nowhere; since we will be changing music a lot based on different situations, we will need a system that makes smooth transitions between these songs. Something like a cross-fade, you know? Where the current music slowly fades out and the next song fades in.

Yeah, that sounds great!

That's it, but I need that to happen in the simplest way possible, because if I have to manually animate these transitions on each place where we will change the background music…it will be troublesome if I decide to change how that works.

Let's do it! We are close to having a functional prototype to promote some playtest sessions!

Thanks, yours truly."

Isn't it cute how the game designer is always pushing the project to new milestones with new features? That matryoshka doll analogy for the Decorator pattern was very cool by the way. But let's focus on the current request.

Our game designer needs a system that they can use to make some kind of cross-fading between current and newer songs. Well, if the request was just about playing background music, we would already have this done by using an `AudioStreamPlayer` singleton. In this case, it needs to be a singleton due to the cleanup that Godot Engine does when we load new scenes. We talk about that in *Chapter 5*.

However, the requested feature is more complex than simply playing songs. It also needs to fade them in and out. On top of that, many parts of our code base will need to perform such a procedure, which is a typical example of a service. Well, at this point, it's not a secret that the Service Locator will be the solution to this demand. But before we dive into action, there are some things we should understand about this pattern so we are mindful when using it.

Besides being one of the simplest design patterns around, it can be tricky to use the Service Locator correctly. Being able to have the discernment about when to use it and when to simply turn a service into a component and use dependency injection to supply such service to user classes, for example, is key to preventing abusing this pattern.

One significant drawback of the Service Locator pattern is that it often performs operations that can interfere with instance creation and the management of instance references, potentially leading to issues with instancing and storing object references correctly. If we are not cautious with how we play with that, a user class may reference an instance that got freed from memory for some reason, ultimately breaking our code. This is due to the typical Service Locator's life cycle, as it is always available and locates services on demand.

Because the Service Locator is a creational pattern that takes out the responsibility of handling dependencies on user classes, we also need to be aware of the fact that we are coupling these user classes to the Service Locator itself, making it a dynamic dependency that will need to be available everywhere together with its user classes, this includes other projects. So we should always be careful about that; this is also true of the Singleton pattern. This is why people usually advocate for dependency injection over the Service Locator.

So why are we going to use it here? Because the specific scenario of playing music, where multiple classes can modify the currently playing track, is an ideal case for applying this pattern, as it presents minimal drawbacks. That said, in the following sections, we will implement our `BackgroundMusic` service locator to allow anything in our code base to fade in new songs on our project.

Creating the BackgroundMusic Service Locator

At this point, we already understand that a Service Locator is nothing but a centralized service provider. Some people go to extremes making a single monolithic service locator class with a variety of services: UI animation, saving and loading settings, game state management, achievement management, and so on. Instead, I recommend you create a Service Locator for every service you want to provide to your code base. This way, porting it and maintaining it gets simpler.

In this section, we will create a service locator singleton that handles music transitions, fading out the current song, and fading in the next song. For that, let's follow these steps:

1.   Create a new scene using `Node` as the root node and rename it `BackgroundMusic`.

2.   Save the scene as `res://Game/BackgroundMusic/BackgroundMusic.tscn`.

3.   Add a new `AudioStreamPlayer` node as a child of the `BackgroundMusic` node.

4.   Toggle on the `AudioStreamPlayer` node's **Autoplay** property so it starts playing as soon as we enter the game.

5.   Then, as the default music, let's pick the `res://Assets/Juhani Junkala [Chiptune Adventures] OGG/Juhani Junkala [Chiptune Adventures] 1. Stage 1.ogg` file.

6.   Since the music will be pretty loud by default, let's change the **Volume dB** property of `AudioStreamPlayer` to `-18 dB`. The `AudioStreamPlayer` node settings should be as follows:

Figure 12.1 – The AudioStreamPlayer node properties in the Inspector

7. Attach a script to the `BackgroundMusic` node and save it as `res://Game/` `BackgroundMusic/BackgroundMusicLocator.gd`.

8. Then, in the script we just created, let's start by exporting a variable that will represent the fading time between the current song and the next song with the default value of 0.3 seconds:

```
extends Node
class_name BackgroundMusicLocator

@export var fade_time := 0.3
```

9. After that, we will create a variable to store the current `AudioStreamPlayer` instance playing a song. As a starter, it will take the `AudioStreamPlayer` node we created in the scene, but after playing a new song, this will change to the most recently created `AudioStreamPlayer` instance instead:

```
extends Node
class_name BackgroundMusicLocator

@export var fade_time := 0.3
@onready var current_player:
  AudioStreamPlayer = $AudioStreamPlayer
```

10. The major feature of this class is its capability of playing cross-fading songs. This is something it will do automatically, so user classes only need to pass the `AudioStream` resource and, optionally, a custom fade time to get what they need from this service. To do that, we will create a method called `play()` that asks for `AudioStream` as an argument, and it will also accept a custom fade time, but by default, it will use the `fade_time` property:

```
func play(new_song: AudioStream,
  _fade_time: = fade_time) -> void:
```

11. Inside this method, we will create a new `AudioStreamPlayer` and configure its `stream` property to be the new song, set its volume down to just 10 percent using the `linear_to_db()` built-in method, add it as a child of the `BackgroundMusic` node, and play the current song by setting its `playing` property to `true`:

```
func play(new_song: AudioStream,
  _fade_time: = fade_time) -> void:
    var new_player := AudioStreamPlayer.new()
    new_player.stream = new_song
    new_player.volume_db = linear_to_db(0.1)
    add_child(new_player)
    new_player.playing = true
```

12. Then, we will seek the position of the current playing song, so the songs don't keep on restarting every time we play them. This will try to help with variety and prevent repetition when fading songs, especially when fading back to the previous song when necessary:

```
func play(new_song: AudioStream,
  _fade_time: = fade_time) -> void:
    var new_player := AudioStreamPlayer.new()
    new_player.stream = new_song
    new_player.volume_db = linear_to_db(0.1)
    add_child(new_player)
    new_player.playing = true
    new_player.seek(current_player
       .get_playback_position())
```

13. At this point, we have two songs playing, which is not desirable. So we need to fade out the volume of the currently playing song and fade in the newly created `AudioStreamPlayer`. For that, we will create a new *Tween* using the `get_tree().create_tween()` method. We will also store the volume of the current playing song to maintain the overall volume of the songs:

```
var target_volume = current_player.volume_db
var tween := get_tree().create_tween()
```

14. Then, we will call the `Tween.tween_property()` method on `AudioStreamPlayer` but on `current_player`, we will tween it down to `0.0` using the `linear_to_db()` built-in method and the `_fade_time` argument:

```
var target_volume = current_player.volume_db
var tween := get_tree().create_tween()
tween.tween_property(current_player,
  "volume_db", linear_to_db(0.0), _fade_time)
tween.tween_property(new_player, "volume_db",
  target_volume, _fade_time)
```

15. Since the old `AudioStreamPlayer` is essentially muted after this tween is finished, we will wait for the `Tween.finished` signal to be emitted and remove the old `AudioStreamPlayer` from `SceneTree`. After that, we inject the new `AudioStreamPlayer` in the `current_player` variable so it now becomes the current `AudioStreamPlayer` waiting for the next cycle of cross-fading songs. The complete `play()` method implementation will be as follows:

```
await tween.finished
current_player.queue_free()
current_player = new_player
```

The complete `BackgroundMusicLocator` class will be as follows:

```
extends Node
class_name BackgroundMusicLocator

@export var fade_time := 0.3
@onready var current_player:
  AudioStreamPlayer = $AudioStreamPlayer

func play(new_song: AudioStream,
  _fade_time: = fade_time) -> void:
    var new_player := AudioStreamPlayer.new()
    new_player.stream = new_song
    new_player.volume_db = linear_to_db(0.1)
    add_child(new_player)
    new_player.playing = true
    new_player.seek(current_player
      .get_playback_position())

    var target_volume = current_player.volume_db
    var tween := get_tree().create_tween()
    tween.tween_property(current_player,
      "volume_db", linear_to_db(0.0), _fade_time)
    tween.tween_property(new_player, "volume_db",
      target_volume, _fade_time)
```

```
await tween.finished
current_player.queue_free()
current_player = new_player
```

With this done and ready, we now need to make this service available globally so other classes can take advantage of what we just implemented. For that, we will turn this scene into **Autoload** called `BackgroundMusic`, as shown in the following figure:

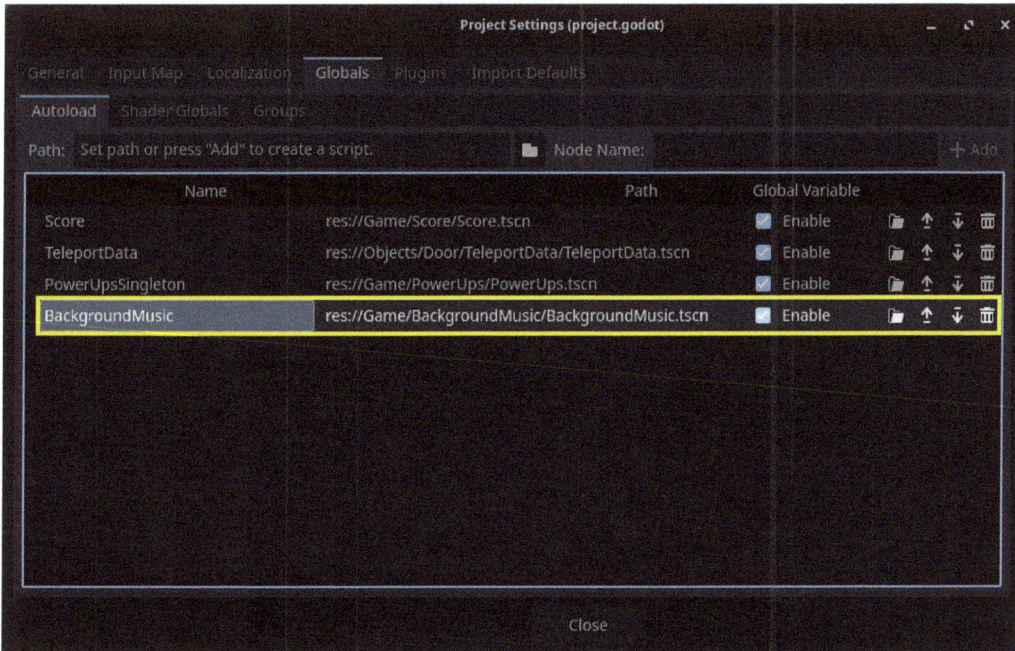

Figure 12.2 – Autoload highlighting the newest created BackgroundMusic autoload

With that, we effectively made our class globally available, like a singleton. Here's a good place to mention a core difference between the Singleton pattern and the Service Locator pattern, now that you understand what a service is. In *Chapter 5*, we implemented the Singleton pattern to be able to maintain the global states of one specific system of our game per singleton. They were used as a bridge between classes so that they all had access to consistent data that needed to be carried and available to user classes of the same domain, for instance, the score-related classes. But the singleton itself (in this case, the `Score` singleton) didn't provide a general commonly used service; it was specific to the score-related classes of our code base.

The Service Locator pattern, on the other hand, can spread its influence all over our code base as it provides a centralized hub of commonly used services to many unrelated classes. This will become clear as we move on to the next section where we are going to use the `BackgroundMusic` service locator on multiple classes on our code base.

Using the BackgroundMusic Service Locator

Now that we have a service located, it's time to use it! In this section, we will make use of the BackgroundMusic service locator to change the song playing in the background depending on a variety of situations in our game. Let's start from the beginning! The MainMenu scene is the first thing the player will face when playing our game. Let's get started with the steps:

1. Open the res://Screens/MainMenu/MainMenu.tscn scene and open the script attached to the root node. Then, add an exported variable of the AudioStream type so we can pick a new song for MainMenu. Then, in the _ready() callback, call the BackgroundMusic.play() method passing the exported variable we just created:

    ```
    extends Control

    const CONTROL_SETTINGS_FILE_PATH =
      "user://control_settings.json"

    @export_file("*.tscn") var start_scene_path =
      "res://Levels/Level1.tscn"
    @export_file("*.tscn") var controls_scene_path =
      "res://Interface/InputRemap/InputRemap.tscn"

    @export var background_music: AudioStream

    func _ready():
        $VBoxContainer/StartButton.grab_focus()
        load_input_map()

        BackgroundMusic.play(background_music)
    ```

2. Then, drag and drop a piece of cool music to the **Background Music** property on the **Inspector** panel. You can find a variety of songs in the res://Assets/ folder. I'm going to use res://Assets/Juhani Junkala [Chiptune Adventures] OGG/Juhani Junkala [Chiptune Adventures] 1. Stage 1.ogg for MainMenu. The following figure showcases the new property in the **Inspector** panel with the song properly set:

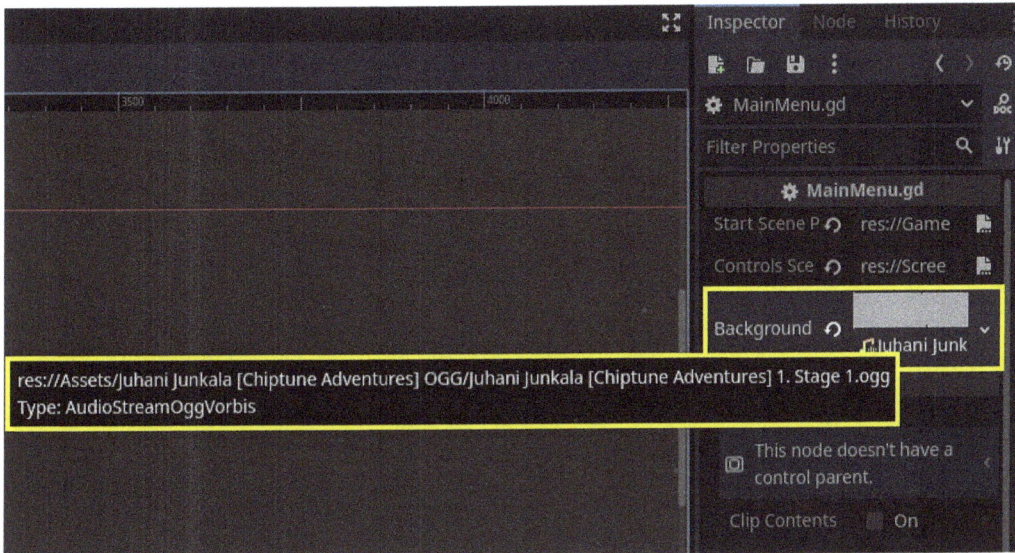

Figure 12.3 – The MainMenu scene's Background Music property populated with an AudioStream file

3. We can do the exact same thing on the `res://Screens/InputRemap/InputRemap.tscn` scene, but, of course, using a different song. I used `res://Assets/Juhani Junkala [Chiptune Adventures] OGG/Juhani Junkala [Chiptune Adventures] 4. Stage Select.ogg` for this one. The changes in the script are as follows:

```
extends Control

const CONTROL_SETTINGS_FILE_PATH =
    "user://control_settings.json"

@export var background_music: AudioStream

@onready var fade :=
    $CanvasLayer/ColorRect/AnimationPlayer

func _ready():
    find_child("RemapButton").grab_focus()
    fade.play("fade_in")

    BackgroundMusic.play(background_music)
```

4. Next up, we can also do that to the `Level` class, as requested by the game designer, since each level will have its own theme. Repeat the process and set a default song on the `res://Levels/Level.tscn` scene. Since each level will have its own theme, we can change that using the **Inspector** panel later on. The changes in the `Level` class script will be as follows:

```
class_name Level
extends Node2D


@export var background_music: AudioStream

@onready var player = $PlayerCharacter2D
@onready var fade =
  $CanvasLayer/ColorRect/AnimationPlayer

func _ready():
    player.global_position = find_child(TeleportData
      .target_portal_name).global_position
    player.fade_in()
    fade.play("fade_in")


    BackgroundMusic.play(background_music)
```

Now, something the game designer also asked for is some way to change the background music on specific areas of the levels. For that, we can create a new `Area2D` node that will be responsible for creating an atmosphere in specific parts of the level. We can call it `AmbienceArea2D` and all it is going to do on top of carrying an `AudioStream` node is carry a reference to the previously playing song so that when players leave it, the previous song that was playing before the players entered the area will play again. Well, for that, let's do the following:

1. Create a new scene using an `Area2D` node as the root node and rename it `AmbienceArea2D`.

2. Save the scene as `res://Areas/AmbienceArea2D.tscn`. We put it inside the `res://Areas/` folder because it is going to be used on areas inside a level.

3. `AmbienceArea2D` is supposed to only interact with the player's `InteractionArea2D`, node so we will change its **Collision Layer** and **Mask** properties so it only looks for collisions in the **Interaction** physics layer:

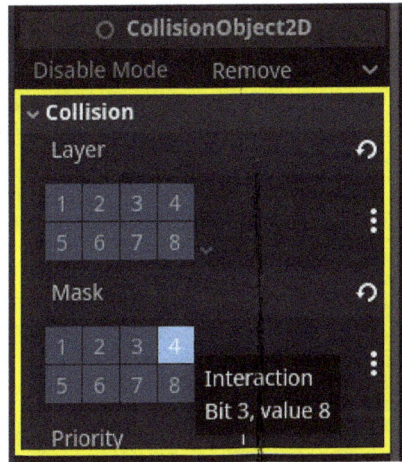

Figure 12.4 – AmbienceArea2D's Collision settings with no layers
and only the fourth bit of Mask toggled on

4. Then, attach a new script to the `AmbienceArea2D` node and save it as `res://Areas/AmbienceArea2D.gd`.

5. In the script, we will export a variable to hold the song that should be played once the player enters `AmbienceArea2D`:

```
extends Area2D
class_name AmbienceArea2D


@export var background_music: AudioStream
```

6. We will also create a variable to store a reference to the previous song that was playing before the player entered the area:

```
extends Area2D
class_name AmbienceArea2D


@export var background_music: AudioStream


var previous_background_music: AudioStream
```

7. Then, we will use the editor to connect its `area_entered` and `area_exited` signals' respective callbacks in the `AmbienceArea2D` script:

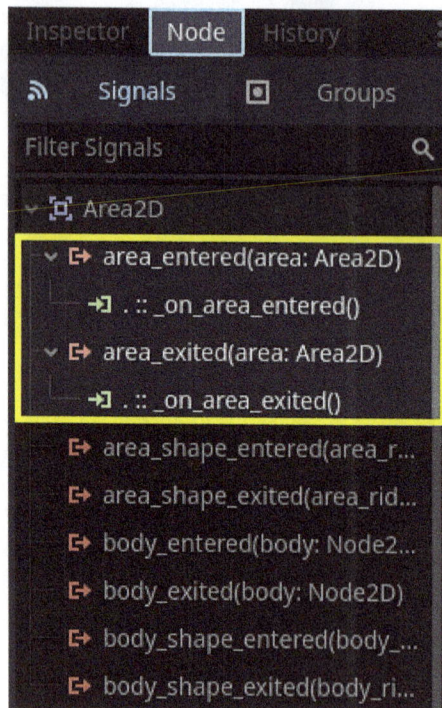

Figure 12.5 – The AmbienceArea2D signals connected to their respective callbacks

8. Back to the script; in the `_on_area_entered()` callback, we will store the currently playing `AudioStream` node in `previous_background_music` and then play the new song passing the `background_music` variable as an argument in the `play()` method of `BackgroundMusic`:

```
func _on_area_entered(area: Area2D) -> void:
    previous_background_music =
        BackgroundMusic.current_player.stream
    BackgroundMusic.play(background_music)
```

9. As for the `_on_area_exited()` callback, we will call `BackgroundMusic`'s `play()` method, passing `previous_background_music` instead, effectively playing the previous song once the player leaves the area:

```
func _on_area_exited(area: Area2D) -> void:
    BackgroundMusic.play(previous_background_music)
```

And that's it! Now, we can use different songs once players enter specific areas in our game's levels! If you are curious about how we can use that, check out the `res://Levels/Level1/Level1.tscn` scene where we have multiple `AmbienceArea2D` instances spread around the level setting different moods depending on what we want to convey.

With that, we have multiple user classes all around our code base using the cross-fading background music service we just created. We will now have to be cautious about how we maintain that throughout the further development of our project! That said, let's see what we learned in this important advanced project!

Summary

In this chapter, we learned how to implement cross-fading transitions in background music using the Service Locator pattern in Godot Engine. The Service Locator pattern is useful when we need to centralize access to services in a way that decouples user classes from the specific implementations of those services. We explored how the pattern provides a centralized access point to shared services, making it easier for various parts of the game to perform operations such as playing or managing background music without directly interacting with the underlying `AudioStreamPlayer` nodes.

The core of this chapter focused on creating a system that can handle smooth transitions between background music tracks, a feature often needed in games to adapt the atmosphere based on gameplay events. We began by designing a service locator class, `BackgroundMusicLocator`, which was responsible for managing cross-fade transitions. This class dynamically controlled the `AudioStreamPlayer` nodes, fading out the currently playing track while fading in the next one, ensuring a smooth transition without sudden interruptions or overlapping sounds. The implementation also handled music positioning, ensuring the new track continued seamlessly from where the previous one left off.

We explored how the Service Locator pattern simplifies code by removing repetitive tasks from user classes, allowing them to rely on a central service for playing and managing music. This decoupling allows user classes to call simple methods to handle music transitions without worrying about the underlying details of the management of `AudioStreamPlayer`. On top of that, the Service Locator offers flexibility for future changes, as updating the music transition logic only requires changes in one place, making it easier to maintain.

We also saw how we could implement specific cases where the service locator was used, such as transitioning music in different areas of the game, including the main menu, individual levels, and special locations within levels. For that, we created ambient zones with the `AmbienceArea2D` custom node, where background music would change dynamically depending on the player's location in the game world. This added a new layer of interactivity and immersion, as music transitions helped convey different moods and gameplay situations.

In the next chapter, we will explore how to enhance the game's overall feel. We will implement a system Event Queue pattern to store a temporary history of keystrokes, allowing for features such as input buffering. This system will enable players to execute buffered jumps and other actions more smoothly, preventing frustration if they press a key too early before an action gets registered.

Get This Book's PDF Version and Exclusive Extras

UNLOCK NOW

Scan the QR code (or go to packtpub.com/unlock). Search for this book by name, confirm the edition, and then follow the steps on the page.

Note: Keep your invoice handy. Purchases made directly from Packt don't require an invoice.

13
Improving Game Feel with the Event Queue Pattern

One fundamental aspect of a platformer game is the player's movement. It is through this feature that players can explore the game's world and maneuver through the game's obstacles, which is exactly what a platformer game does.

Games under the action genre, like platformer games, are all about the player's ability to deal with time, especially their reaction time and hand-eye coordination. Precisely reacting to events in the game world is fundamental in this genre and subgenres, but it is tricky to get it right.

Good game design isn't about punishing players for not following our design exactly. Instead, it's about making them feel that they are making progress so that if they do something we strongly discourage, we can apply appropriate consequences without it feeling unfair. In game design, this is called forgiving design, where we offer many mechanisms for the player's mistakes to help them get into the real challenges.

You've probably already heard of the famous coyote jump, also known as coyote time, right? Where a player can still perform a jump after just leaving the edge of a cliff. It's inspired by that cartoonesque moment where Wile E. Coyote from the Looney Tunes series chases Road Runner. At some point, the character blindly runs off a cliff and floats for a moment until he realizes he is about to fall, and only then does he fall. Based on that, many game designers implement what is known as coyote jump, where, after falling from a cliff, the player has a very brief moment to still perform a jump. This helps players reach further ground and pass through some challenges that were, ideally, meant to be done by forcing the player to jump from the very limit of the cliff.

Forgiving design takes the perspective that players are not expected to be perfect but rather it's expected that they stay within a tolerance window. This boosts the game feel by allowing a greater range of actions by the player that will still lead them to success even if they don't do exactly what the designers planned.

In this chapter, we will learn how to use the Event Queue pattern to create an input buffer that will allow us to implement yet another forgiving design feature, known as jump buffering, to allow players to compensate for small anticipations in their jumps and even compensate for some input lagging.

We are going to cover the following topics in this chapter:

- Understanding the Event Queue pattern
- Spotting use cases for the Event Queue pattern
- Implementing the Event Queue pattern in Godot

Technical requirements

To follow this chapter, access the project files in the `13.improving-game-feel-with-event-queue/01.start/` folder. If you encounter any confusion, bugs, or errors while working through the *Implementing the Event Queue pattern in Godot* section, refer to the files in the `13.improving-game-feel-with-event-queue/02.finished/` folder. Any issues can be reported using the issue tracker at `https://github.com/PacktPublishing/Game-Development-Patterns-with-Godot-4/issues`.

If you haven't downloaded the repository files yet, you can get them here: `https://github.com/PacktPublishing/Game-Development-Patterns-with-Godot-4`.

We'll start with exploring the key principles of the Event Queue pattern, including how it works, its advantages, and how to effectively implement it in Godot to enhance game feel and responsiveness.

Understanding the Event Queue pattern

In most applications, it's a common practice to abstract special "happenings" in the form of events. For instance, when the player presses keys, when the game loop updates, when a button is pressed, when a character reaches critical health, when the player talks to a non-playable character, when the player loots an item, when the player defeats an enemy, and so on. We saw in *Chapter 6* that we can trigger these events as signals, and this is one of the most common approaches. It even leads to what is known as the Event Bus pattern, another design pattern that uses a singleton to host signals that other classes can emit. It's a mix of the Singleton and the Observer pattern for event-driven architectures.

But emitting notifications, or signals, is not enough. Sometimes we need to store these events so we can handle them later on. The Event Queue pattern is made exactly for that. I decided to put this pattern in the *Advanced Patterns* part of this book due to its level of versatility. The pattern itself is very simple; you create an array and store instances of events inside of it. An event can be anything, as demonstrated in the previous paragraph.

It's up to us to decide the relevant data that we want to store on each event. One good example of an event system is Godot's InputEvent class and subclasses. Since they are meant to represent input events, there is essentially one main piece of information: the device that emitted the event. When we get into subclasses, things get more interesting. For instance, InputEventKey provides information about whether the input event is about the pressing or releasing of a key, which key it relates to, and even whether it was pressed with other modifier keys, such as *SHIFT* or *CTRL*.

By implementing an event queue in our system, we are able to decouple these events' creation from their handling. This is crucial in complex systems, especially in games, where various subsystems generate and respond to events such as user inputs, physics interactions, AI decisions, and rendering. The event queue not only decouples the events from the classes and systems where the event happened, but it also decouples them from the time these events happened, allowing us to do all sorts of manipulations on the chain of events if we need to.

Imagine that you are making a **Tactical Role-Playing Game** (**TRPG**) and in the game's combat system, players can create a queue of actions that will resolve at the end of the turn, after all actors in the game have also made their action queues. Now, one of the actor's skills is to randomize the final action queue before it resolves. This can easily be solved with an event queue, Players would insert their actions in the action queue that would be resolved at the end. We check for the presence of any special actions that need to be resolved in a special order and execute them. In this case, the other actions should be shuffled before resolving them at the end of the turn. See? We decoupled the time when the player performed an action from the action execution itself and even decoupled the very order in which the events happened.

We can also do the opposite of that by ensuring that events happen in a specific order. For instance, it's common to use the event queue to correctly process internal engine events, such as physics collisions, rendering, input handling, and sound playing. This way, we can order the correct sequence of events, ensuring that we don't play a sound on the next frame if the collision that generated it happens in this frame. In that example, we would store and sort physics events first, ensuring that they would be processed before audio events.

The Event Queue pattern is so common and powerful that it even originated its very own programming paradigm, known as event-driven architecture, which essentially allows us to create systems that transmit events through loosely coupled components. This is not a common architecture to create whole games, but can be useful for specific systems of a game. This is because games are hard to abstract as a definite sequence of events due to games' intrinsic dynamic and emergent nature. We never know what players will do, so we can't abstract games as a chain of predictable events, with an immutable chain of cause and effect.

A core advantage of using an event queue in games is that it capitalizes on the speed of event processing. In many cases, games don't handle events at the precise moment they occur, allowing the queue to efficiently manage and process them in quick succession.

So, the Event Queue pattern allows us to handle these events asynchronously. For instance, in action games, the player may rapidly press buttons to perform multiple actions in quick succession. Without an event queue, the game could miss some inputs or process them out of order, leading to a frustrating player experience. The event queue allows these inputs to be stored and processed in sequence, ensuring that each action is handled as expected, even if there's a delay between input and processing. We are going to see exactly that in our game, so keep that in mind.

This pattern is not called a "queue" for no reason. The idea is that as soon as an event gets processed, it is removed from the queue, typically in first-in, first-out order. This is important because if we have a one-to-many system where multiple objects handle events from the same queue, each time an event is handled, the next object should handle the next event in the queue, ensuring that an event is not handled twice.

Something interesting about decoupling events from the time they happen is that we can also set an expiration time for them. This allows us to create a range of interesting game mechanics. This prevents old, irrelevant events from being processed later, maintaining a sense of responsiveness in the game. Expiring events help keep the event queue manageable and ensure that only recent and relevant inputs are processed, which is especially useful for online gaming experiences. We don't need to process that a player walked left 0.2 milliseconds ago if the player got killed already. Yeah, lag sucks.

Now that you, hopefully, understand how the Event Queue pattern works and its benefits in decoupling systems and handling events asynchronously, it's time to dive into some real-world examples. In the next section, we'll explore some use cases where this pattern is applied in game development. From managing player input buffers to synchronizing complex AI systems, these examples will showcase how the Event Queue pattern can streamline event handling and improve both gameplay experience and development efficiency.

Spotting use cases for the Event Queue pattern

As we saw in the previous section, there are numerous examples of the Event Queue pattern in game systems. Since it is a versatile pattern that allows us to create abstract queues of events, where events can be anything in our game, the usage of this pattern becomes clouded by its potential. In this section, we will see some concrete use cases so things become clearer for us. Maybe one of the following examples is exactly what you are looking for in your next project!

The Event Queue pattern plays a core role in games like turn-based strategy titles by making sure that turn resolution happens in a predictable order. When players in a strategy games issue commands such as moving units or attacking, these actions trigger a series of events such as animations and sub-events that occur as a consequence of these main actions. This provides a clear structure for players' strategies, allowing the game to resolve each event step by step, from animations to game state updates, maintaining the pace of their turn system.

Figure 13.1 – XCOM 2 player plotting their strategy during their turn.
Image taken from RabidRetrospectGames YouTube channel. Link:
`https://www.youtube.com/watch?v=wVHO_0PS36A`

Similarly, the combat action queue in real-time RPGs allows for fluid combat by queuing up player and enemy actions based on parameters such as speed or priority. In games such as *Final Fantasy XII* or *Dragon Age: Origins*, both players and AI characters engage in combat by selecting abilities, techniques, magic spells, and other actions, which are placed into a queue, sorted, and processed in sequence. This makes combat remain fluid while maintaining a sense of order, as characters' actions unfold in a way that respects their speed and attack timing. This queue system also allows players to issue commands while other actions are still being resolved, which improves the pacing of combat, especially in real-time systems where immediate reaction may not be feasible.

Figure 13.2 – Final Fantasy XII's combat with members of the player's party queueing their actions for execution based on their speed. Image taken from 30 Something Gaming's YouTube channel. Link: `https://youtu.be/Eq_1LSDDGpg?si=ALDBp7Ui89JNI0qH`

In crafting systems, especially those featuring conveyor belts, the Event Queue pattern can be a good approach to resolve the crafting logic. In *Rogue Galaxy*, players manage a factory where items are crafted by assembling various components, with conveyor belts transporting materials between machines. As items are produced, their progress is queued for subsequent crafting steps. In the same way, *Factorio* showcases this pattern on a grand scale, as players build extensive factory systems using conveyor belts to automate the gathering and processing of resources. Events are queued in such systems as resources arrive at different machines, at different times. The management of these queues and the timing of production steps are fundamental to implementing this kind of crafting system.

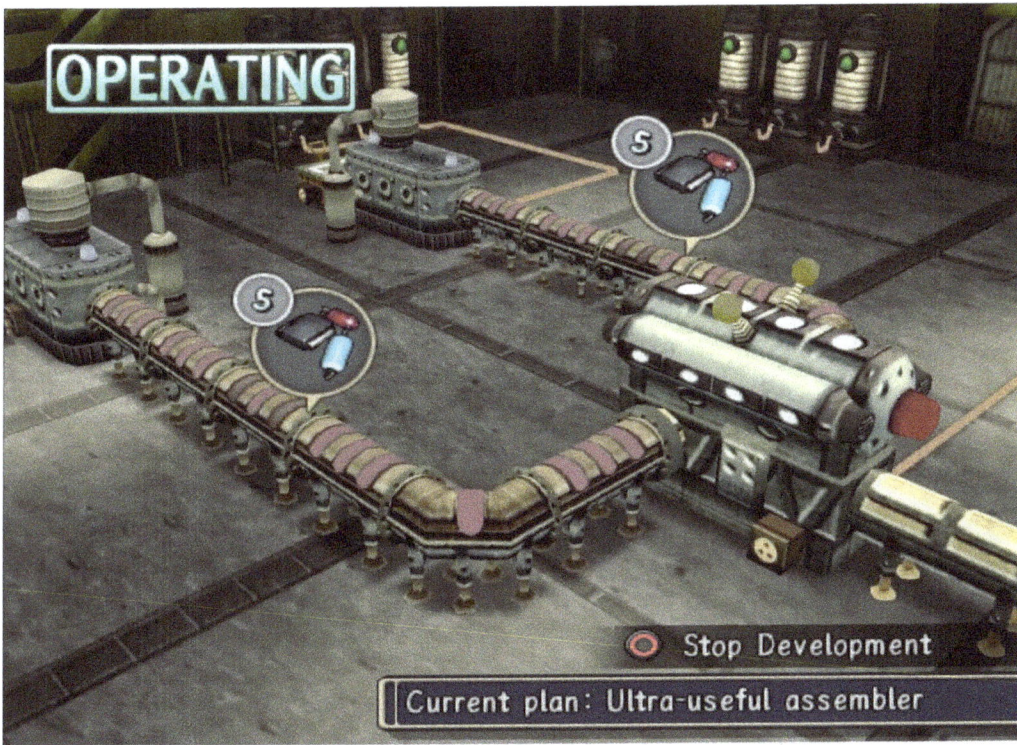

Figure 13.3 – Rogue Galaxy's Factory system with two ingredients being processed before getting combined in the assembly line. Image taken from VideoWulff's YouTube channel.
Link: `https://youtu.be/sfvdLaTXXD4?si=q5MtwsdxvM2Nqcp_`

Finally, input buffering in fighting games allows for the execution of complex combos by queueing up input events and processing them in the correct order, even when inputs are given in quick succession. In titles such as *Street Fighter* or *Naruto Shippuden Ultimate Ninja Storm Revolution*, the Event Queue pattern allows players to input a series of moves that the game will process as the character finishes each animation. This prevents missed inputs and ensures that combos execute fluidly, even when timing is tight. Input buffering also allows us to execute special moves, such as casting a special skill like *Hadouken* where multiple buttons need to be pressed in a specific sequence. With an input buffer, we can check for a specific sequence of inputs within an input event queue and cast special moves accordingly. In these cases, the event queue would also implement an expiration time to prevent undesired processing of inputs as special moves.

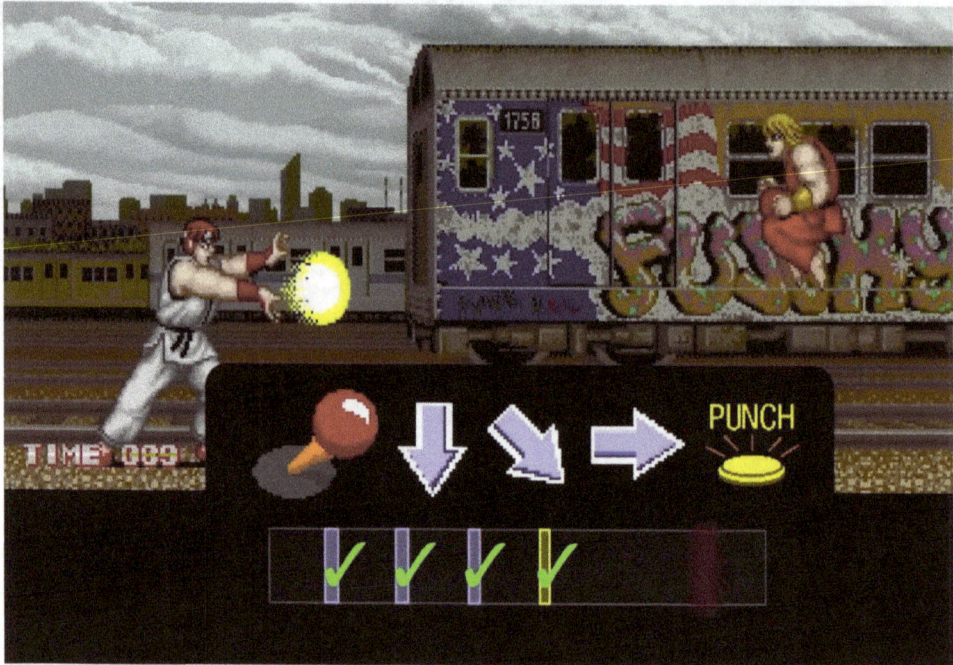

Figure 13.4 – Street Fighter's tutorial teaching players the input combination to cast a Hadouken. Image taken from Core-A Gaming's YouTube channel. Link: `https://youtu.be/b4Kc1p6Iat8?si=tRDhEGBPED1i_5U6`

In the next section, we'll implement an input buffer that can be used for a jump buffer, giving players a brief window of time before they hit the ground to input a jump, improving our game feel!

Implementing the Event Queue pattern in Godot

As you can see, the Event Queue pattern is a powerful tool to have in our hands. We can use it in many systems of a game, both locally and globally. For instance, we can create an event queue singleton to hold events that multiple other classes would process. Or we can create an event queue to handle local events, such as the character's next animation in a combo.

Note that, ideally, anything can be abstracted as an event. It will depend on your context. This means that we could create something like an `Event` class with relevant properties, or be more specific and create a `MovementEvent` class that would create objects that represent the character's movement such as if the character jumped, moved left, moved right, stopped, or grabbed something. You could be even more specific. For instance, in the `GrabbedObjectEvent` class, we could store a reference for the object that was grabbed. In these cases, we could create a `MovementEventQueue` class that would store these movements in case, for instance, we want to replay them.

In this section, we will rely on Godot Engine's built-in input system, which provides `InputEvent` objects with information about events related to all sorts of inputs. In our case, we are specifically interested in `InputEventKey` objects. We are going to store and process them to check whether the player pressed the jump button moments before landing. In our current implementation, a jump can only happen if the player's character is currently in contact with the floor. But our game designer has an interesting request for us that makes this implementation not ideal. Let's see the game designer's thoughts about it

Ahm, hey!

I was making some playtests lately with our player character, the King Pig. See, recently we've been making some improvements to make the game more action-oriented, right?

One of the things I noticed that can be annoying for the player's experience is the fact that we are demanding a lot of accuracy from them, which makes the game unforgiving of players' minor mistakes. These mistakes are not relevant to the game experience, so I thought about being less demanding.

One of the things I noticed that could improve the game feel a lot is implementing a jump buffer for when players miss the timing of a jump. Currently, our game is mostly set on the floor and we don't have many acrobatic sessions. For instance, I want to make some moving platforms action puzzles where players will need to quickly jump from one platform to another.

During one of the tests for the design of such puzzles, I realized I was missing the jump not because I didn't press the jump button, but because I pressed it too many times…before landing on the floor.

For an action-based game, it's better that the player presses the action many times before necessary than to press it only once when necessary. We are going towards a game with a high actions-per-second count and accuracy is not a big deal. We want players to press the attack and jump buttons a lot, even though the game won't immediately process every action. But it will be as soon as possible! That's the thing.

So I need you to implement a way to keep those actions stored for a brief moment before we process them in the game. Can you do it?

From yours truly,

Fictional Game Designer

In this request, two main concerns from our beloved game designer take the spotlight. The first thing is that the game designer wants to specifically store the player's input events. We can be even more specific and say that they want to store when the player presses the jump and the attack buttons. The reason for that is so that these input events can be processed later on, when the time is right. The second interesting thing is that they don't want to keep these events stored for long as this would cause the player's character to perform actions at a time that may not be convenient for the player. This indicates an expiration period for these actions.

Well, implementing the Event Queue pattern with a timer to pop events on a timely basis sounds like the perfect solution for that! In the following sections, you will see that the pattern itself is simple, but how we use it and other features that we will aggregate to it can be more thoughtful. In the next section, we will implement our very own input buffer following the requirements from the game designer!

Storing input events with an input buffer

With the overall abstraction of the problem, we understand that the game designer's request demands that we implement something like a custom Event Queue pattern that stores input-related events. Fortunately, in Godot Engine, we already have an input event system in place, so we can take advantage of that. In this section, we will implement an input buffer, an object that stores and processes a queue of input events. Let's get started! Open the project inside the `13.improving-game-feel-with-event-queue/01.start/` folder and let's go through the following instructions:

1. Create a new scene, and add `Node` as its root node. Rename it as `InputBuffer`.

2. Add a `Timer` node as an `InputBuffer` child.

3. Save the scene as `res://Actors/KingPig/InputBuffer.tscn` as this will be used specifically by the `KingPigPlayer2D` class, so we will store it inside the same folder.

4. Attach a new script to the `InputBuffer` node and save it as `res://Actors/KingPig/InputBuffer.gd`.

5. Open the script and let's start by exporting a variable that we will use to represent the expiration time in which each event will be stored:

    ```
    extends Node
    class_name InputBuffer


    @export var expiration_time := 0.1
    ```

6. Then, let's store a reference to the `Timer` node so we can use it when an action is stored:

    ```
    extends Node
    class_name InputBuffer

    @export var expiration_time := 0.1

    @onready var timer := $Timer
    ```

7. Now, it's finally time. The waiting is over. All that build-up has come to a climax. We will implement the Event Queue pattern! For that, create a variable that is of type *Array* and is a typed array. It will only store `InputEvent` objects:

```
extends Node
class_name InputBuffer

@export var expiration_time := 0.1

@onready var timer := $Timer

var event_queue: Array[InputEvent] = []
```

8. To store `InputEvent` objects in our event queue, we will override the `_unhandled_input()` callback method. Inside this method, we will first check if the current event being handled isn't an `InputEventKey` object. We don't want to store every type of `InputEvent` object; we are only interested in keys pressing and releasing. So, if we are dealing with anything other than an `InputEventKey` object, we return from the function:

```
func _unhandled_input(event: InputEvent) -> void:
    if not event is InputEventKey:
        return
```

9. We also don't want to store multiple instances of the same event if it's just an echo. An echo is an `InputEvent` object emitted when we hold a key or a button, which essentially means that between two frames the key was still pressed. To prevent flooding our event queue with this type of unnecessary information, we will check if the current event is an echo, and if so, we will also return from the function:

```
func _unhandled_input(event: InputEvent) -> void:
    if not event is InputEventKey:
        return
    if event.is_echo():
        return
```

10. Finally, if the current event is something that is actually interesting for the context of our `InputBuffer` class, we will append it to the `event_queue` array:

```
func _unhandled_input(event: InputEvent) -> void:
    if not event is InputEventKey:
        return
    if event.is_echo():
        return

    event_queue.append(event)
```

11. Then, we need to start the expiration countdown. Here, we should make sure that we don't keep on restarting it because, if we do, it won't ever expire until the player stops pressing new keys. Is that a tip based on an empirical mistake I made while writing this code? We will never know. But the idea is to check if the `timer` node is already running, or rather, if it isn't stopped, and if so, we start it using the `expiration_time` variable:

```
func _unhandled_input(event: InputEvent) -> void:
    if not event is InputEventKey:
        return
    if event.is_echo():
        return

    event_queue.append(event)

    if timer.is_stopped():
        timer.start(expiration_time)
```

12. As a queue, we need a method to obtain and remove – in other words, pop – the first entry of the array. This is the main difference between a simple array and a queue. In a queue, the items of the array are always handled in first-in, first-out order. Keep that in mind. We will create a wrapper method for that to allow user classes to get the first element of the `event_queue` variable without knowing it is an array or of its very existence. For the outside world, the `Inputbuffer` node will just give the user classes an `InputEvent` object. Let's call this method `pop_next_event()` and it will return an `InputEvent` popped object from the `event_queue` array using the `pop_front()` method:

```
func pop_next_event() -> InputEvent:
    return event_queue.pop_front()
```

13. User classes need an interface to check a specific action is present on the `InputBuffer` object. Remember, `InputEvent` objects are created on the go. They are events, and each one of them represents an instance of an event, thus each one of them is a different instance. This means we can't, conveniently, check for a specific `InputEvent` object inside the `InputBuffer` object, and even if we did, it would only match this specific instance, even though the player may have pressed the jump key multiple times. So, instead, we need to check for the presence of the jump action within the `InputEvent` objects stored. For that, we will create a method called `has_action()`, which will receive a string as an argument representing the action name and will return a boolean value telling us if the action passed as an argument matches any `InputEvent` object:

```
func has_action(input_action_name: String) -> bool:
```

14. By default, we will presume that the action is not present in the event queue. Then, we will loop through all the events in the `event_queue` array and check if any of them represents the action matching the `input_action_name` argument. If we find any, we will change our assumption, which will now tell us there's such an action in the queue. Then, we break the loop, because there's no reason to keep looking if we already found one instance matching the action:

```
func has_action(input_action_name: String) -> bool:
    var has_action := false
    for event in event_queue:
        if event.is_action(input_action_name):
            has_action = true
            break
    return has_action
```

Something important to keep in mind is to ensure that events that were already processed do not stay in the queue anymore. This means these events may not be at the queue's front but in any position. This is because we are not making a queue specifically for handling only jump-related events. We are storing any `InputEventKey` object, so we will have many other events related to other keys in the `event_queue` array. We could implement an event queue just for jump-pressed events, but since the designer also wants to check for attack-related events, let's keep it generic.

15. For that, we will create another method, called `process_by_action_name()`, which will ask for a string argument representing the action's name and will return an `InputEvent` object:

```
func process_by_action_name(input_event_action:
    String) -> InputEventKey:
```

16. Inside this method, we will first, find the index of the first event representing the action. For that, we will increment an `index` variable ranging through the event queue array's current size. Then, we will check if the element in the current index relates to the desired input action. If so, we store the current index and break the loop:

```
func process_by_action_name(input_event_action:
    String) -> InputEventKey:
    var event_index: int
    for index in range(event_queue.size()):
        if event_queue[index]
            .is_action(input_event_action):
            event_index = index
            break
```

17. Then, we will return the `InputEvent` object to the position we found through the loop we just did:

```
func process_by_action_name(input_event_action:
  String) -> InputEventKey:
    var event_index: int
    for index in range(event_queue.size()):
        if event_queue[index]
          .is_action(input_event_action):
            event_index = index
            break


    return event_queue.pop_at(event_index)
```

18. Last but not least, we will use the editor's interface to connect the `Timer` node's `timeout` signal to the signal callback in the `InputBuffer` class called `_on_timer_timeout()`.

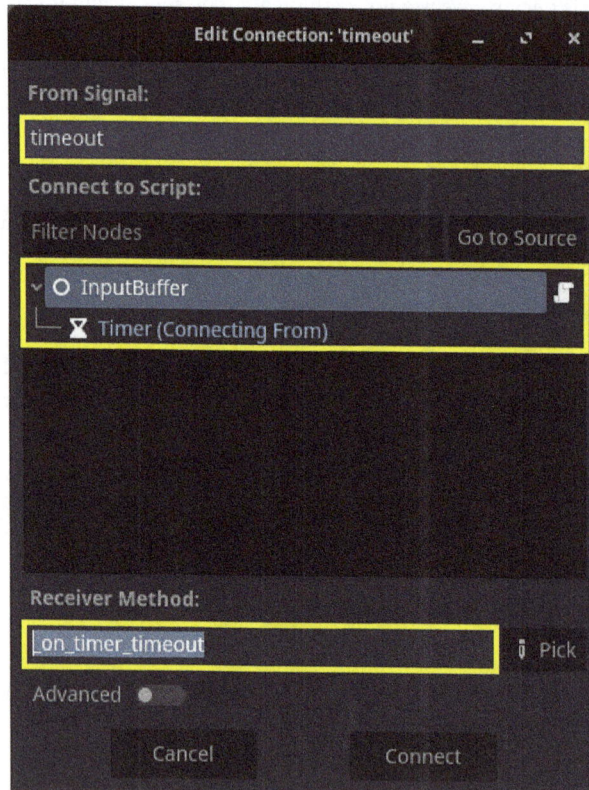

Figure 13.5 – The Timer node timeout signal connection on the InputBuffer node's _on_timer_timeout() method

19. Then, in the `_on_timer_timeout()` callback, we will check if there is any entry in the event_queue array by checking if its size is greater than zero. If so, we pop the next event from the queue. Otherwise, we stop the timer, as this would mean there's nothing to expire, so it doesn't need to tick anymore:

```
func _on_timer_timeout() -> void:
    if event_queue.size() > 0:
        pop_next_event()
    else:
        timer.stop()
```

There we have it! Our very own input buffer that allows us to store and process InputEvent objects. With this power in our hands, it's time to use it responsibly. Currently, the only user for this class is the KingPigPlayer2D class, so in the next section, we will implement the necessary steps to allow it to take advantage of the features we just implemented.

Buffering and processing jumps

Now that we can check for the presence of input events that match the jump action, we can use that to buffer the player's jumps, allowing King Pig to perform a jump if the player presses the jump button within a time window before landing on the floor. For that, let's open res://Actors/KingPig/KingPigPlayer2D.tscn scene and follow these steps:

1. The first thing we will do is to instantiate the InputBuffer scene as a child of the PlayerCharacter2D node.

2. Then, open res://Actors/KingPig/KingPigPlayer2D.gd, and let's start by creating a variable to store a reference to the InputBuffer node right before the fall_speed variable:

```
@onready var input_buffer := $InputBuffer
```

3. Then, in the _physics_process() callback, we will look for the conditional statement that checks if fall_speed is greater than 0.0 and the character is on the floor. This means that it just hit the floor after falling, which is exactly what we are looking for to execute a jump if there's a jump buffered. Inside these conditional statements, we will check if input_buffer has an instance of the jump action:

```
if fall_speed > 0.0 and is_on_floor():
    if input_buffer.has_action("jump"):
```

4. If this is the case, we will also check if InputEvent that we found is related to the jump action being pressed. This is because if it was released, there's no reason to perform a jump. We will also check if the jump action is still being pressed, because otherwise, the player may not actually want to perform a jump. If all these conditions are true, we will execute jump_command():

```
if fall_speed > 0.0 and is_on_floor():
    if input_buffer.has_action("jump"):
        if input_buffer
            .process_by_action_name("jump")
            .is_pressed() and Input
            .is_action_pressed("jump"):
                jump_command.execute()
```

5. Now, if there's no instance of the jump action in input_buffer, we will just set the animation property to "ground" as it was before:

```
if fall_speed > 0.0 and is_on_floor():
    if input_buffer.has_action("jump"):
        if input_buffer
            .process_by_action_name("jump")
            .is_pressed() and Input
            .is_action_pressed("jump"):
                jump_command.execute()
    else:
        animation = "ground"
```

That's it! We just implemented our jump buffer based on the presence of a jump action being pressed. I recommend you play a bit with the InputBuffer node's **Expiration Time** property on the **Inspector** tab so that you can find a good time window for this feature. It can be tricky to find a good spot as too much time would mean that the player may perform an undesired jump, and if the expiration time is too short, it would mean the player doesn't have enough room to mistakenly press the jump button before hitting the ground.

Now that you've implemented your first event queue, and are able to see immediately how it has a direct impact on a player's experience, let's review this chapter, the final chapter of the book!

Summary

In this chapter, we learned about the Event Queue pattern and how it can be used to enhance game feel, especially in action-based games. We started by exploring the importance of player input and how precise timing can make or break the experience, particularly in high-action sequences. The Event Queue pattern allows us to store events, such as player inputs, as a queue to process them later, ensuring that no inputs are missed, even if they happen slightly before or after the optimal time. This concept of buffering events allows for forgiving design features, such as jump buffering, making gameplay more responsive and player-friendly.

We explored the benefits of decoupling events from the exact moment they happened, which is especially useful when things happen in quick succession. This pattern ensures that actions are processed in order without losing important inputs. By implementing an event queue, we also created a system where the game can handle inputs asynchronously, allowing players to press buttons rapidly without the game missing their keystrokes.

Another key aspect we covered was the ability to set an expiration time for events in the queue. By defining how long an input remains valid before it is discarded, we ensured that the game remains responsive without storing outdated inputs. This expiration system prevents the player from performing actions that no longer make sense in the game's context. We saw how this can be applied to other mechanics, such as combat systems and crafting systems, where the sequence and timing of actions are critical.

We also implemented an input buffer in Godot. By storing `InputEvent` objects in a queue, we allowed the player to press the jump button slightly before landing and still perform the jump, compensating for minor mistakes in timing. This system is especially useful for platformers, where players often need to time jumps perfectly. The buffer gave the game a smoother feel, as it forgave slight errors in timing, allowing players to press the jump button within a brief time window before hitting the floor and still perform the jump.

As we conclude this chapter, the Event Queue pattern proved to be a powerful tool for improving the overall feel and responsiveness of our games. It allows us to manage player inputs effectively, ensuring that even fast-paced actions are handled accordingly and in the correct order.

Congratulations on completing this book! You've come a long way through the fundamentals of programming, object-oriented design, and basic and advanced patterns of game development with Godot, learning how to structure your projects efficiently while also enhancing gameplay experiences. I hope the concepts and patterns covered in the book will serve as valuable tools in your development journey, empowering you to create games that resonate with players worldwide. Thank you for purchasing this book and for coming this far. Your dedication and passion for learning will pay off, and I hope this book becomes a stepping stone to achieving your dreams.

On a personal note, I want you to think about every line of code you write as being a chance to create something beautiful, something that can inspire others and bring joy to the world. I hope you continue on this path of learning and making games. As a Christian, my efforts and success are for the glory of my Lord Jesus Christ, who surely has an amazing plan for your life too. Keep striving, keep creating, and may you always find strength and inspiration to pursue your dreams too. And as always, keep developing. Until the next time!

Get This Book's PDF Version and Exclusive Extras

UNLOCK NOW

Scan the QR code (or go to `packtpub.com/unlock`). Search for this book by name, confirm the edition, and then follow the steps on the page.

Note: Keep your invoice handy. Purchases made directly from Packt don't require an invoice.

Index

A

abstraction 6
    used, for simplifying complex systems 20-22
Autoload feature 62, 75

B

BackgroundMusic Service Locator
    creating 245-249
    using 250-255
behavior 5
    converting, to component 49-52
Brain class
    cleaning up, with strategy
        executions 202-205
Bumping Pig brain
    designing 181-187
BumpingPig commands
    creating 168, 169

C

Callable type 156
class 5
code pollution 40
Command pattern 155-158
    implementing aspects 157
    implementing, in Godot 160, 161

use cases, spotting 158
Command pattern, in Godot
    Bumping Pig brain, designing 181-187
    BumpingPig commands, creating 168, 169
    commands to buttons, mapping 177-180
    commands with buttons, using 169-171
    concrete commands, implementing 171-176
    game designer's changes, evaluating 161-168
Command pattern, use cases
    actions, backtracking in tactical
        RPG battles 160
    queuing, in real-time strategy games 159
    strategic encounters, creating in
        role-player games 159
    template behaviors, making in RPGs 159
    using, as undo/redo in level editors 158
complex scenes
    creating, by composing with nodes 48, 49
complex systems
    simplifying, with abstraction 20, 21
composition approach 46, 47
Composition Tree design pattern 47, 52
concrete commands
    implementing 171-176
container variable 102

D

Decorator pattern 212, 213
  implementing, in Godot Engine 215-217
  use cases, spotting 213-215
Decorator pattern, in Godot Engine
  Diamond objects, using to add
    power-ups 232-237
  properties, turning into Stats class 217-223
  StatsDecorator class, creating 224-226
  Stats, wrapping with power-
    ups Singleton 227-231
Dependency Inversion Principle (DIP) 36
Diamond objects
  used, for adding power-ups 232-237
duck typing 31

E

encapsulation
  used, for scoping properties
    and methods 22-25
Event Queue pattern 258-260
  implementing, in Godot 264, 265
  input events, storing with
    input buffer 266-271
  jumps, buffering 271, 272
  jumps, processing 271, 272
  use cases 260-263

F

Factory Method 101
Factory pattern 95-97
  implementing, in Godot 99, 100
  Node2DFactory class, creating 100-104
  Node2DFactory, using 104-112
  use cases 97-99

find_parent() method 102
first-person shooter (FPS) 195
FSM, with animations
  Advance expressions, establishing 132
  animation transitions, creating 128-131
  AnimationTree node, setting up 125-127
  implementing 123-125
  transition conditions, establishing 132-135

G

game designer
  changes, evaluating 161-168
games
  creating, by composing with scenes 52, 53
Godot
  Command pattern, implementing 160, 161
  Observer pattern, implementing 87, 88
  player's health interface, integrating 89-92
  State pattern, implementing 121
  Strategy pattern, implementing 196-198
Godot Engine
  Decorator pattern, implementing 215-217
  design, turning into object 10-16
  Service Locator pattern,
    implementing 243-245
Graphics User Interface (GUI) 37

H

hierarchical state machines 162

I

inheritance
  used, for extending object's behaviors 25-30
interaction strategies
  implementing 205-208

InteractionStrategy family
creating 198, 199
interface segregation principle 36, 49
used, for creating components 40, 41
used, for making high-level
abstractions 41, 42

L

Liskov Substitution Principle (LSP) 36
used, for ensuring compatibility 39, 40
LootBumpingPig
creating 53-56

M

mutation 5

N

nested state machines 162

O

**Object-Oriented Programming
(OOP) 19, 35, 217**
basics 4, 5
principles, complying with 6, 7
used, for game designing 8-10
objects 5, 192
behavior, extending with inheritance 25-31
Observer pattern 84, 85
implementing, in Godot 87, 88
use cases, spotting 86, 87
Open-Closed Principle (OCP) 35
used, for object extraction and
maintenance 38, 39

P

player's health interface
integrating, with Observer pattern 89-92
polymorphism
used, for maintaining compatibility 31-34
power-ups Singleton
Stats, wrapping with 227-231
properties 5

R

Real-Time Strategy (RTS) game
commands, queuing 159
strategic encounters, creating 159
template behaviors, making 159
Remote Procedure Calls (RPCs) 157
role-playing game (RPG) 98, 194

S

score system
creating 68-72
diamond's scoring responsibility 73-78
serialization 157
Service Locator pattern 240, 241
implementing, in Godot Engine 243-245
use cases, spotting 242, 243
Service Locator pattern, in Godot Engine
BackgroundMusic Service Locator,
creating 245-249
BackgroundMusic Service
Locator, using 250-255
shatter() method 111
signals 87
Single Responsibility Principle (SRP) 35
used, for unbloating objects 36-38

Singleton pattern 62

implementing, in Godot 66

use cases, in games 63

Singleton pattern, in Godot

designer's request 66-68

multi-door teleporting system,
   implementing 78-81

score system, creating 68-73

Singleton pattern use cases, in games

background music, playing
   without interruptions 65

engine built-in features, accessing 66

players' data, maintaining 63-65

third-party APIs and plugins, using 65

Spawners 98

StateMachine 161

State pattern 118, 119

implementing, in Godot 121

use cases, spotting in games 119, 120

State pattern, Godot

designer's requirements 121, 122

FSM, implementing with animations 123

**state-specific behaviors, handling
   with State pattern 136-139**

concrete states, creating 141-145

context behaviors, extracting 139, 140

damages, dealing with 148-150

dead state, used for killing
   character 152, 153

hit state 150-152

runstate, used for navigation 145-148

Stats

wrapping, with power-ups
   Singleton 227-231

Stats class

properties, turning into 217-223

StatsDecorator class

creating 224-226

Strategy pattern 192, 193

Brain class, cleaning up with
   strategy executions 202-205

implementing, in Godot 196-198

interaction strategies, implementing 206-208

InteractionStrategy family, creating 198, 199

target object, using 199-201

use cases, spotting 194, 195

sub-state machines 162

T

Tactical Role-Playing Game (TRPG) 259

actions, backtracking 160

target object

using, to provide strategy 199-202

Trigger 49

‹packt›

www.packtpub.com

Subscribe to our online digital library for full access to over 7,000 books and videos, as well as industry leading tools to help you plan your personal development and advance your career. For more information, please visit our website.

Why subscribe?

- Spend less time learning and more time coding with practical eBooks and Videos from over 4,000 industry professionals

- Improve your learning with Skill Plans built especially for you

- Get a free eBook or video every month

- Fully searchable for easy access to vital information

- Copy and paste, print, and bookmark content

Did you know that Packt offers eBook versions of every book published, with PDF and ePub files available? You can upgrade to the eBook version at packtpub.com and as a print book customer, you are entitled to a discount on the eBook copy. Get in touch with us at customercare@packtpub.com for more details.

At www.packtpub.com, you can also read a collection of free technical articles, sign up for a range of free newsletters, and receive exclusive discounts and offers on Packt books and eBooks.

Other Books You May Enjoy

If you enjoyed this book, you may be interested in these other books by Packt:

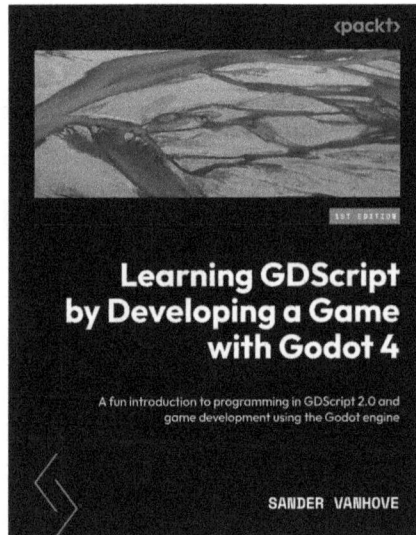

Learning GDScript by Developing a Game with Godot 4

Sander Vanhove

ISBN: 978-1-80461-698-7

- Develop your GDScript 2.0 programming skills from basic to advanced, emphasizing
- code cleanliness
- Harness Godot 4's integrated physics engine to control and manipulate in-game objects
- Design a vibrant and immersive game world by seamlessly integrating a diverse array of assets
- Master the art of processing input from various sources for enhanced interactivity
- Extend the reach of your game by learning how to export it to multiple platforms
- Incorporate simple multiplayer functionality for a dynamic gaming experience

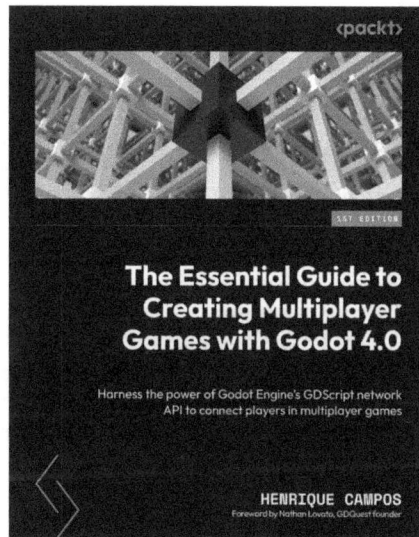

The Essential Guide to Creating Multiplayer Games with Godot 4.0

Henrique Campos

ISBN: 978-1-80323-261-4

- Understand the fundamentals of networking and remote data exchange between computers

- Use the Godot game engine's built-in API to set up a network for players

- Master remote procedure calls and learn how to make function calls on objects remotely

- Enhance your GDScript proficiency to get the most out of this powerful language

- Explore industry-standard solutions for common online multiplayer challenges

- Improve your networking skills and discover how to turn single-player games into multiplayer experiences

Packt is searching for authors like you

If you're interested in becoming an author for Packt, please visit `authors.packtpub.com` and apply today. We have worked with thousands of developers and tech professionals, just like you, to help them share their insight with the global tech community. You can make a general application, apply for a specific hot topic that we are recruiting an author for, or submit your own idea.

Share Your Thoughts

Hi,

I am Henrique Campos author of *Game Development Patterns with Godot*. I really hope you enjoyed reading this book and found it useful for increasing your productivity and efficiency.

It would really help me (and other potential readers!) if you could leave a review on Amazon sharing your thoughts on this book.

Go to the link below or scan the QR code to leave your review:

`https://packt.link/r/1835880290`

Your review will help me to understand what's worked well in this book, and what could be improved upon for future editions, so it really is appreciated.

Best Wishes,

Henrique Campos

www.ingramcontent.com/pod-product-compliance
Lightning Source LLC
Chambersburg PA
CBHW081054220326
41598CB00038B/7091